MY SON: THE 7/7 SUICIDE BOMBER

D1581727

A FATHER'S ANGUISH

by Mahmood Hussain Mir

First published in 2019

This book is copyright under the Berne Convention. All rights are reserved. Apart from any fair dealing for the purpose of private study, research, criticism or review, as permitted under the Copyright Act, 1956, no part of this publication may be reproduced, stored in a retrieval system, or transmitted, in any form or by any means, electronic, electrical, chemical, mechanical, optical, photocopying, recording or otherwise, without the prior permission of the copyright owner. Enquiries should be sent to the publishers at the undermentioned address:

EMPIRE PUBLICATIONS
1 Newton Street, Manchester M1 1HW
© Mahmood Hussain 2019

ISBN: 978190936067-9

Printed in Great Britain.

CONTENTS

On Thursday July 7th 2005, four bombs were detonated in London killing 52 people, including the bombers, and injuring a further 700.

It was the first successful suicide bomb attack on British soil and the biggest terrorist atrocity since the 1988 Lockerbie bomb which brought down Pan Am flight 103.

The four suicide bombers were named as Mohammed Sidique Khan, aged 30 of Beeston, Leeds; Shehzad Tanweer: aged 22 of Leeds; Germaine Lindsay: aged 19 from Aylesbury, Buckinghamshire and Hasib Hussain, 18, from Holbeck in Leeds.

Hasib Hussain was my son.

MY PERCEPTION OF HASIB

THIS BOOK WAS WRITTEN over the course of the last fourteen years. That is a lot of time for your perception of a person to shift, even when that person is your son. Initially, such was my horror and grief at losing Hasib in the 7/7 bombings that I couldn't accept that he was gone and this is reflected in my thoughts during this book.

I often question the official line of various investigations into the bombing. True, there are obvious discrepancies between the official line and the evidence provided. However this is not the place to go into it here. All I will say is that the lack of an official inquiry into the bombings has left a vacuum into which doubt over the sequence of events has been allowed to creep in.

I have finally and reluctantly come to the conclusion that my son was involved, made a conscious decision to plan the attack, helped construct the bombs the four detonated and even went into a branch of WHSmith when his battery initially failed as he was supposed to bomb a tube train rather than a bus. That is the uncomfortable truth. And it is a truth I have wrestled with over the years.

Hasib must have perceived his victims as faceless strangers, rather than people with loves, lives, families and careers, to do what he did. They had done him no 'wrong', rather they represented something that was alien to him and that he felt so strongly about that he decided to commit suicide in the most spectacular way and take a dozen people with him. Why he did this I will never understand.

At no point did Hasib express a viewpoint extreme enough to suggest that he was either capable of performing such an act or expressed sympathy with this type of action. Remember, suicide bombings were quite common at the height of the US/UK invasion of Iraq, yet Hasib never expressed approval of this type of action.

To my wife and I Hasib was a very quiet, conscientious son of whom we were immensely proud. So the shock of his death, the premeditated manner of it and our 'guilt' at not being able to spot a change in him that could have prevented it, only added to our grief in the aftermath. Then there was the intrusive media attention and downright lies concerning Hasib which only served to add stress to an already catastrophic situation. They labelled him illiterate, a petty thief and a religious zealot. Part of the reason behind this book is to tell the world that this media portrait of him was untrue.

A couple of years after the attack my wife and I went on a pilgrimage for Hasib to Saudi Arabia. There we saw a 'doppelgänger' of our son in Makkah not far from where, just a few years before, Hasib had completed his Hajj. We were momentarily convinced this was our son, even though the man in question spoke no English and had a wife and family. At that time we were still not convinced that the our son's involvement in the 7/7 bombing was a terrible nightmare and that, like real nightmares, we'd wake up and discover that Hasib was alive and had nothing to do with the attack. I suppose at some level we had to believe in this false hope to maintain our sanity...

Looking back, perhaps there were clues on Hasib's previous visits to Saudi Arabia. He was fascinated with martyrs and he knew the stories behind them, his knowledge was better even than that of my wife and I. On his Hajj he would visit the martyr sites alone. At the time I just put that down to him appreciating the sacrifices those figures made in the name of Islam but perhaps it was a clue as to how Hasib was thinking. The honouring of martyrdom is a key tenet of Islam but it can easily be turned into something more sinister.

The press have claimed that Hasib was transformed by his Hajj in February 2002. Coming just six months after the 9/11 bombings, it may be that Hasib's perception of martyrdom was strengthened by his visit at a time when the 9/11 terrorists were being lauded by Islamic extremist groups. He certainly became more devout afterwards and expressed a clear view on certain Islamic customs that he derided as unorthodox. Hasib was a fundamentalist. This is not a slight on my son, far from it, because to me he practised Islam as it is supposed to be practised. He also thought about his religion a lot and was dedicated to it. As a father I was proud of his dedication while my other son was completely different. On reflection this may have endorsed his 'fundamentalism' and helped him cross the line separating a devout Muslim from a fanatic without my wife and I realising it.

Above all, perhaps the most upsetting aspect of the bombing was the coldness with which Hasib decided to end his life and those of his victims. There was no sense of nervousness about him in the days leading up to the attack and he had never hinted that something big was about to happen. His conversations were very ordinary and he was planning his future the last time I saw him as we discussed his education, marriage and what he planned to do for a living.

It is Hasib's lost future that pains me most – what could he have become if he had dedicated himself as fully to life as he did to death? He came from a close, loving family, he was relatively well off, he had a university education to look forward to and was planning to get married. It really is mystifying and tragic.

Instead he will go down in history as a fanatic and the 'youngest bomber' who killed a dozen people and part of a terror cell that took 52 lives in the first suicide bombing in the UK. Why did he seek this notoriety? Did he convince himself he would be rewarded?

Finally, from a narrow personal point of view I am most angry at Hasib at what he has put his mother through. In deciding to end his own life he showed her no mercy and she is a changed woman. It's a miracle our marriage has survived but we no longer enjoy life, we exist from day to day.

She hasn't laughed or smiled since 7th July 2005.

AN ORDINARY DAY

THURSDAY JULY 7TH 2005 should have been an ordinary day. I got up early on that morning as I had an appointment with an eye specialist at 9.25 am. Turning on the TV there was news of what was described as an 'underground electric fire' in London. Some channels were saying that tube trains had caught fire. The news was repeating that fire had broken out underground. Although my son Hasib had told me he would be in London, it didn't cross my mind that he may be in trouble.

He had told me that he was going to the capital with his friends sight-seeing the night before and enjoying a couple of days there. He had always been a conscientious son and, with his education now complete, we were making preparations for his marriage to a Pakistani girl. A little later, my wife got up and watched the news with me but she didn't express concern for Hasib. We didn't think he would have any connection with an 'underground electric fire'.

I went to the hospital for my check up. It was a coincidence that my appointment was at 9.25, a few minutes before Hasib would board a bus in London that would lead to his death and the deaths of many others and change our lives forever.

The specialist checked my eyes. I am a diabetic and I had gained good control of my sugar levels because a few weeks before I had very painful laser treatment in my left eye. At one stage I was scared that I might lose my eyesight. She checked my vision at about 9.45 and this was the time when the No 30 bus blew up.

On returning home, the shocking news about the bus didn't concern me immediately. The rolling news coverage seemed confused as to what had actually taken place in the capital that morning with conflicting reports of electrical fires and an exploded bus in Tavistock Square, right in the heart of the city. But to us it was still just 'news' – it didn't affect us directly...

That evening, my wife and I went to a friend's house to offer our condolences as their relative had died. Prior to this, my wife,

Imran and most of the other relatives who knew Hasib's mobile number rang it but there was no response. It was only then that I started to worry and I couldn't help thinking something awful had happened. My main concern was that he might be trapped underground in the various electrical fires reported on the news. I was blaming myself thinking that I should have asked for an address where he was staying and got his friend's phone number. By that night I was really very worried. That evening as I was sitting with friends, my thoughts were really in London with Hasib and my friends could see my disquiet.

Sadly, this was only the start of our family's nightmare. As the hours passed and we had no word from our son, it became clear that Hasib had been caught up in these attacks and was either severely injured or dead.

On the following day, after Friday prayers, I trawled our district, Beeston, in panic in an attempt to find my son. A series of conversations led me to discover Hasib's friendship with two other men who, it would soon emerge, had also met their deaths in London. Known locally as 'Sid' and 'Kaki' – Siddique Khan and Shehzad Tanweer were later portrayed as the masterminds of the four-man terror cell who wreaked havoc in the first Islamic terrorist attack on British soil. Within days police informed me of my son's death and, worse, that he was responsible for the attack on the Tavistock Square bus.

In the 13 years since the attack I have mulled over the same questions – was Hasib, just 18 on 7th July 2005, used by 'Sid', who was 30 at the time of the attacks, as some kind of patsy to detonate his bomb? Or was he involved in a role-playing game gone wrong as has been suggested by conspiracy theorists?

Or was Hasib entirely aware of what he was doing and if so, what inspired him to blow himself up? If so how was he radicalised? Could I have done anything to spot my son's radicalisation?

Our family changed forever on 7th July 2005. We were a proud British-Pakistani household. My wife and I had lived and worked in Leeds for decades and raised a family; two sons and two daughters. In an instant we were transformed into the parents, brothers and sisters of a monster by the British press and our lives were never the same.

In the years since the attack I have kept my silence about the background to our son's role in the UK's biggest ever terrorist attack. Newspapers, television and radio from around the world have offered huge sums for my story but out of respect for my son's memory I have stayed silent, you cannot put a price on your son's memory. Now, however, I believe it is time to speak for my family, we were victims of this bomb too...

PART 1 – FAMILY LIFE

1. NATURE'S MIRACLE!

IN LATE 1985 my wife told me that she would like another child, preferably a boy. We already had two daughters and a son. I did not give any reply but a few days later she repeated her wish and this time she was adamant. I reminded her that she had already had two operations and we should be happy with what we have got and that, in my opinion, three children was enough. The doctors had also told us that a fourth child could be dangerous for her health. But my wife would not listen to me and insisted. I told her many times not to forget the doctor's warning but she refused to listen to my advice.

Now, I dearly love my wife. On the one hand, I did not want her to suffer but, on the other, I wanted her to be happy. So, after some hesitation, I agreed we would try and see what Allah brings us. At that time my eldest son, Imran, was about six years old and I really worried that another pregnancy may be dangerous for my wife.

A month or so later we were in the small bedroom when she gave me the good news that she was pregnant. She told me that it felt like someone has sat in her womb like an angel with a live spirit. This spirit was Hasib. Then, after a few days, she told me that she had been pregnant for a month after tests. I was still frightened regarding her health but she was over the moon and telling everybody that she was pregnant again.

This same room where my wife told me that she was pregnant with Hasib was the room where my son went to London on 6th July 2005. He lived his whole life in this room. He would pray, read and sleep there. This room is full of precious and unforgettable memories. It is like a shrine for us. I also pray and sit in this room and spend my time there now and again. Hasib used to pray there and his knee marks are still there indented in the carpet. I feel close to him whenever I go to his room and offer prayers. I am unable to describe how I feel. Everything is as he left it. Sometimes I touch his clothes and they are full of nice and unusual fragrances. I feel he is around me and listening. I feel he is in his room looking at me. I can hear his voice and he is talking to me. It's a very quiet and peaceful place. I feel close to him spiritually and I sometimes sit there for hours. Many times I have felt that Hasib was sitting with me and saying that he is happy where he is and God is happy with him and he is in paradise. I pray for him. May Allah have mercy on him and grant him the highest place in heaven.

Despite my anxiety, my wife's health was very good before and after Hasib's birth. She was very happy and proud that another child was on the way. We had no clue whether it was a boy or a girl. I do not think we were able to find out the sex of the child before it was born back then but in any case we did not ask. We thought if we have a boy then our family would be perfect, as we would then have two of each. I was so happy; I often put my ear on my wife's tummy and listened to the baby's heartbeat.

My wife never complained that Hasib kicked her. She went to see a specialist and came back happy, there were no complications. Everything was fine and she always had good news when she returned from hospital after the usual check ups. Time was running very fast. I was very busy at work and often worked long hours. I was diagnosed diabetic and was feeling tired but I had no choice but to work long hours because of my family.

We had been told by hospital that Hasib's birth would be by caesarean section and we were aware of the dangers and possible complications. This would be my wife's third such operation. She was called into hospital one day before the due date. She was admitted to Leeds General Infirmary and given a bed in ward 56. Clarendon Wing where most women went to give birth.

My wife and I both hoped for another son. Our God listened to us and Hasib was born on 16th September 1986 and, if I am right, it was a Tuesday and in the early hours of the morning, about 4.30am. He was over 6 pounds in weight and healthy and beautiful. We were both very happy as were our other children. I used to take my other three children to the hospital and the nurses were very kind. There was not much security in those days, like we face now.

We usually stayed with my wife and Hasib for two hours or so.

Hasib was very beautiful; his cheeks were pink and he had golden hair. I was very grateful to my Allah for this precious gift. We congratulated each other. She said "it looks like he is not my son!" I asked her what she meant. She replied "Hasib is white with pink cheeks and golden hair, but our hair is black not golden". She was just joking! My wife was very happy and emotional at the birth of Hasib. A lot of relatives came to see the baby and my wife. Some came with flowers and some with fresh fruit and drinks.

On the evening of 17th September 1986, I went to hospital with my children and some other relatives. My sister in law was also with me. There were a lot of visitors and they took their turn to see baby and mother. When all the visitors left after seeing mother and baby, we also came out of hospital about 8.15 p.m.

It was dark. When we were near the main door a young man was standing there. He was alone. He didn't talk to me but he started talking to my sister-in-law. He asked her "would you do me a favour!" We thought he might need something. It was not in our thoughts that he may be a beggar. In those days we would see very few beggars like we see these days in the city centre. You may have come across such people, who beg to fulfil their drug or drink habits. My sister-in-law asked him "what do you need?" The man replied, "Please leave my country!" We all started laughing at his insulting behaviour. We were thinking he may need something or he may need something for his children. We did not react to him at his racist behaviour except by laughing. I did not intervene otherwise something serious could have happened.

Hasib's mother came home from hospital after 10 days. All the doctors and nurses were very caring and had done their job very well. My wife was very weak and pale but she seemed glad after having another son. I took a few days off work. Taking time off was very difficult because other workers were very jealous and full of racial hate because they did not want a Pakistani man having a good job. It was unfortunate when I told my Manager that my son had been born, he said something which I do not want to repeat here. I just ignored his remarks because I did not want to put my job at risk. All my life, I lived by good principles and I never tried to hurt anybody deliberately. His remarks were very hurtful but I ignored them. I had worked for almost 18 years for this particular firm and took time off twice. Once, when Hasib was born and another time when my uncle died. I worked very hard for this firm. I always respected my managers and other workers but unfortunately I had suffered from a lot of racially hatred there. I was not alone and I am sure other workers at other factories experienced racial discrimination during this time. In my experience, most employers got away with this type of discrimination. I took a few days off work. My other children were at my mother-in-law's house. I took time off because of my children, but she was looking after them, so I decided it was better for me to go back to work.

I had named my other children with the help of my wife but this time I left the decision entirely to her. Although I had given her some advice she had already decided the baby's name. She reads the Qu'ran often, and in the Qu'ran there is the name 'Hasib' and she liked it very much and this is one of the names of Allah. We decided to keep the baby's name Hasib Hussain Mir; Hasib is one of Allah's names, Hussain is my surname and Mir is my father's name.

I was very happy and over the moon but I cannot express the happiness and joy I had when he was born because it hurts my soul and body. The love of my life, the happiness of my soul and body has gone. He will never come back. There are some times when I can not write anymore because it is very upsetting and hurtful…

Following Hasib's birth our family was complete, we now had two daughters and two sons. We were very happy. My wife was over the moon when Hasib was born. It was my wish to take my children to Pakistan to meet their grandparents and other family members. I asked my wife's advice about going to Pakistan. She agreed. We both started to get ready and planned our visit during the holidays. I was concerned about my job as it was very difficult to get time off work. I couldn't risk my job and the wages I was earning so we decided to go to Pakistan during the official holidays.

I informed my father that we were planning to come to Pakistan. He was happy and looking forward to seeing us. Going to Pakistan for just two weeks was such a short time. I was thinking of having two more weeks off from work and go to Pakistan for 4 weeks but unfortunately the firm where I was working was very racist and would not even consider compassionate leave. Non-white workers were denied time off, even if somebody's father or mother died. You could leave the company when personal time off was needed but compassionate leave was not an option at all. It was dreadful for some workers but unfortunately, that's how it was in those days. There were no black faces in management, most Asian and Black workers were doing the undesirable jobs and unsocial hours. I only kept my job because no white person wished to do a 12 hour night shift.

Anyway, Hasib was about 9 and half months old when he first went to Pakistan and our extended family was very happy to see us. I was happy that my parents had met my children. I was thinking that in this way I would keep in touch with my family in Pakistan and provide a sense of belonging to my children. During the flight, Hasib was very quiet and we had no problems at all. My other children were also happy and well behaved during the flight. As soon as we reached Islamabad airport and boarded the bus to the main terminal and came to the immigration section, I was shocked and angry when I experienced unnecessary delays and demands for bribes. After this, we came out of the main building and my father was waiting for us. We greeted each other and sat in his car. We hired another taxi for our luggage. We got home safely. The weather was very hot and humid. This part of Pakistan had not had rain for weeks. We realised that we were going to have power cuts and, of course, there were millions of Pakistani born and bred mosquitoes waiting for us. The electricity was off almost every day because of the burning of a local transformer or short circuit. Imagine children who came from England with no electricity in that humidity and hot weather: it was unbearable for them.

My father's neighbours didn't bother to report these power-cuts to the local electric station for repairs because they knew my father would report it and bring electricity workers and pay them to repair the transformer. My father knew some of the workers and they would come straight away as they knew they would be treated with tea, biscuits and maybe some money. I am ashamed and disgraced to say this practice is still going on in Pakistan and some workers will not repair electric faults without a bribe or some kind of favour. As my poor mother was making tea for the workers, they put a new fuse in the transformer and soon they left after tea and biscuits. I heard one of the workers saying to my father "you shouldn't be coming to the station to report the faults you should send a message with a child and that would be enough." My father was a sympathetic man. He would not want others to suffer in that scorching heat. He would always help the neighbours. As I mentioned, my children came from England where the weather was relatively cold. It was unbearable for my children to stay in Pakistan for a long time. Some of my children became ill and started to cry but Hasib was quiet and patient.

As we were just settling down after the power cut, we all started to feel ill because of the water. I'm not sure if it was because the water was dirty or just different. I became sick myself and badly dehydrated. One of my old Christian school teachers came around to see me and he suggested eating bananas, isapghol husk and a yogurt mix. I felt better after a few days and took care of myself and the others with this treatment. Everybody knows that some children, who are from England, when they travel abroad, suffer stomach problems. They are a bit soft and delicate for the Pakistani climate and it is understandable that some British Pakistani children do not travel to Pakistan for this reason. There is no pure and clean water and on top of that there is a chance the electricity will go off and sometimes there is no gas to cook with.

Suddenly, Hasib fell ill. He was suffering from a stomach bug. He was crying. I gave him that mix I had when my stomach rumbled but Hasib was only a little baby and it did not work on him. I became very worried about Hasib. It was the second night of his illness and hearing his cries made me very upset. After a very bad night when neither my wife or I got any sleep, Hasib's mother gave him some milk and he felt a little bit better. We took him to a local doctor that morning, who was also my father's physician. He was a good doctor and a child specialist. His name was Dr G Ahmed and his practice was at Committee Chaowk Rawalpindi. He asked me to give Hasib a mixture and some ground up tablets. I took Hasib home and kept giving him the medication and he felt a lot better after a short time. Dr. Ahmed was an old man then, I always pray for him and remember him. I do not know if his practice is still there and who is in charge. In 1994 I went to see him after my father died suddenly and I wanted to know if he had any knowledge of his illness prior to his death. He told me my father was suffering from hypertension.

Anyway, Hasib was better after taking his medication. He was a happy child. All the neighbours loved him. Children often took him and he would stay with them for some time and they would bring him back home for feeding. He loved going with other children and we hardly saw him most of the day. While in Pakistan, Hasib used to play with animals, birds and little dolls. He would point to an animal or bird and say something in his own language. Seeing a bird or animal, he would clap with excitement. One day a boy brought a baby goat. Hasib was sitting on a bed and this boy put the goat on his bed, he started crying. I was there and I took a photo. That is a very precious picture of Hasib for me now.

I spent two weeks in Pakistan and came back to England for work. I left my family there. A few days after getting home I was missing them; telephone calls to Pakistan in those days were very costly. As my wife and children were in Pakistan I thought they should visit my elder sister who was living in Karachi. Although it was very expensive to fly to Karachi, I thought it was worth it as my children would see the rest of the family. I asked my wife and my father about this and they agreed. They stayed there for nine days.

Back in Leeds, I had never felt anything like this loneliness. The experience of being alone for the first time in ages was really sad and I was blaming myself for it. I phoned my wife to ask if she could come home sooner. I asked my father to send them as soon he could arrange a return flight. He wanted to keep them longer but he eventually agreed and made arrangements to send them back. I love my family and the house was like a ghost town.

For the record, that was the first and last time that Hasib went to Karachi. He was about 9 months old. It is necessary for me to add this here because after 7/7 a Pakistani police officer rang me and asked me if Hasib had visited Karachi in 2004, more than that he was pressurising me to admit that Hasib was in Karachi in 2004. Hasib never travelled to Karachi in 2004. The only time he went to Karachi was when he was a baby. yet this officer insisted that Hasib travelled to Karachi with me in 2004! I am not sure who asked him to find out about Hasib and Karachi. Perhaps it was the British police or MI5? We found out later that it was another Hasib who travelled to Karachi in 2004.

That police officer made me very angry – my family and I were devastated and our life had been turned upside down. We had lost our son and he was threatening me to say that Hasib went to Karachi in 2004, which was completely and utterly untrue. The reason I must write this here is that most Pakistani people know about Pakistani police behaviour. Not all Pakistani police officers are corrupt. There are some nice people that I honestly believe are honourable and respectable police officers in Pakistan but unfortunately, most police officers are corrupt and take bribes. When they stand before their Creator, what would they say? There will be no bribe and favours there! You reap what you sow! I can express my views, but I am unable to change the world and some Pakistani police officers are dishonourable.

Anyway, my family returned from Karachi to Rawalpindi after 9 days. I was worried about my children's health. I always asked about Hasib's health and his well being and my wife told me he was fine. Our other children were able to say something to their mother but Hasib was only a baby and he couldn't express his illness or pain apart from by crying. He used to sit in a pushchair occasionally and his mother would take him to the local shops. We hardly used that pushchair and my wife left it there in our house. When Hasib came back from Pakistan his stomach had ballooned and his whole body was full of mosquito bites. I was shocked. His face had become dark. His belly was also full of bites. I tried to pick him up but he clung to his mother. Our other children were fine. I was really very upset as I was thinking maybe my parents did not look after my children. But I can't blame them as it was not their fault. It was the weather and climate. As soon as he returned from Pakistan, Hasib was trying to stand up and walk. He was also climbing steps but unfortunately he fell down and broke his leg!

★

Hasib recovered quickly from that accident and before we knew it he was ready for nursery. It happens like that with children, one minute they're in nappies, the next they're getting married! Obviously, most parents do their duty to bring up their children in a way so they can thrive in society. When it comes to a child's misbehaviour, most Asian parents say that there is too much freedom in this country, but there are many other factors regarding these problems. The society and environment we are living in also plays a big role in their lives. I think parents should bring up their children according to their abilities and the sensitivity of the times. For example, a child who is living in the Middle East with his parents is getting an education in an Arab country, it is clear he would learn Arabic and will mix with Arab children and that environment is bound to have an effect on them. So you cannot just blame a child but also the environment they are living in. He or she would read, speak and talk in Arabic. Similarly, in England, a child would learn within the environment he or she is in. Due to society changing and wherever you live, there would be positive and negative affects on your child.

When I came to this country, I started worrying about my children. I used to hear from my elders that television was bad for children. Asian parents used to take children out of schools as soon as they became 16, especially the girls. At the beginning what I had experienced made me very careful and very sensitive about the issue of bringing up children. I think that's why I didn't buy a television for a long period of time, fearing it might bring negative effects on my children. When I bought a television, I kept it in our bedroom so the children could only watch it before 9 pm because some programmes were unsuitable for them. When we watched television at the weekend, especially in the evening, we parents would always be there. But you cannot control or protect what they learn from the outside. We tried to guide our children but we were not always with our children, although we did the best for them. I do not think it is fair to blame everything on the culture or environment we live in. For those people who always blame this culture or sometimes the country, in my opinion they should not live here. It is not fair on the country that provided shelter to millions of immigrants over the decades from all over the world. Where would you go; Pakistan or the Middle East? I personally think the environment and culture we are living in is for everybody.

You cannot escape some of the bad things in Britain but they are far outweighed by the good. It can seem like us Muslims are living in dark times at the moment and sometimes it seems that if we come out of it safely we'll have been lucky. However the alternatives are far worse. The Pakistani environment is far perfect – talk about lawlessness! Who feels safe in that country? Most are trying to get rich through corruption. Where have their principles gone? I often tell my friends that Britain is the best country in the world. We have a lot of opportunities and freedom. We have no fear if we are in a masjid or any religious place but look at what is happening in Pakistan. You do not know when you would be shot at, even (or especially!) in supposedly secure religious places. The only condition this country asks of us is to obey the country's laws. That is why, in comparison with other countries, this is the best place to live. You would not find a better education system anywhere else.

Anyway, I was talking about Hasib's education and drifted a bit off the subject. When Hasib returned from Pakistan after his first visit, he was approximately 10 months old. One day, as usual, he was playing in the dining room and crawled towards the stairs. His mother followed him but very quickly he climbed a few steps and fell down very badly and broke his leg. His mother and I took him to the local hospital. Initially we waited a bit but he was seen by the doctor who said straight away that he'd broken his leg but we needed to do x-rays to make sure he needed plaster. We came home after a nurse put the plaster around his leg. I still remember the nurse was talking to my wife saying it was the first time she had to put plaster cast on such a small baby.

Despite the injury and pain, Hasib did not cry as other children might. He was very calm and patient. After a while, the plaster was taken from his tiny leg. The white plaster was full of sympathetic messages. That plaster is still with us and my wife kept it as a souvenir.

Hasib always played either alone or with his cousin. He was a very calm child, and never made a fuss while playing with his toys and he rarely cried. When eating he loved milk and always chewed his food. He always slept with his mother and me regardless of it being winter or summer. There was a special place on the first floor in one corner where he used to sleep in his cot. This cot is still with us in his room behind his bed. In the same corner on the first floor where he used to sleep when he was baby, there is a settee. When he was young he always sat on this settee listening to music or reading. Imagine seeing him as a baby lying down in his cot and then a young man sitting down on the settee, it sends shivers down my spine.

It was Hasib's habit to go to bed early and get up very early the next morning. He often played in bed when we were sleeping. Most of the time he would wake us up. We had a big bed and I slept on one side and my wife on other and Hasib slept right in the middle. My other son was also little and both enjoyed a warm and cosy bed. Sometimes Imran embraced his mother and Hasib clung to me. As I have written earlier, Hasib's cheeks were red and when he slept with us in a warm bed, his cheeks became redder and sometimes flaky.

Hasib was very young when he was circumcised. I think he was about one month old when I called a very well known doctor in those days, Doctor Khan. I still remember very well I paid £50 for this religious job. Although it was a lot of money in those days I paid him with real happiness. When Doctor Khan was performing sugary on Hasib, I was holding his legs and his mother was holding his shoulders. Hasib cried and screamed so much it was unbearable for me and I started crying. I remember his mother was quiet, but I carried on crying, and could see him in pain. How could I have not felt his pain? The table where Hasib was laid down for circumcision is the same table where I write his life story.

It is important to write about Hasib's habits before he joined nursery. He would often play with his cousin. She was a big baby. Sometime she started crying for no obvious reason. Hasib would not cry even if she snatched his toys away. Hasib and his cousin's innocent relationship carried on from childhood until he passed away and she got married. His cousin did not have a brother and because of this, she always loved him as a brother. We have got a lot of precious memories in the form of photos and videos of them playing. If he had nobody to play with, Hasib would play alone and never lose interest in his toys. My working hours were very long. His mother would leave him at his grandmother's when she went out shopping. Hasib would always be very happy and excited when I came home from work. He would cling to me and embrace me. I missed my children because of working long hours. He would blow candles and play with balloons when we celebrated his birthdays. He loved the company of other children and receiving many gifts from our relatives. When he was able to speak, he would copy his mother and say "La Ilaha Illah Allah Mohammed Ur Rasool Allah". He would copy some other Urdu words like Ubba and Umma. He would copy his mother when she offers her Salah and I often laughed to see him doing his actions. Hasib was growing up slowly. He was a very quiet and patient child, and if he could not find anything to play with he would just sit and be in his own world.

His mother applied for him to join a local nursery. It was

very easy to find nursery places in those days. Hasib's sisters were educated at Ingram Road Primary School and after this school, they transferred to Matthew Murray High School. Both schools were very close to our home, just a few streets away. Hasib's nursery was also very close and it was ideal for us. Looking at his education record and my diary, he joined nursery on 16th November 1989. Primarily his mother stayed with him at school but gradually, after settling down, she would come home leaving him in school. He would come home smiling and happy. He would bring his art work and other papers with him. He would be very excited and happy to show me his pictures. Each morning he would come out of our home and start running to school. It is very important to say that since his nursery and up until 5th July 2005, he kept all his nursery, school and college certificates and annual reports and any other educational achievements. They were all very neatly organised and put away in a leather case in his room.

2. MY UPBRINGING

PERHAPS NOW I have outlined the circumstances behind Hasib's birth I'd better to go back a bit and explain how my wife and I came to England.

I was born in a very sacred village in Azad Kashmir called Dhangri Sharif. It is situated in the Mirpur district in northern Pakistan. I lived in this village until I was about 8 years old. My father had moved to England when I was only a baby so I was brought up by my mother and grandfather. One day I overheard my mother saying that my father was returning from Walayat (England) soon. I was very happy and looking forward to meeting him. Unfortunately he found it extremely difficult to adjust to village life because he had become accustomed to living in a city in England. Life in rural Pakistan was a bit of a contrast! Many times I heard him telling my mother and grandfather that he would move to nearby Rawalpindi or Islamabad and start a business there. My grandfather wasn't happy at all because he would be left alone.

After returning to the country of his birth, a lot of his old friends came to visit my father. He had returned with a few things that were hard to get hold of in Pakistan – the main ones I can remember were a camera and an old gramophone, the type from the HMV record label, and a pair of binoculars. He took our photos and showed me how to use the binoculars. I used it many times and I could see faraway hills and mud huts on the horizon. When he took our photos he used big bulbs for the flash and I remember being very scared of it. Funny how you remember these things as a child!

My father started making plans to set up his transport business. He had arranged for several buses to be shipped to Karachi and he was making arrangements to bring them to Rawalpindi. He had no plans to start a transport business in the village so there were a lot of arguments between my mother, grandfather and father. It's understandable and very unfair to an old man and a father who now was facing isolation and further hardships. There was no one in the village that could look after the family. I was very close to my grandfather and he loved me to bits. I was very upset and didn't want to leave him. I was very scared, especially overhearing the bitter arguments between my father and the rest of the family. My dad would always lose his temper and it wasn't nice to witness. The family feud tore me apart and it affected me very badly.

When my father was in a good mood he would tell his friends about his time in England. He had burned his passport and kept telling everyone that "Goray" (white people) were very racist and some English women beat their husbands or lovers with high heeled shoes, this is a huge insult in Arabic culture. My father and his mates would laugh about their time in England but I also heard of a sinister side to life there. My dad talked about unfair treatment at work places and in everyday life. I was listening one morning and he said he had been attacked on the way to work by a "Goray" who beat him up and left him for dead at the roadside. He ended up spending weeks in hospital.

Some aspects of my father's experience in England were terrible. he had shared a room with his workmates and all ten of them would share each other's beds according to their shifts, there were no proper facilities for bathing and no inside toilets and they shared the bathrooms with other householders. He said that "Goray" people would say bad things about them and call them "Paki bastards" without reason or just to provoke them. They would spit on them when they were in the street or just for standing on their doorstep. "Goray" people would knock your door down or hurl abuse at you if they smelled curry. Many Pakistani Muslims were beaten by "Goray" Gangs because they didn't like the smell of curry – which is quite ironic given how popular Pakistani cuisine is nowadays in Britain! My father was very scared and often feared for his life when he went outside. His "Goray" supervisor always gave the Pakistanis the worst jobs for less money. He was frightened to return to England because of hatred, fear for his safety and the colour bar.

Despite all this and his frequent warnings, I still wanted to visit

England. When I was about 13 years old my uncle, who was already in England, sent a letter to my father and asked if he would agree to let me visit him as his son. My uncle had added my name on his tax papers to get a rebate as a lot of other people were doing this at the time, it was a well known dodge. My papers were put forward for a visa at the British Embassy in Rawalpindi. I was interviewed but the visa clearance officer rejected my application on the grounds of age that I was out of the legal band required. I think a son was allowed to join his father in England if he was under 14 years old, but a doctor in Rawalpindi working for the British Embassy, Dr Mola Bakash Minhas, asked for a bribe from my father and he wouldn't pay, so this doctor sent an unfavourable medical report to the Embassy. In his opinion I was over 14 as he had checked my arm bones. Funnily enough, it was during this process that my surname was altered from Mahmood Sultan to Mahmood Hussain. My father's surname was Sultan and my uncle's name was Hussain. I was very upset when I was told that my dreams were dashed. I thought I could have had a good education in England and that was the main reason I wanted to join my uncle there.

Soon, my father started his transportation business in Rawalpindi. He was a very successful businessman and he was a very well known, well-liked and respected member of the community. I joined a local school soon after we settled in Rawalpindi, it was a very reputable establishment. I loved my education and my teachers and I stayed there until I had passed my examinations. I came first in the whole city and it was an extremely proud time for my teachers and school, of course not forgetting my parents. This was a Christian High School run by Christian Missionaries. Apart from religious education, all the other teachers were of Christian faith. All my teachers were very kind and helpful to me and I will respect them from the bottom of my heart until the day I die. A female teacher used to take me into a nearby church and showed me how they pray. I am very grateful and humble for her kindness.

A little later my father suffered a downturn in his business and was unable to pay school fees because his business partner was deceiving him. Most times he was unable to pay the monthly fees but my teachers were very kind and did not let this affect my education. I remember very well that one of my Christian teachers paid my fees and helped me in many other ways. Unfortunately I eventually had to stop my education due to a lack of money but I started to do some odd jobs and carried on getting an education from private colleges.

After being rejection for a visa I was a very unhappy child. I went to a masjid (Islamic school) to seek help. One day my Urdu language teacher, a devoted Christian, poet and very well known Urdu calligrapher, asked me if I could help him. He is buried now in a Gora graveyard in Rawalpindi and may God bless him as he was a father figure to me. His wife was just as good to me and always treated me like a son. Whenever I got the chance to go to Pakistan, I went to see her. I always sat at her feet and asked her for her blessing. She had lost her sight because of diabetes.

I'm definitely not a perfect person but these two people made me into a reasonable human being. I had very neat handwriting and my Urdu teacher wanted me to help him by practicing more, so at age 13 I became an Urdu and Arabic calligrapher. I started by writing Pakistani voting lists and soon I was doing well and participated in his other projects; writing posters and magazines and helping him with some of his books. He trained me to be one of the best calligraphers in Pakistan. As a married man, who worked full time as a teacher, the calligraphy was often too much for him. He was very skinny and you could even count his facial bones. I used to go to his house and return home late and then I had to go to school very tired the next day having had very little sleep. I was falling behind in my lessons but I soon caught up. He was also teaching Urdu to our class and he never punished me as he knew I'd had very little sleep and was often unable to do my homework.

I was soon earning a little money by helping my teacher. When I got my first wage my father was ill with TB and his business had failed. I went straight to the clothes shop and bought six meters of blue material for his Shalwar Kameez outfit and a half dozen handkerchiefs and gave him 30 Rupees in cash. He smiled and I could clearly see my father thinking, "I am not alone as I have a son who will look after me" which made me very proud. I dreamt that one day my own child would go to work and he or she would give me his or her first wages but that never happened. Hasib promised to send me £10 a week if I went to Pakistan and live there.

There was a very popular Urdu magazine called *Jehan-Niswan* (Women's World) and I used to do the calligraphy for that. Then there was an Urdu weekly newspaper called *Mashriq* which was published in London in the 60's and the beginning of the 70's. I also used to work for this paper and our client would send art work from Pakistan to London.

Around this time Pakistani politics became very volatile. In the build up to the war between India and Pakistan a printer asked me to do calligraphy for a book called "Jab Indra Jawan Thi" (When Indra was young). I calligraphed that book and it took many days and nights. It was a short but very effective book and it became a best seller in a few days. The printer and I were later arrested and we were only released when we promised not to do it again.

I was only 16 when I was arrested again in Campbellpur because I calligraphed a poster which belonged to a Shia Sect and a Sunni Sect didn't like it. I was taken to Campbellpur District main Jail and spent a few days there. The jailor was nice to me but I don't know about the others. I remember people would tell a story of a well-known local villain and that once his mother came to visit him in jail and he bit his mother's ear off from inside the metal gate because, according to him, she didn't provide him with a proper education and upbringing! Anyway one of my Doctor's friends who I would write Urdu prescriptions for bailed me out and whilst I was sitting with him at the jailor's house, the jailor asked me if I would marry one of his seven daughters! I promised I would but later ran away. He was a good man, sorry sir!

I carried on helping my teacher and also learned about book binding. Urdu, Arabic and Persian calligraphy is my passion and hobby. It is in my blood and I always kept it as a hobby. I produced some masterpieces of which I am very proud.

3. HASIB'S TRIPS TO PAKISTAN

AFTER 7/7 there was a lot of ill-informed talk about Hasib's trips to Pakistan. Many journalists made a connection between Hasib's radicalisation and his behaviour after returning from Hajj in 2004. I feel compelled to put the record straight here and explain exactly what went on during these trips because if you believed everything you read, you would assume that my son was in Pakistan for terrorism training!

As stated earlier, Hasib's only visit to Karachi came when he was nine months old. It was part of a visit to my home country to see relatives. He travelled to Pakistan a second time with myself and his mother in July 1995. Let me make it clear, Hasib never travelled to Pakistan or any other country alone.

I had visited Makkah for my first Umrah in December 1994 and when I came back I was diagnosed with kidney cancer. I had been told by the kidney specialist that one kidney had to come out. I was devastated and thought it was the end of me. It was a very difficult and most upsetting time, not only for me but also for my family. I was shattered, very down and couldn't believe what I was experiencing. I was also told by the doctor "if your kidney cancer spreads to other parts of body, then there is nothing that can be done to minimise your cancer". A few months earlier I had lost my job and now I was suffering from cancer. I was in a very troublesome and unfortunate situation. I was responsible for my wife, four children, parents and six brothers and sisters. My doctor suggested I make a will. I was in emotional turmoil; few people could withstand it easily.

I had my operation on 18th April 1995. I was admitted to the local hospital for 9 days. My kidney was taken out and after 5 days I was told that the cancer had not spread to any other parts of my body but that they were keeping an eye on me. I stayed under observation for almost 5 years. I am very grateful to my GP, my surgeon and his team. May Allah give them a long life with good health! I will never forget the care that was provided by the nurses. One of the nurses really touched my heart. She was an angel of this world. May Allah give her more ability to serve humanity and forgive her mistakes and sins!

When I felt better, I asked my GP if I was able to travel to Pakistan to see my family and he gave me permission to travel for a short time. I had asked my sister if she could stay at my house and look after our three children. She was happy to help. I went to Pakistan with Hasib and my wife, leaving the other three children with my sister. My father had died in 1994. We flew to Pakistan and stayed in our own house. My brother was also staying with us. Hasib was very close to his uncle and I let Hasib sleep in his room. Hasib was about 9 years of age. He was always quiet and busy with his animals and birds. He was very happy to play with other boys of his age. He made a few friends and they would come to our house and play together. He was a healthy child and because of the hot weather, his cheeks were always red.

We have a water fountain in our garden in Pakistan. He would stand under the water and cool himself down. The weather was very hot and extremely humid. It was the season for a variety of fruit and fresh vegetables. Hasib loved mangoes and they were in season. You could buy all types of mangoes very cheap. I love gardening but my physical capability was limited. I wouldn't even try to do any heavy physical work. Hasib always tried to help me when our garden needed sorting out. Hasib would eat mangoes every day and he liked the outer part of the seed in particular. He used to ask me or his mother what to do with the big seed and sometimes he would throw them in the bin and sometimes he would plant them in the soil. One day he planted a stone and it grew to a small plant, and one of them eventually became a huge tree. That tree is still in our garden in Pakistan and almost every year it gives us so much fruit. Once we were there and a lot of mangoes fell down from this tree after a short but powerful hurricane. Although the mangoes were green they were very sweet. They were the kind of mangoes which are naturally green in colour but very sweet. I hope and pray this tree will stay healthy so people can enjoy the fruit. Sometimes neighbours ask us for unripe mangoes to make mango pickle and sometimes kids go up and steal them but we don't mind at all. It's a joy and pleasure to listen to people saying "we went to pick mangoes from Hasib's mango tree".

While we were there we saw a cat in our garden. It was very small and weak. My wife fed her first and then washed her. She was very hungry. She put milk in front of her and she would drink it straight away. We could not let her go in this condition and kept in our house. Hasib loved this little cat and started to look after her. He always kept her with him. He would feed her and within a few days she was back to her full glory and put some weight on and looked very healthy. She would run after Hasib and play with him and sometimes she would lay down with Hasib in his bed and snore. She always followed him. Hasib was very caring towards animals and never hurt them.

My brother wanted to buy some vegetables and household things for himself and asked me, my wife and Hasib to come with him to a local Jummah Bazaar. We went there and looked around. We didn't find anything interesting and pleasurable except for one thing. A man was selling different coloured hen chicks. Hasib became angry and upset. He started to ask a lot of questions about those poor chicks that were in a very small cage and crying for water. He asked me if I could buy them and set them free. I told him it was not possible for me to do that because the man would just bring some more, it was a never-ending cycle. Hasib then asked his mother if she could buy them but my wife's answer was the same. Hasib then requested if he could have a few. I bought 2 chicks of his choice and took them home in a big card board box, but one of them died soon after we returned home. The remaining chick was very cute and loving. Now we had a problem; a cat and a chick in the same house! It was not wise to keep them together. But we were very lucky; we didn't have any problems with either of them. The kitten would play with the chick and the chick followed the kitten all over the house. Their friendship was adorable. It may be possible that the kitten was not yet familiar or experienced enough to kill a chick and they got along very well.

Unfortunately this yellow chick was following Hasib in the kitchen one day and Hasib had no idea that the chick was very close to one of his feet. As Hasib turned back, the chick was crushed and died instantly. I was out of house when this incident occurred. When I returned home, I saw both my wife and Hasib and they looked as though somebody had died. I asked them what happened and why they were so sad and my wife told me what happened. Hasib was very upset and full of sorrow. I told him not to worry; I would get him another next Friday telling him that "it's an accident and you should not be so unhappy." He liked that chick very much. He was blaming himself as it was his fault, and he should have been more careful.

While we were in Pakistan my wife wanted to visit her elder sister who had arrived from England and still lived in the village where my wife and I had grown up, near Mirpur. We hired a taxi and, really, it was too much for me because I was still recovering from the operation. As we approached our village the road was very bumpy. I was not feeling well and noticed that some blood was coming from my wound. It was too hot and I didn't want to put a plaster on it because it might cause more problems and maybe get infected. When we got there Hasib asked his mother where we were born. I could not point out the exact place but showed him a particular room where I was born. As I have mentioned before, Hasib was very keen on collecting small items. He picked up some stones near our ancestral house and kept them in his bag. We were not aware of this. As we were making plans to return to Rawalpindi we decided to visit the Khari Sharif Shrine. I was ill and unable to travel but had to go with other family members.

After that we went to see our relatives who were living near the shrine. This whole area had changed and looked very different. There are some very interesting and beautiful irrigation systems which were built under the British Raj. The structures are old but the building work is so strong that it still looks like new. Unfortunately a bridge which was a lifeline for Pakistan and Azad Kashmir was still standing at the time but has since collapsed following a sudden heavy and forcible flow of dam water. We were told that the bridge was very strong but it collapsed because of negligence from the dam management company and killed a lot of people and livestock. The Kashmiri Government built a new bridge where the old bridge was but it's not as strong as the old one. Unfortunately, more money has been spent on memorials to Kashmiri politicians than the bridge. This bridge is now very dangerous and may collapse again soon but who cares? There is no value for human life in that part of world.

As mentioned, I found out later when we reached home that Hasib had picked up a few small stones from where his mother and I were born. I am not sure why Hasib picked up those stones. Were they a souvenir? We returned and a few days later we planned to visit our local Shah Faisal Masjid. Hasib's uncle had a pistol and Hasib used to play with that. Of course it was always empty. It was made in China and he said it was just to scare people around where we lived. There were a lot of crimes and thefts going on and he bought it for protection. But in my opinion, this wasn't the reason. He terrorised his family members with it more than anything else! Hasib was not allowed to touch it, if it was loaded. My brother also had a key ring with a small pistol attached to it. I think it's the type that's available from a locksmiths' shops or hardware store.

Anyway, we went to see Shah Faisal Masjid as planned. My brother was driving an old car which belonged to my father. Hasib and his mother were sitting on the rear seats and I was in the front passenger seat. There is a long road when you travel to Islamabad. As we got very close to the masjid a Pakistani policeman stopped our car. This was usual for us but not for Hasib. My brother got out of the car and approached the policeman. Obviously the policeman wanted some money from my brother. His papers were up to date but he still wanted to fine and charge him. It was very hot and Hasib's face was red hot. He couldn't stay in the car. He asked me a few times why the policeman had stopped the car. I eventually said that Pakistani policemen are crooked and they just stop cars to get bribes. A few minutes later my brother was free to go and he told me that he had paid 50 Rupees. He had to tell me all this because I was responsible for the money.

When Hasib's uncle told me how much he had paid, I turned back and told my wife and Hasib. My son was upset at this treatment and said "Allah will curse him and I don't think they are Muslims at all" before saying "Abba! You always told us to visit your country and I think the policeman was crooked. These policemen are supposed to keep the law, not break it. Shame on them." I was ashamed by his harsh comments but he was completely right. I wondered why I brought him to Pakistan where such practices are commonplace.

We went to a place called Shaker Parian National Park next to the Rawal Dam. It was late afternoon and still hot and humid. We went up to Shaker Parian. There was nothing special there, just a fountain. This place was badly treated by the management. There were some dried wood and dirty water flowing out of the fountain. My son was looking at me as if to say, "Father, why did you bring me here?" After this boring trip on the hilltop, we came down and walked down to Rawal dam. We sat in a small boat with other "joy riders". As the boat went into deep water, I started to panic. It looked like the boat was sinking. I was very scared but Hasib and his mum enjoyed it. I knew Hasib would love it because he loves playing and messing with water. After this terrifying experience we sat down at a café (accompanied by a lot of flies) and my brother, who was very hungry, had a lot to eat. We then went to the lower part of the dam where there were a lot of huge gates. This part was very lush and green and on the way we saw some goats and water buffalo as well as mud huts and a lot of crops. When Hasib saw goats and sheep he became very excited and wanted to touch them. He went near them and started stroking the baby. They were white and beautiful. I think he tried to feed them but their mother also came along and snatched the food from Hasib's hand. We were very happy to see Hasib in a good mood and enjoying himself.

Hasib was very excited and asked me if I could buy a baby goat for him. I told him I am happy to buy one for him but the problem is that, firstly the farmer may not sell it and secondly, who was going to care for the goat after we had gone back to England. He spent some time with one particular baby goat and I took some photos of him playing with it. Hasib was very used to playing with animals and he had no hesitation in looking after them. He always approached them with kindness and care.

We then went to see the huge gates of the dam. There was some water flowing from the dam's doors creating a small stream. The stream was full of stones. I was thinking about how these huge stones had arrived there. It is a very beautiful, peaceful and natural place. Hasib was unaware of any danger and I warned him to be careful as there were a lot of slippery stones.

We saw a newly-wed couple sit down on a big stone, lost in their own world. They were splashing water at each other. The girl asked me if I could take their photo. I took some snap shots. I was very happy to do that and they started talking with us. We had seen their innocent, passionate and lovely relationship. One of them asked me which city we came from. I told them our whereabouts and the Bride said "your son is speaking English." The Bridegroom whispered to her and pointed out to Hasib and then his Bride's pink cheeks changed to red. They both wished to have a child like Hasib. The couple left holding hands.

Hasib played in the water wearing his Shalwar Kameez, which dried very quickly afterwards. We came back after a short while to the garden. It was nearly late afternoon and the sun was going down. It was a very lovely view. The birds were flying above our heads and going to their nests after a long day. It was nearly dark when we came back after an enjoyable day.

The time we spent at Rawal Dam was very enjoyable. Hasib particularly enjoyed it. He loved stroking the goats. He even tried to catch some fishes when he went in to water. He laughed and became very excited when he noticed some fishes in the stream. The goats were small and are known as "Sindhi goats". I remember my Grandfather kept a few and my mother was also very keen to breed them as their offspring brought good money if they were sold at market. I noticed that Hasib would run if an animal came running after him, but when he approach them himself he would do it in a very calm way, or slowly follow them.

We spent most of our time at home sorting our things out.

We went to see our relatives, and once or twice to a local garden called Liaqat Bagh. Some children came to play with Hasib and were friendly towards him. He was offered ice cream and sweets. I told Hasib that his grandfather had once run a very successful transport business in Liaqat Bagh where his bus station was situated before we moved to the main road close to Gawal Mandi Bridge. I pointed out to Hasib the space where our 5 buses used to park. Due to the hot weather, Hasib sometimes felt very hot and his cheeks became red and flaky. He would turn the water fountain on and cool himself down under the water. He would sometimes climb over the fountain. This big fountain was built by my father in our house for his grandchildren.

We have so many videos of Hasib in our house in Rawalpindi. After the 7/7 incident, I saw a short clip of him in a video wearing shorts and climbing on top of fountain. I became very upset and asked my wife not to show me them again.

My father had planted some small trees in our Rawalpindi house and they were growing rapidly. One of our neighbours had a big black goat and a baby goat. I was cutting some tree branches and somehow that goat was outside our house and waiting for fresh green leaves. I gave some to the goat and it started eating them. Hasib came out of the room and asked me if he could feed some more leaves to the goat. He became very hysterical and excited and kept feeding them. Then he started to bring goats inside our house and fed them. He loved stroking them and a few times he tried to milk one of them, but failed. There were a lot of flies if food was not covered properly and Hasib would try to catch them in his hand. There were some frogs and other insects in our garden but he would never hurt them or cause them any harm. He would put a little frog in his hand and play with it.

Hasib was closer to his mother than me. He was quiet in his childhood and also in his youth. He always talked in a respectful manner. I really never found anything wrong with him but if I had to tell him something, he would listen very carefully and take notice. I never had to stop him from doing anything as a child because he wouldn't do anything wrong in first place. He was very careful and responsible as a child and as a young man.

Nowadays it's not easy to get permission from school to take your child abroad. It is possible that unauthorised time off could result in your child being expelled from school. But I am talking about the good old days when you could take your child abroad for long holidays. I always informed school and brought my children back very soon if they went abroad as I always put their education first.

We planned our return; our seats were confirmed and we started to pack our things. My mother-in-law was in Pakistan and she came to see us in Pindi. My operation wounds were getting a little better. My wife wanted to travel to see her mother and sister as my wife didn't know when she would see them again. I thought Hasib would enjoy seeing our ancestral home again. We hired a taxi again and returned to Mirpur. We stayed there for a couple of days. My wife went back to our village of Dhangri for the first time in 35 years. She was almost three when she had emigrated to England with her parents. She had returned to Pakistan since but always stayed with her parents in Mirpur city and had never visited her ancestral home which was about an hour from Mirpur. She had stayed there with her parents in rented accommodation and then married me in 1974. Travelling back to Pakistan in 1969 was a sad story but I have no space here to add anything about that.

So Hasib, my wife and I returned to Mirpur for a second time. This village used to be called Dhangri Bala but now for some religious or spiritual reasons, it's now been changed to Dhangri Sharif. My mother-in-law and sister-in-law looked after us very well. The old house had been demolished and rebuilt and now it had some modern features such as electricity, running water, a flushing toilet and there were some shops nearby. The house was bigger than before with a huge garden, a lot of fruit trees and some livestock. The grounds were a lush green with different kinds of birds singing. One distant relative was also living there and enjoying free food and British money. Three days later his son also appeared and stayed there. There weren't any power cuts while we were there and the electric fans carried on spinning. But the most natural thing was as soon as fresh winds picked up, the trees were also buzzing. It's like the air condition was working. We did not feel the heat here as we had in Rawalpindi. This was a huge, open and green place and we enjoyed the fresh, pure air.

Sometimes it made my wife and I angry when the man who was living there started demanding not only food but money as well. Then his son came back from Saudi Arabia and he was also a scavenger. I did not like it at all. I felt a little bit sorry for my mother-in-law but it was her business and I couldn't intervene. Perhaps she was tolerating them as she was alone in that big house or may be it was something else, I really don't know. I didn't want to put a burden on her and asked my wife if we could go home early but she insisted on staying longer.

My mother-in-law had a huge garden; I would say it was a big field which was full of oranges, mangoes, bananas, lemons as well as fig tree and guava trees. The guava fruit was delicious and I ate a lot of them. I forgot that guava is a laxative and the water change made my stomach upset. My mother-in-law was an excellent cook. She had a clay oven and she would make fresh chapattis with home grown wheat. I noticed that she had burned her arms when she baked chapattis in the oven. She would not allow my wife or her sister to help. I felt sadness towards my mother-in-law as she had 9 children and was living there alone protecting her ancestral property. It was a remarkable struggle. I am sad and ashamed to talk about it as some Pakistani people occupy the properties and lands of people who emigrate to England. The police and the justice system in Pakistan are a disgrace, with unimaginable crooked behaviour.

One example: a woman was struggling to get back her ancestral land from wicked people in her village. Although she did manage to get back some land from the occupiers, she died there while protecting her property. After her death, the Government of Pakistan and also the so-called Independent Government of Jammu and Kashmir, decided to upgrade Mangla Dam so the house and the land would be submerged in water. The irony was that her sons were not capable of managing or interested in keeping the ancestral home and land. They are British-Pakistanis. They wouldn't bother about the house and land. All they wanted was their share but no responsibility. And unfortunately this will happen to most of us who are settled in England. We will suffer unimaginable heartache and consequences. It's only a matter of time. It also includes me. My mother-in-law did what she could to please us and personally, I am very grateful for her kind hospitality. To please us, she baked millet and maize chapattis. She put some butter and cane sugar on top. The butter was the purest you could get freshly made from cow's milk. It was delicious and a real taste of village life.

We made plans to go to the Indian border. We hired a taxi but as we were half way there, we heard that a massive landslide had blocked the road. We were right at the top of a hill and could see the stunning views. It's like heaven on earth; big mountains with trees and greenery everywhere. We saw a big masjid and a shrine at the top of the hill. It was a very quiet and peaceful area and we loved it. Hasib wanted to go up to the border area but we abandoned our plans because of the danger of further landslides. It had been raining a day before our travel. We have seen nature very closely and that was enough for us.

We had to return to Rawalpindi because we were due back in England. My wife's sister was due to fly back a day before us and she came to visit our house with her mother and some relatives. While we were in our village in Dhangri Sharif, my wife and I went to see a mango tree near our house. When we were little, we used to sit under the tree and pick ripe yellow mangos. There were some children there and they were doing the same. Sometimes we fought over the quantity of mangoes. My wife and I were pleased to see that mango tree again. We took some unforgettable photos and we talked about our precious time together there. This tree was still very big and healthy. We were told that this mango tree was still very popular and people came from all over to take its ripe mangoes.

We couldn't take Hasib with us because it was raining and muddy. The man who was looking after our house had a long wooden stick and two barrelled shot gun. It was old but enough to scare people. Hasib was playing with that gun when we returned.

The old man had inserted two real bullets and Hasib aimed at the tree and fired both shots. He laughed and Hasib asked him to fill the gun again but the old man was not prepared to do that as I stopped him. Hasib was only a small child and should not play with guns especially with loaded guns. It was too dangerous. There were also different types of birds and they would sing and make beautiful sounds. They were colourful, extra-ordinary and eye-catching. Hasib always pointed out where the birds were sitting and singing. We have a small jungle near our house and a lot of trees. I went there with Hasib to see the birds and different type of trees. Hasib loved every minute and had a very good experience of village life.

The political situation in Pakistan raised its head a few times. I was in Dhangri Sharif and I had to go to the local masjid for Friday prayer. I had been reading my daily prayers at home because of illness. I took Hasib with me and slowly walked to a nearby mosque. We met a man who had come from England. This masjid is attached to a graveyard. As we entered, the Imam was speaking out against the then leader Benazir Bhutto. Instead of preaching faith and telling people to be good and look after other people and not to occupy other people's land and homes, he was swearing about this particular politician and saying bad things against her and her party. I was shocked. He was a Kashmiri political leader more than a religious preacher. I later found out he was not only an Imam and political leader, he was also the owner of the masjid. A shrine was attached to this masjid. Someone told me that nearly half of this masjid was built on a cemetery. People complimented the imam saying that he was a very influential person with connections in England so he could do whatever he likes. I was just there to read my Friday prayers.

As soon as I came out of the masjid a few men were shouting and telling worshippers to visit the shrine adjacent to it. A person took us to the shrine. I saw some people kissing the grave and asking for something in their prayers. Some were standing at the side of the grave and bowing down and kissing it. The marble grave was huge, it must have cost thousands of pounds to build. I saw one old man putting his forehead on the grave as if he was asking something from this dead person. Hasib and I were shocked as to why these people were kissing the grave. It's fundamentally and religiously wrong in my opinion. A dead person cannot give you anything. There is no basis for this in our faith. If they think a dead man can give something good to them, it's their luck. I have no intention to say anything against them. It's just that I was not brought up like that so I have different beliefs regarding this matter.

Unfortunately, the majority of Kashmiri people are under the influence of these so called "Religious Leaders" who are fundamentally wrong and take advantage of them. Most Kashmiris are divided into a caste system and they have no collective interest just personal interests. On top of that they are also divided by Sects and again, unfortunately, all these things bring hate among lower and higher castes. The politicians and religious leaders take advantage of these divisions and make their living. I just read some Qu'ranic verses and asked Allah to forgive the man his sins and came out of the shrine. When I came out I read a small calligraphic marble stone which was fixed to a wall, I realised that the shrine was dedicated to a religious teacher who taught me as a child. He had lived near our ancestral house when I was small. Now, after his death, he had become a saint like figure and people worshipped him. May Allah forgive his sins and others!

As I have mentioned earlier, my sister-in-law wanted to come with us to Rawalpindi as she had to fly back from Islamabad airport. We returned to Rawalpindi with her and a few other relatives. She stayed with us for 2 days and flew back to England. When we were coming back to Rawalpindi, the police stopped our van many times and asked for tea money or I would say bluntly, police tax. The van driver had to pay and that extra cash came out of our pockets. Hasib asked each time why we were stopped and I explained to him what was going on. It was not only the police that stopped us, there were some beggars also after our money. It's a good business. Once we were sorting out the business with the police, a beggar asked for money from a passenger who was travelling in a car. He shouted at him and said "You thief" and told him to push off. The beggar shouted back and told him off and said "you are a bigger thief than I am. You stole money from UK's tax department, Social Security, VAT and all your money invested in your big bungalow!" He nearly hit him with his stick. We were amazed and laughed at his blunt reply. He was saying something which was true and applied to some people. Of course most people are law abiding and hard working. Most of the Mirpuri beggars would ask for a few coins. It was the same at Islamabad Airport.

My wife started packing. It was very hot and sometimes she would work all day and pack. I also asked Hasib if he could start packing his things, and to keep his personal things in his hand bag and the rest in our suitcases. Hasib's hand bag was open and there was only one string, you could pull it and the bag closed. We didn't know what he was packing. We thought it would be his usual things. We had to pack our household items away like kitchen utensils, furniture, fridge and other small and big items. I think most Pakistani and Mirpuri people would experience this and they have to pack and put them away safely because people do not care for them. My brother was also with us and he didn't do anything. My operation wound meant I was unable to lift heavy items but I still helped my wife. Hasib did what he could. He helped his mother and sorted a few things for her. I was very upset because both my brothers disappeared on this day when I needed them most. We had to manage by ourselves. My wife and I are normally self-sufficient and we do not rely on others, but I was ill so I needed the help. They never missed an opportunity to grab money from me and my wife but now they just did not want to help.

The story of the building of our house in Pakistan is strange. When I came to England in 1976, and as usual, I had experienced a few things which I did not like at all. There was too much freedom and children not listening and all other things which I hope most Asian people would know now. I thought, if I have my own house in Pakistan I could take my children regularly and they would be able to understand our culture and the way we live in Pakistan. I asked my father to buy a small piece of land but he bought it very near to our old house. Although I didn't like that place at all, I kept quiet because I dare not hurt my father's feelings. I asked my father to build enough rooms so we could stay there for a few weeks; two bedrooms, a kitchen, a bathroom and a sitting room – that would be enough for us. If I needed more space, I would deal with it in the future. I never had any need for a big house. I am a simple person and I would not waste money to please others or show off. So I drew up a simple plan and sent it to my father and agreed to pay the costs and sent all the money up front. But he spent all the money to make a very big house. I asked him after a couple of months how it was progressing and he said he needed a lot of money to finish it off. I never asked him to build a huge house and spend all that money! He wanted to build according to his own plan and I was stuck now and had no choice other than to send more money. It was a considerable amount.

There were some of his friends who were pushing for him to build an even bigger house as they were saying to him, "your son is in England and you do not have to worry about money" and my father carried on listening to them or may be there was another reason, I'm not sure. My father completed the building work. He fell ill many times during this time and workers did not build the house carefully and some problems accrued which I had to put right later. When the house was completed, the only person living in that house was my father. Although he kept it very clean, well decorated and looked after it properly, it was too much for him as he was an old man. I had another problem, my brothers and some other relatives were jealous of this house and they thought I had become superior to them and they started causing trouble for me. My father was an old man and not feeling well. Maybe my father thought he did the best for me, however he told me once that he needed at least two women to clean the house! He would stay in that house every day and sleep alone despite his 6 children who lived nearby in our old house.

A year later, unfortunately, they found him dead in my house after he got up for his Fajr prayer. After his tragic death, I would need to write another book but I will just touch on this topic in the form of a very short story to explain what happened. Thank

God, my house is still there and Allah has put it in good use and hopefully after my death it will be used in a better way. I have tried to sell my house many times but I have been unsuccessful. My brothers tried to destroy me and some other relatives as well, but I'm still here and so is the house. My older brother "looked after" the house just to grab money from me. Then my younger brother asked me if he could have that house and use one room. I paid all the bills and repair costs for more than 9 years. I spent a lot of money for repairs because he wouldn't do anything and I had to go to Pakistan to do it myself. After Hasib's tragic loss, I went to Pakistan and I was shocked to see the state of my house and told him if he could not look after it properly I would kick him out. He answered that I never gave him anything and that was enough for me – I kicked him out. He was not only making a good living out of my house but he built another house of his own with the income he earned there. He was still not happy. Soon after leaving my house, he lost everything and his business. Sometimes you learn the hard way.

Another example after Hasib's loss was when I returned to Pakistan. One of my brothers came to my sister's house where I was staying and brought a crooked woman asking for money. Instead of showing any sympathy towards me, he was asking for money. This was the brother who was swearing to my dead mother and father. I will not forgive him. My parents were happy with me and I had done everything in my capacity to please them and I am satisfied that when they went they went happy with me. I had very hard times and I am still in very difficult circumstances, but I believe my creator always tests me and He will be the one who gives us rewards afterwards.

I was honoured by Allah that he gave me the ability to perform Hajj for both my parents. I am very honoured that my Allah gives me more ability to do good deeds for them. I had a dream once, my father was saying to me "son I have built a house in Pakistan for you and also a house where our prophet Mohammed (pbuh) is buried" after that sign, I do not need anything. If my house is near to our Prophet Mohammed's (pbuh) burial place then what else do

I need? I am a humble servant of Allah and I tried hard to fulfil my duties according to my faith and I am very grateful and appreciate fully what I have in my life.

People who have emigrated to England, in my opinion, have lost a lot but gained very little. I am sure we will never be able to recover from this damage. Our decisions will affect future generations. Most Pakistani and Kashmiri people know what I am talking about. We are in a very difficult position and most of the next generation are in trouble and do not listen to their parents. We came here for a bright future but we have lost it. I will give you an example. A while ago, a well known author wrote that when the British left India almost two hundred thousand workers went with them, soon after those émigrés also lost their identity. In my opinion, I may be wrong, but this is a fact that will also happen to us. Not many people return to Pakistan and become successful there, eventually they have to return to England. The kids who travel to Pakistan get a lot of hassle from their relatives and they don't like to go back. The reason for writing all this is that we take our children to Pakistan and Kashmir and they get a very rough deal from their relatives and local people. Sometimes they treat us as though we are from other planet. They see us as wallets to be picked!

I have been living in England since 1976 and truthfully, I never return from Pakistan happy. If our relatives have spared us, then at the airport we are robbed and humiliated by officials. If a shopkeeper finds out that you are from England, then you lose your skin. It is shameful! Hasib was no exception. He saw everything and was not happy at all. He had a very bad impression of Pakistani police and Airport authorities. Bear in mind, it's very possible, despite building huge homes for them; our new generation would not want to know Pakistan in the future.

The importance and the reasons for me to write about these circumstances are that we Pakistani and Kashmiri immigrants face a lot of difficulties when we go back and visit our country. Almost every year the Pakistani Government makes it more difficult to travel here. Pakistani passport, ID cards and on top of that our national airline, which never showed any profit in its history, take advantage and raise fares. If we compare this with other airlines, for example Indian airlines, they fly further than Islamabad but their fares are very cheap and Indian children can visit India by paying a lot less than PIA.

Most Pakistani travellers will know what happens at Islamabad airport and how they have been treated by customs and immigration officers. It is disgusting. Pakistan became independent over 60 years ago and previous generations gave their blood to that land but what have we achieved? A customs officer cannot differentiate between bribe and charity. He has no understanding of Halal and Haram. Of course, there are good officers, but I have not found many!

Now I come to an unexpected, disgraceful and shameful experience. An innocent Pakistani British child travels to Pakistan with his parents and goes to see his parent's birth place. He picks up a few stones as souvenirs and plays with a very small pistol type key ring and innocently takes one empty casing of bullet with him and puts it into his hand bag and takes it to a local international airport. We did not know that Hasib was carrying these items with him at the airport. He had the pistol key ring from England and an empty bullet case from Rawalpindi from his uncle. Hasib did not have a pellet bow or cross bow, otherwise it would have been even more difficult for us.

Islamabad airport is not far from our house. Firstly, custom officers ask us to open all our suitcases. I opened them despite it being a big operation. I got some help from Hasib and his mother but that was not enough. Our suitcases were searched along with the other passengers. The other passengers were looking at our items and of course, we were not blind and obviously, we had our eyes on their stuff too. We passengers were all in the same situation and I found it very humiliating and felt as if we had been stripped naked. There was no privacy at all. To put this in context, I have never been asked by a British custom officer to open my suitcase since 1976!

Anyway, Hasib was a little boy and he was ordered to go through customs with his mother. Unfortunately, I was carrying about 4 kg of mangos for my children. He told me that I cannot take the mangos with me. The custom officers reminded me that I needed an export licence to take mangos abroad. I laughed. I told him I was taking them for my children not to sell in a market. I also saw that other passengers were taking boxes of mangos with them. I told him again that I don't eat many mangos as I am diabetic but these are for my children. He insisted and eventually I told him to keep them and give them as a present to his family. I think it was enough for him and he said I could take them with me. I do not know how much money he made from other passengers by just telling them they needed a licence to take mangos abroad.

My wife and Hasib were being searched. The uniformed lady custom officer was very arrogant. She called me and asked me to follow her along with Hasib and his mother. She took us in a room where there was a very senior customs officer sitting in a chair, he had stars on his shoulders. The lady custom officer was carrying Hasib's hand bag. I was looking at my wife suspiciously and she was worried. We were all standing before a Pakistani senior customs officer. The lady informed him that she had found precious stones, a bullet and a pistol in the child's hand bag! I nearly collapsed at this point. She told him that she had found weapons in the hand bag but now "all the weapons were in her control". I thought, maybe someone placed them in Hasib's bag, but I was sure that nobody else had touched my son's bag. I tried to keep my nerve. I asked them what kind of weapons they had found. The senior customs officer told me he had to write a report and I must sign it. He handed over a blank piece of paper to me and asked me to put my signature on it as on my passport. I told him that before I did that he had to let me see the illegal weapons first. He shouted at me and informed me that all weapons have been confiscated and they are now Pakistani government property. He asked me again to place my signature on a blank piece of paper. I refused and insisted on seeing the weapons. Then he started writing about the pistol, bullet and precious stones and then again ordered me to sign. I refused again. He shouted and said "you are going to miss your flight."

I shouted back and said "To hell with the flight I am not in a rush and the plane will not leave without my family. Let me see the weapons first. I am not going to sign your paper!"

Luckily the office door was open and the other passengers could hear me shouting and most of them started looking at us. He said "I am telling you for the last time, sign it, otherwise I will arrest you, your wife and your child."

When I heard this I lost my temper and shouted at him as loudly as I could and told him off in way that he will remember for the rest his life. Perhaps he had a conscience because when he saw my anger and refusal to pay him a bribe, he backed off. I reminded him about his shitty behaviour in front of my son and wife. I will never take this abuse. It doesn't matter where I am living, in England or Pakistan. I told this idiot custom officer (who was trying to frame me and Hasib so he could get a lot of money from me), "I do not care if the flight is getting late or I am not going back home, I will never give you money for a bribe."

I then asked Hasib and he told me that he had got a few little stones, a pistol type small key ring and an empty bent bullet shell in his bag and the lady took them. He told me how he got those and he was taking them to England as they were not dangerous items. I now realised what the matter was. I told Hasib and my wife not to worry and I will deal with the officer. I told him it was in his best interests to return our stuff. He was still asking for my signature and I told him to get stuffed and sign himself. He then said we will settle this matter very easily as he had not arrested me or Hasib, and all I needed to do was to just make this woman happy and give her something. I shouted again and refused to do that. "You are a dishonest customs officer and also your colleague." I demanded all my things back and swore at him. He left saying something to his colleague and soon after she returned the items including the handbag. This was the most disgraceful behaviour I ever seen and Hasib experienced it all in front of the other passengers.

Hasib was upset and frightened to lose his things but now he was happy to get them back. We were very tired, and as soon as we sat down on the aeroplane we all nodded off. Islamabad airport is only a mile or so from our house. I feel very sorry for those passengers who travel from far away to catch flights and then they get this sort of treatment from customs and immigration officers.

I have also experienced this at Karachi airport. The customs officers have the same mentality, they just make a passenger's life hell. I have been going back to Pakistan regularly for over 40 years and I have not seen any improvement.

The improvement is not building huge houses or having a good life style by taking bribes and living on immoral income. Improvement is looking after your fellow human beings; morality, working hard, gaining respect for your country and being an ambassador for your country. Look what is going on in Pakistan! We are not treated well because we have lost our morality and dignity.

Hasib joined school when he returned from Pakistan. He stayed with us for 3 weeks in Pakistan and I bet he learned a lot from it. As I have said before, we never had complaints about Hasib. His teacher asked him about his experience while he was in Pakistan and as he told me he was happy and if he got another chance, he would like to go to again.

4. MARRIAGE AND MOVE TO ENGLAND

WHEN I WAS about 19 years old, my wife to be returned to Pakistan with her family. At the time I was working at a military base as an Auditor. My wife's parents were not initially interested in me because they had wanted their daughter to marry someone else who was from a rich family (this is a very long story of family horse trading) and my father became very upset when he heard these remarks and backed off but suddenly my wife's parents changed their minds and agreed to give their daughter's hand to me. I was over the moon because my wife and I had always liked each other since we were little when we had played together as children. We were somehow very attached to each other despite her moving to England with her family when she was a teenager.

From the start it was obvious that I wanted her more than she wanted me. Nevertheless, I was so excited that I told everybody that I was going to marry my childhood sweetheart. My wife and I got married in 1974. We were very happy.

Not long after my in-laws and their children wanted to return to England. All the Pakistani airports were shut due to tension between India and Pakistan. My father had made arrangements to take them to Afghanistan by crossing the Pakistani border, and they flew back to England from Kabul airport via the Soviet Union. My wife was very upset when she said goodbye to her parents. However she was very happy with me and I tried my utmost to look after her. Our financial circumstances were not good at that time but we managed. She would stay at home and I travelled to another city to work and every weekend I would return home for the weekend and go back to work on Monday morning. Nothing in this world is perfect. I love my wife and I will carry on loving her until my last breath. There are millions of reasons to love her but now I love her more because she is Hasib's mother and he is no longer with us.

One day I came back from work and heard that my wife was pregnant. I was very happy and so was my wife. My father was happy too and it was the first time I had seen a smile on his face for a long time. In fact, he looked happier than the rest of the family. My in-laws wanted to bring my wife to England when they heard this news. They were worried about her health. I wasn't happy at all about my wife returning to England. My wife was upset too and my father was under huge pressure from my in-laws so he decided to send my wife back to England. However, when my father checked her passport he found that it had expired sometime ago. In fact, she had overstayed and she had to reapply for an entry clearance visa if she wanted to go, so it wasn't easy at all. She went to the British Embassy with my father and was interviewed by the Embassy official and she was granted a visa. At that time my wife was heavily pregnant with our first child, and she was weak too. I was devastated when she got her visa, but slowly I managed to control myself and thought about my daughter's future, and I also thought about following her to England later. I had to swallow that bitter pill for the time being. Although it was very upsetting for us to separate, my wife was ready to go, and I assured her that we had a bright future to come even though it broke my heart.

My wife and my unborn child left me on 17th December 1974 at 12.05 am from Islamabad airport bound for London. When we were at the airport she wanted to embrace me, and I wanted to hug her in a way that nobody on this earth would try to detach us, but she was snatched away from me. It still tears me apart when I remember that horrible time. It was a long time ago but those memories are still fresh. I walked home because the airport was only a short distance from our house. The flight left at 2.30am and I saw the plane flying right over our house knowing my sweetheart was on it.

"I reached home safely" was the first telegram I received from her. She had arrived on 17th December 1974 and joined her parents. It was like someone had cut me in two. I became very lonely, isolated and depressed. I couldn't settle and was unable to go to work for a while. With my wife back in England, I had no idea when we would see each other again. I started writing letters to her. We were apart for 1 year and 8 months. I would write two letters a week and she would reply to me the same. We wrote more than 216 letters to each other during this period. Each letter was unique, full of love and of course very private.

I came home from work one day and my father informed me that he had heard that spouses who came to Pakistan and got married there but move to England can call their husband or wife to join them. He had also heard that the British government was making some new immigration rules, but he wasn't sure when. In early 1975 I applied for a Pakistani passport. Naturally, I had to give some bribes to the passport office to ensure I was successful, I then went to the British Embassy in Islamabad with my father and handed in my application. I think mine was the first test case. The Embassy said that they would write to me after receiving clarification from the Home Office. An interview date was sent to me by post of August 1977. I was shocked and dismayed at the time-scale! Of course, even after waiting so long, there was no guarantee of getting a visa, it could be rejected again. As I said, I was the first husband who applied for a visa to join my wife in England and I had received an interview date almost two and a half years away! It was like a prison sentence. Now I had very little chance of seeing my wife. I became more upset when I heard the news that our beautiful baby girl was born on 21st March 1975 knowing I wouldn't see her until she was at least two years old.

I become very depressed and the British official (Mr Osborne) who issued the long interview date had a job to handle me. I started writing letters to him asking for a review of the interview date to see if they could bring it forward. I had no problems typing my letters because I had a typewriter in my office. Mr Osborne (God rest his soul) answered my letters and explained about the new immigration policy for newly-weds. I think he and the British Home Office knew that this was the most inhumane immigration policy. For goodness sake, come to your senses - how could newly-weds stay apart for two and a half years? Why do they always apply this sort of stupid immigration policy to Pakistani, Bangladeshi and Indian people? Would you apply these policies to a white man and woman? Of course not.

At the end of my constant letters to Mr Osborne, or perhaps because of some policy changes, he brought forward my interview date to 17th July 1976. I have still got carbon copies of the letters I wrote him. I also kept all his replies. My wife also wrote to him requesting an early appointment. Now, despite the date being a year earlier, I kept writing to Mr Osborne until the day got nearer to my interview date. As I have mentioned above, it wasn't guaranteed that I would get a visa.

At last the day came and I went to the British Embassy in Islamabad with my father and a dear friend of mine. One of my cousins had also applied for a visa and was due to be interviewed, I saw him at the Embassy. I was interviewed by Mr Osborne himself in the presence of an interpreter. After some formalities, Mr Osborne asked me if I had my wife's letters with me. I opened a bag and took a huge pile of letters out and put them on his desk and suggested he read whichever he liked and he's free to take his time. As he picked one up, I opened a one meter long birthday card which my wife sent me and I laid down this on the table too. Mr Osborne laughed and said "hand over your passport and fee" I then thanked him and came out of the room. I paid a 60 Rupee fee and came out of the Embassy building with a stamp on my passport which said "granted entry clearance to join wife in England".

I arrived in England to join my wife and daughter leaving my father, mother, brothers and sisters behind on 15th August 1976. I will always be grateful to England and Mr Osborne who provided me with the opportunity for this bright future. Now I was ready for a new life in a new country with a new family. I was a young man looking toward a bright future, but it wasn't easy at all. Unfortunately, my new family weren't so considerate. My uncle, who had once tried to bring me to England, and another older uncle invited me for dinner and gave me about £22, which I immediately sent to my father. I was billeted at my in-laws which was already overcrowded. They gave me my marching orders after a month! I started looking for a job and visited various work sites with my uncle day and night. I wasn't aware of the word "Paki" but some "Goray" people called me a "New Paki" on the street. I asked my uncle "how do they know that I am clean?" "Paki" translates to me as "clean". My uncle laughed and explained, and that's how I come to understand what they meant when the "Goray" said "Paki" to me again.

Fortunately I found a job in a steel foundry a month after arriving in Britain. Each day at work was different. I worked alongside a large number of first generation Polish workers and some English too. The Poles would call me a "Paki" and call the black men "Nigger". Now knowing the offensive meaning of "Paki", I always kept my cool because I couldn't risk starting a fight with any of them for fear of losing my job. I knew if I did anything wrong I would be sacked. I needed the money and it was a crucial time for me. I was now responsible for my wife and child as well as 8 more people who were relying on me back home. Swear words, calling a Muslim a Paki and treating other coloured workers in offensive terms, was normal in 1970s Britain. Some Polish men were extremely rude to me when I went to my locker room and showered. At the same time as getting this job, I had to find somewhere to live having been kicked out from my relative's house. So, I was always conscious that if I said anything to any of them I would be in deep trouble and out of a job with nowhere to stay.

When I started earning money I opened a bank account and started looking for my own place. My wife was always with me and we decided to buy a house near to my in-laws. As we were looking for a house I saw a small board inside the window which said "House for sale, no blacks or Asians". I was shocked but my wife ignored my concerns because she had lived for some time in England and was used to this sort of hatred. She was only 3 years old when she came to England with her family and she was educated at a local school and worked for a short time. She also suffered with racism in the work place and on the streets of Holbeck, even though she has lived there all her life. "Paki bashing" and racially motivated hatred was a normal thing for her.

As we were looking to buy our first house I visited many banks looking for a mortgage and they all refused. One of them told me privately that his bank would not give loans to people of Pakistani origin. I won't disclose the names of those banks who discriminated against me and my wife! I then went to the bank where I had opened my bank account. They also refused and said something awful to me. Then I went to a private lender who told me that he only provides loans to "his own". When my wife asked for an explanation, he said "We give loans to Jewish businessmen and market traders". It is worth remembering I was working nights and during the day I was mortgage hunting and so I wasn't getting enough sleep. It was awful. In the end,I managed to get a loan from a local building society and we bought our first and last house.

When we moved in we weren't exactly welcomed with open arms – one of my neighbours was a white man who immediately put his house up for sale the day we moved in. Then he refused to sell his house to a coloured family. Their behaviour towards us was very discriminatory. They complained to us many times about the smell of curry and even suggested angrily that we should shut our doors and windows when we cooked. Eventually he and his family managed to sell their house and left. They always gave us a dirty look on the rare occasions when they saw us on the streets, so we always avoided them.

Being a Muslim, arriving from Pakistan and trying to settle in England was a struggle and one of the most difficult tasks I've ever had to face. I was working 12 hours a day or more. It felt like slavery at times - the white people at my place wouldn't work more than 8 hours a day! The treatment from some Polish and white workers was horrendous. Both Polish and white men were the same for me, their racist behaviour was the same. They wouldn't say anything to each other but they terrorised me a lot. Some German men also worked with me and often called me a "Paki" and openly said bad things about Jews and used to make some gesture about them. Of course, I had no idea what they were saying but they would continue with their humiliating gestures toward Jews, even though no Jews worked in the factory! They would say a lot against Islam and Muslims as well so they weren't just anti-Semitic.

Aside from the abuse, conditions at the foundry were pretty grim. There were no tea or lunch breaks and we had to push hard to get any kind of break. If a white man sat down for tea or lunch, it was acceptable to management but when a Muslim worker sat down it would be a different story. I always feared for my job so I kept some dried food in my pockets and ate it whenever I was hungry, I dare not eat curry in front of white workers. A South African supervisor was very disrespectful to me and other Muslim workers. He would never call us by name. He would always say something irritating and disrespectful. Calling us "Paki" and using abusive swear words was a normal thing for him. If someone dared to complain to the department manager, then the excuse was that it was "Industrial Language" and there was the chance he would be transferred to another job the next day, or got even get the sack if he persisted.

Each year we could never take a day off for Eid. Many Muslims workers had been sacked for just taking a day off for Eid prayers. If someone asked for a day off then the answer would be "take the day off and stay home". To be honest with you, and I swear by God, I never took a day off for Eid for fear of losing my job. I was aware of the financial hardships and I couldn't put my family here or in Pakistan in a difficult position. The other problem were the shameful arguments between Indian, Pakistani and other Asian workers. Some of them hated each other. The Indians and Pakistani didn't like each other because of the war. I was fighting on all fronts! I faced a lot of racism from Indians. It's funny but an Indian worker would also call a Pakistan worker a "Paki" in anger because he is from Pakistan. It was very hard for me to adjust to this kind of racist environment.

I worked non-stop and then one day in 1993 I came home from work to be told that my father was very ill, this was obviously very upsetting. If I dared to take leave from my job, there was a good chance I'd lose it so I decided to wait until the 2 week July holidays knowing that I may lose my father before then. I talked to my supervisor about his illness and asked for an extra week with my holidays but he refused and suggested to me that I should take "Compassionate Leave" which I did. I was granted an extra week without pay and I was asked to report back to work on my due date. Written permission was given to me but when I returned to work, my job had gone to somebody else. I protested and reminded them about the letter but nobody was prepared to listen to me. I was threatened by the departmental manager who had given me permission. He told me off and made remarks about my father. I reminded him of the agreement saying that it's unfair and he must behave like a manager, but he continued to threaten that he had the power to sack me there and then. I lost my temper and told him that I would take him and his racist company to an industrial tribunal. In turn he kept calling me a "troublemaker Paki" and sent me home on that day and asked me to come back the next day. I went back to work the next day and complained to a union rep. He also started shouting at me and humiliating me in front of management, the next day I stopped paying my contributions to that union and joined another. I was under huge financial pressure; I had just bought a house and other things were on my mind so I had no choice but to accept another job.

By the way it was my uncle, my father's brother, who had taken my job while I was in Pakistan and he conspired with the manager, union man and the departmental manager because he provided a lot of skirts, trousers and dresses to their "Mem Sahibs" as he was also running a market trading business at the time. Tell me, how can one man fight a traitor and corrupt management at the same time? I accepted a new job but it affected me a lot. I lost a lot of weight and suffered from stomach ulcers. I kept working despite all that because I needed the money for my family. I had started working for this company in 1976 and worked with hardly a break until 1993. I had worked day and night tirelessly. I became a diabetic and in June 1993 I had an accident at work. Both my legs were badly burnt because a shell mould had burst as soon as molten metal was poured in to it. Again, I was very scared because if I took time off, I may lose my job. I kept working 12 hour shifts and it got better after three months. I still have some scarring on my thighs. I was offered £800 compensation by the company's insurance and I accepted that very low amount as my sisters were getting married and my father needed the money.

I had helped my brother and sister to settle in England but they wouldn't help my dad and, as I was the eldest son, I was solely responsible. I have no regrets at all – my father had stuck by me and I had no hesitation whatsoever to continue to help him.

This was the background to our family settling in Leeds. It was tough, but no tougher than the average experience of Pakistanis in England.

5. HASIB'S EDUCATION

IN THE AFTERMATH of the 7/7 bomb it was widely reported that Hasib was 'poorly educated' and a 'below average student'. This was far from the case. In this chapter, I will look at some of his educational achievements at nursery, school and college. I will summarise them because the details would take up too much room.

Hasib was a very good student, almost all his teachers praised and commended him for his work. In his 1991 school report his teacher M. Passman wrote, "Hasib can write his name and tell the difference between colours and can count from 1–8 without any hesitation. He can draw and make pictures with different kinds of colours. He takes a full interest in class and is keen to learn different skills. Hasib enjoys drawing with different colours and uses chalks. Hasib plays and take part in various games with his cousin and spends most his time with his cousin. Hasib finds it difficult to speak in clear English and his mother had been asked to help him to speak English. Hasib's personal and social skills are extremely good and are developing very well. Hasib is doing very well in English, maths, science, art, environment, PE, personal and social skills. He works very hard in those subjects and takes a lot of interest. All teachers are satisfied with his educational progress and he is doing very well in all subjects.

In Easter 1992, when Hasib joined the higher class, all the teachers were happy with his progress, educational and social development and praised him for doing good work in all subjects.

1992/93: Hasib has improved his writing skills and is doing very well and completed his school homework. All his teachers praised him for his good work in English, Maths, Science, Technology, Geography, History, Arts, Music, Physical and Religious Education. They wrote satisfactory reports. In his yearly report it was stated that Hasib had taken 34.5 days off from school without prior school permission. It continued, "Hasib was well spoken and a responsible student. Hasib can recognise his skills and abilities. Hasib has written his personal comments regarding school that 'he is going to school to do work'." Hasib had signed his name beneath the comments.

Hasib's teacher praised him for his educational skills and achievements and written "well done Hasib." Continuing, "Hasib is doing well in his class and relates well with other classmates." They wrote good comments about Hasib's education and skills. All teachers are satisfied with him.

1994/95 report – year 3: "Hasib is doing well in English, Maths, Science Technology, Geography, History, Music, and Physical and Religious education.

In the religious section the teacher has written that, "Hasib has a good knowledge in more than two religions. He has taken part in school assemblies and also took part in a drama and successfully acted as a Roman policeman."

In the history section his teacher wrote that "Hasib has a very good knowledge of current and past history. Hasib also has a good knowledge of British history and knows a lot of British historic events after 1930."

In the section of physical education, his height is noted. "He is a lot taller than his peers but he didn't experience any difficulties playing with his school friends. He gets on with everybody and enjoys their company." The report was signed by his class and head teacher.

1995/95: "Hasib is a very quiet person and he talks to others with great respect and dignity and his manners are extremely respectful. His relationship with his classmates is warm and affectionate and he has special bonds with his peers. Hasib is good in Maths and he always presents his school and homework neatly and with great care. He is very conscientious in Technology and loves learning about History. He is eager and enjoys playing with others and willing to take part in the games." Hasib got 4 merits cards and has 31 merit awards on them. Each merit shows why they were awarded to him and each merit has got the signatures of his teachers. One of his teachers said on his report that he enjoys Hasib's artwork.

1997/98: "Hasib worked extremely hard this year and has shown a very good progress in different skills, especially in technical skills but still he was asked to work hard to make improvements and concentrate on his overall learning skills. Hasib has a lot of potential and takes his school work very seriously."

The reports from Ingram Road Primary School contain very good remarks from his teachers. He was praised for his school work, educational development, behaviour and was seen as a good personality. We were happy to read his reports and fully satisfied regarding his upbringing. My wife and I signed all Hasib's reports.

After completing his education at Ingram Primary School, Hasib joined Matthew Murray High School in 1998, this school is also very near to our home. At the start of his schooling, Hasib's mum would take him to school and bring him home. I would also go to school if I had time. Hasib loved playing with other children especially with his cousin. The other family kids had a very good and warm relationship with Hasib. He would love to go to their birthdays and loved inviting them to our house. Although he enjoyed playing alone, when he played with other kids he would share his toys and other things which he had.

Hasib used to play with battery-operated toys. He would sometimes take the battery out and make something else. He would eat and drink on time and sit with us and share and enjoy his food. His brother and sisters liked him very much, they adored him. He was not a stubborn or crying child. He was very well behaved and extremely quiet.

When Hasib started attending Matthew Murray High School, my wife would take him and bring him back. We were aware of the school's reputation and for his safety we thought it would be good if we took him to school, even though the school was not far from our home.

Hasib loved food. He loved all kinds of food. His mother always cooked for him but sometimes he would make some of his own food or sandwiches. He was well mannered at the table and would never talk loudly or misbehave like some kids do when they are eating. One day, as usual, we were all sitting around the table and eating and there was a little mince meat curry left on Hasib's plate. He couldn't eat it and threw it in the bin. I was watching and become a little angry and told him not to do that again, as it was against our religion. He was a little bit scared but I told him not to worry. He said, "I am sorry."

I swear to God Hasib never gave us any trouble in his life. His mother was very happy with him. He never disrupted us in any way. I do admit that I might have said something to him in the heat of the moment and for that I am sorry. I would ask for his forgiveness. I am a father, his parent. It is possible that when you bring up children and are under pressure, you may say something to a child that you do not mean.

Hasib liked playing football and cricket. He also played snooker and would watch matches on TV. He often took his mates to the nearby field and played cricket. Hasib was a tall young man but most of his mates were small. Although he was tall and well built he was gentle with the other boys and as far as I know he never started fights or hurt anyone. Once I brought some cricket equipment from Pakistan for him and he took good care of it. He would take his friends to a local playing field and play with his mates and share his cricket gear. One of his best habits was to keep everything tidy and in order. He would never leave his belongings in a disorderly manner. He never left his things lying around; he would keep them in good order. He was a perfectionist when he was little and he was still a perfectionist when he was a young man. He was an orderly and responsible man. I have got the same habits as Hasib. When I look back at Hasib's short life, his habits were the same as mine. He was full of sincerity, clean and very neat. He had very humble principles and he always stood by them.

I would not comment on all his educational reports because a short insight will be enough. I have got all these reports and all of his teachers were happy and praised him for his educational efforts and achievements.

Not a single teacher said that Hasib was weak in his education on any subject, on the contrary, he was praised by all his teachers. He was that ordered in his life that he kept all his reports and certificates in a safe place. I wanted to share my son's high standards which made me copy the contents of his reports, and I am very humbled and proud that my son was a perfectionist as a young man.

Summary of Matthew Murray High School Reports

1998/99: "Hasib has got a lot of potential and he should use it fully. He is fully focused on his school work but he needs to do some more hard work."

One of his teachers complained that Hasib was "not following instructions and he is less interested in school and home work." He was given 67%.

He worked well in his Technology and Design subjects.

His French teacher said that Hasib should do more to improve and was given 55% and in speech was given 82%.

In Artwork, Hasib's homework was "very good" and he was encouraged and praised by his hard work and achievements.

In History, his work was excellent and again his efforts were praised by his teacher and he got "well done" written in his book. He was also told by his subject teacher to work hard and put more effort in and to concentrate more. On his sheet with his signature on and dated 17th June 1999, Hasib pointed out on which subject he must work hard at and concentrate more, so he should do better than last year.

2000/01: Most teachers praised him for his hard work and to achieve more, saying he should work harder.

Hasib's PE teacher was "not happy with his progress" and he says in his report that Hasib is "somehow shy and not taking any interest in his subject." Although I will add here that Hasib never liked taking his clothes off in front of any body. Even if he wore a shirt and shorts, he would feel uncomfortable and he never liked showing his body to others. His mother and I were aware of this problem. We don't think that Hasib's teacher knew of or cared about his shyness. Because of this reason, Hasib chose another subject instead of PE.

His annual report was satisfactory and in some subjects he was doing very well and praised by his subject teachers. But again he was reminded to do more hard work and pay full attention on various topics.

2001/02: Again this year Hasib was praised by his teachers for his hard school work. The teachers commented on his work and said that he was doing very well. One teacher said that Hasib was one of the best students in the school. Some teachers said that Hasib could do more and he was asked to put more hard work and attention into some of his subjects. His overall progress was satisfactory.

It is worth pointing out that following July 7th 2005, some newspapers were very dishonest and unreasonable. They falsely accused Hasib of not managing to achieve any grades when he came out of school. The Headmaster of Matthew Murray High School was quoted in an article in the *Yorkshire Evening Post* that I have quoted below.

From the *Yorkshire Evening Post* – 20th July 2005:

[Headmaster of Matthew Murray High School] Mr [Colin] Bell said reports that had painted [Hasib] Hussain as a school failure who never sat his GCSE exams and spread warning leaflets around the school following the US September 11 attacks were wrong. "There has been a lot of misinformation spread about this young man," he said. "He did the GCSEs, contrary to reports in the media, and he did not spread leaflets of hate mail around the school. It's just not true.

"We are as staggered as anyone else that this has happened and there was absolutely no indication during his time here that it would. There has been an element of disbelief and disappointment. Everybody is clear about how abhorrent such an act was, but as a general rule, the school carries on as normal. The children here need consistency, and that's what we are trying to give them. There are children who are certainly more subdued than normal. For the most part they are children from the Beeston community who may have known Hasib."

As his headmaster and teachers said, Hasib was a very good pupil and he had a good education. They describe him as a very respectable and good student of the school. It is very important for me to mention in regards to this fact the Headmaster and Education Leeds because it shows that some newspapers twist the story to sell papers. They did not hesitate to destroy people's lives and cause a lot of distress and suffering. I know they are doing a job but they should do it with care.

Like some other British national newspapers, some local newspapers also printed unreasonable, baseless and completely false stories about Hasib's personality, education and other matters. We all read newspapers, sit in front of TV and of course use the internet. What we read and hear often has no verification. I think they call this 'fake news' now! Most of us enjoy the sensationalism and truthfully don't care whether what we are watching is the truth or not. I think this is where media must take responsibility and tell the truth, not just go for sensationalism.

I also think that the general public is so busy with their own lives that they don't stop to check or they have no interest in checking whether stories are true or not. In summary we just believe what we read, hear and see. Most times they are selling sensationalism, rather than the truth.

A local newspaper also printed some baseless stories about Hasib. The Leeds Education and Matthew Murray High Schools statements are very clear. The school head denied that Hasib left school without any GCSE's; instead they said in school reports that Hasib was 'a remarkable student of this school'. They also denied that Hasib distributed leaflets and encouraged other school children after the September 11th attacks, again this wasn't true.

Playing with other people's lives is a very dangerous business. Journalists and newspapers make a fortune with baseless stories. I have no hesitation to say that the media is targeting Muslims in particular.

Admission to College

After gaining GCSEs from Matthew Murray High School, Hasib chose to go to Thomas Danby College in Leeds. Hasib left school in 2003. I asked him what kind of course he was interested in. I would like to emphasise here that I have never pressurised my children to pick certain subjects. I always encouraged them to have their own choice. If my child was good in arts then why not choose an art subject? I left it to my children but unfortunately it didn't work out with some... Hasib picked a Business Advance course for his next two years at his college.

I drove Hasib to Thomas Danby College. He had passed his GCSEs with good grades and had a Merit for his business subject. He was weak in English. He gained some middle marks in English but he passed it. Hasib was wearing Arabic dress when he went to college for his admission. The lady at the college took a very brief interview with him and Hasib seemed a bit upset and worried afterwards. The English lady was half naked, showing off her upper arms, which might have upset Hasib. I am not sure about that. The lady refused to admit Hasib to the college. When I asked her for an explanation, she refused to say why. When I persisted and demanded explanations, she refused again. Then I asked her if I could see her supervisor. She then went inside a small office and the supervisor came out after a while and sat down with us. I asked her to look at Hasib's certificate again. I showed her the Merit and good marks on his certificates. What else do you want? While I was talking to this lady, Hasib's face was getting red with anger and he was clearly very upset and uneasy and I would say there was some kind of hate as well. I asked Hasib if he would like to go to another college. As soon as I said this, the lady said that she would take him but with one condition, that Hasib will have to take English as well. I asked Hasib about that and he said agreed. His admission went through with a small hitch. The young woman was looking at Hasib's beard and his Arabic dress again and again and my son was getting upset by it. It was clear she was not happy with Hasib's dress. But we were there for his education not his dress sense. In my opinion, if there was a dress code, then it should have been implemented on her, not him. My son was more covered up than this lady with a low cut top and short skirt!

I was rather surprised and upset about her foolish behaviour. She might be upset because Hasib was not wearing so-called "suitable dress" or perhaps something else was disturbing her. To have a very short interview and then be refused admission seemed very unreasonable. The college may be more tolerant nowadays but that was a bad experience. I have studied there for before and I have never experienced such behaviour.

After this Hasib started going to college. He would get up very early and after his prayers, he would eat breakfast then go to college. He had to get two buses to get there. Hasib wore Arabic dress most of the time. I have seen some boys wearing Arabic dress but I am not sure why the admissions lady disliked Hasib's dress? It's a personal choice surely? I am sure colleges are more open now and allow any type of dress. I may be completely wrong but I could only tell from our experience. Hasib gained the following qualifications and received the following certificates from Thomas Danby College in 2004 and 2005: Certificate in English in June 2004 and Certificate in June 2004 in Business. In July 2004, he received a certificate for Computer IT, a certificate for (CLAIT). In June 2005, he received certificates of Business Advance.

I received two certificates on 8th July 2005 in which there were full details of his achievements on the course. He passed with good grades. When I received this envelope on 8th July 2005, I put it on the table in his bedroom so he could open it himself when he returned home from London but of course he never did. Another Business Advance Certificate dated January 2005 arrived on Thursday 3rd November 2005 (a day after Hasib's burial). I was puzzled, astonished and very surprised. One certificate came on 8th July and the second on 3rd November. It's as if Hasib was telling me "Father! I have completed my education"!

6. HASIB'S RELIGIOUS EDUCATION

PARENTS CANNOT IGNORE the religious education of their children. It is a fundamental and basic human right of every child to receive a religious education, regardless of whichever religion they practise. Even parents who don't practice religion, or do not believe, still have a duty to give their children some religious education without believing in a faith.

It's clear that a child who is born in a Muslim household will get an Islamic education and learn the basic teachings of Islam. As parents, we took our Islamic education and spiritual values for our children very seriously. An Islamic education for my children was compulsory. Hasib's religious education started at home. His mother taught him the basic Islamic lessons. When he was a little older he started attending local Islamic classes, first in Matthew Murray High School and then in a local boys club where a religious scholar was teaching Hasib and other boys and girls. A small room was booked for this purpose in Matthew Murray High School and then a hall was hired from a local community centre. It's very unfortunate that some local people didn't like this. It may be possible that out of racial hatred our children experienced difficulties. Hasib attended religious classes in Matthew Murray School for some time. When some local youths, and with regret some adults, started smashing school windows regularly, then the school management said they were unable to provide a room and they could not afford more repairs. The school informed parents and teachers of their decision. The cost to repair the broken windows was £350.

Hasib learned more about religion when he was in the boys club. He also learnt basic Arabic and Urdu writing skills from myself and his mother. It was our daily duty to take Hasib to the boys club and bring him back and the same with school. The boys club was also very close to our house. Hasib gained a good grounding in Islamic spiritual values by learning the Qu'ran and we were happy and satisfied with his education. Hasib observed fasting, even as a child he didn't miss the fasts. He also completed and read all his salats (prayers) which he missed when he was little. Although they were not necessary, he did it and was very happy about it and as parents we were happy. He regularly offered his salat prayer five times a day. He never missed his Friday prayers. He would take time off from school and college and had to go to a nearby masjid and offer his Salat–e-Jummah. He was a very respectable, very well-mannered, very well-spoken and well-behaved young man. He hardly missed a religious lesson when he used to go to the boys club even if he had a cold or 'flu. Hasib read the full Qu'ran twice with his Islamic teacher. After reading the Qu'ran twice, his teacher would not allow him to sit in class because there was an age limit for all boys and girls. But Hasib kept reading the Qu'ran at home. Hasib went to Saudi Arabia when he was just 13 years of age to perform Umrah. I often reminded him that there is a special difference between him and other boys because he had seen Kabbah and Madina where our beloved Prophet Mohammed (pbuh) is buried.

Whenever I saw Hasib reading the Qu'ran, I thought that he was a lot better than other children who were just interested in TV, PlayStation games and chatting on the internet – this young man was completely different...

Our beloved son Hasib performed his first Hajj when he was 16 years old. I'll explain a bit more about the pilgrimage later because many seem to believe that this was the point at which Hasib became radicalised, or at least was made ready for radicalisation.

Hasib had a very good knowledge of Islamic teachings and history. He would never show off in front of people. Although he would discuss any matter regarding any Islamic subject, he was very careful about this. He never liked so called 'mullahs' who he said were just greedy and spread the wrong message of Islamic teachings. Many times he criticised them by calling them greedy. He would observe simple, straight Islam and avoided mingling with different types of Islamic Sects. His views were strong and understandable. He was very critical and if he was against a particular sect, he would say that instead of following one of the mullahs. He would often say "They should look after the poor and needy people in this world". I never interfered or forced my own views on him. I was happy and supported his view about various aspects of Islamic sects. He knew a lot more about it than me.

Hasib also performed and took part in an Itikaff in Ramadan 2004. This involved him staying and praying in seclusion in a masjid for ten days. I tried to stop him because I didn't think he would be able to complete it but he had already got permission from his mother. When I asked him why he wanted to do this, he told me that he just wanted to pray and get more reward. He stayed in a local masjid for the whole ten days and nights. I went to see him every evening. There were some other men with him there. I would sit with him for a short time and I was not allowed to talk about worldly issues. The boys would prepare their own food and eat together as if they were brothers. I didn't know any of them but they were very respectable young men. Some of them were reasonably good cooks and prepared the food for everyone. I never saw Hasib cooking or preparing anything there. Once I asked Hasib if a particular boy could cook and he replied "yes, he could boil an egg" and all the others started laughing.

I stayed in the masjid just for a short time to see if Hasib was alright. A young man offered me a few packets of sweet dates to take home. He told me that every day they got food from Muslim families but they preferred their own food.

Hasib always led me to the stairs and he stayed behind a certain point. He was not allowed to go out because of Itikaaf. It is only possible to come out in certain extreme emergencies. Hasib was very adamant, patient and self-reliant. I was very surprised to see him in this form. Each evening I saw him leaning back against a wall reading the Qu'ran, I felt a bit sorry for myself because I had tried to stop him from sitting in Itikaaf thinking it would be a bit hard for him but he completed it very easily.

I went to see him one day before Eid; he was outside sitting in a car with some of his friends. I didn't recognise him straight-away because of mist on the car window. He wound down his window and told me that they were all celebrating Eid tomorrow. As usual, we celebrated two Eids that year! I wanted to bring Hasib home and asked him to come with me, but he wanted to stay with his mates and one of them told me he would drop him home later. I was happy as he had completed his Itikaaf and it was celebration time. Next day, we both went for Eid prayers and it was unusual to go to the Bengali Masjid, but I went with him anyway. There was nobody there I could relate to. Normally we went to the Islamic Centre, Omar Masjid, and we would meet a lot of friends but there were none at the Bengali Masjid. I was a little bored but I wanted to see Hasib happy. There were a few young men who shook hands and embraced Hasib but I was without friends.

When Hasib was going to college, he would get up very early and go for Fajr prayer. It was his habit to get up about 3 am and go to Beeston Omar Masjid. After prayer, he would come home, have breakfast and go to college. One evening we were all sitting in our front room and Hasib's sister asked him about getting up in the morning and walking down to the masjid. She told him that he must be very careful about his safety. There are two pubs on the way and sometimes people cause trouble. He assured his sister that nothing would happen. She assumed that he was tall and strong and nobody would try to touch him. But he told her that he was going to a masjid, Allah's house, "who would touch me?" he said, "nobody can harm me and Allah will always protect me." I offered to drive him to masjid every morning, but he said he was fine. I was also worried about him walking down to the masjid. I told him that he could read his prayers at home for safety. He then started reading his Fajr prayers at home.

I was going to Saudi Arabia and invited him to join us (me and his mother) for another Hajj, but he told me that he was honoured once and he was happy to perform his compulsory Hajj.

I knew Hasib very well. By that I mean his daily life and his character. He was a very neat and orderly person. What I did not know is what was on his mind. Obviously nobody could even try to guess other people's thoughts. I was sure Hasib was not a religious fanatic or anything else. He was just an ordinary young boy. He never said anything and I never suspected anything bad about him. I believed he was not troublesome to others nor was he troubled as far as I was aware. To me he was just an ordinary well-behaved Muslim child, obeying Allah's commands and following his prophet Mohammed's (pbuh) life style and Sunnah.

For instance, Hasib would never attend a funeral procession. Such as when a person dies, people read the Qu'ran and then eat. He would not attend anything like that. He used to say that these are parties and have no value in our religion. Instead, he said, these people should offer food to the poor people or donate money so they could eat or buy basic things like clothes, water and shelter. He was very strict about that as a basic understanding of charitable Islam.

Once, a relative's mother died in Pakistan. He was a very rich man but did not want to leave his business and go to his mother's funeral. Instead he arranged a big religious gathering at his house and spent a lot of money on food and other things. Despite an invitation, Hasib didn't attend. He went to their house the next day and offered his condolences but did not eat any food.

I never saw him listening to Pakistani, Indian or English music, or any other so called Islamic music like Qawali, which has no basis in Islam. He loved light Arabic music and listened to Sami Yusaf. Whenever he travelled with me in our car he would listen to his Arabic religious songs. Since 7th July 2005 I have never turned on the tape player in my car. It makes me very upset, it's unbearable. I remember once Hasib, his mother and myself were travelling in a car and Hasib turned his music on which made me very emotional and I started to cry. Sami Yusaf's voice was very emotional and the words were going through my mind. Sami Yusaf was submitting himself to Almighty Allah and I couldn't control myself, I cried in front of Hasib and his mother.

★

Most Muslims will be aware that in almost every city in England they have Death and Funeral Committees. They become members and pay a small membership fee to arrange funerals when they die. I was a member of such an organisation. Our organisation has been running since 1999. In case of the death of my wife or any of my children, we were covered. However, any child who reaches 18 should have his or her membership separately. Hasib reached 18 on 16th September 2004. I told him to become a member. I filled an application for him and asked him to sign it but he refused. I pestered him about it a few times and asked his mother to remind him to sign it but he still refused. I told his mother that he shouldn't be worried about his membership fee but he told his mother he doesn't believe in these things. Out of the love of my son, I thought I should hand over this form to our organisation without his signature and pay his fee. However, having thought about, I changed my mind as it was clearly a matter of principle with him. I still don't know why he refused to sign it and why he was reluctant to join the Death Committee membership? I don't think that not believing in funerals was sufficient reason.

As mentioned, Hasib would get up very early each morning and read his Fajr prayer and Qu'ran. He would read his five daily prayers on time. He had some Islamic and religious books. He could not read Urdu very well so he bought books in English. He would try to speak in Urdu if someone spoke to him in that language. I heard him talking to someone in Urdu and he was not bad at all. His knowledge of Islam was a lot better than most young men his age.

One day he was reading an Islamic book. I asked him if I could have a glance at it and he handed it over. I turned a few pages and found out it was written by a converted Muslim. Hasib said "Abba! Did you know that one day Kabbah will be built again?" I was astonished. I did not take this seriously and did not pay any attention, thinking he might be wrong. A few days later a new molvi (Islamic Priest) was showing off a bit and sitting among his followers, so I put this question to him. I just wanted to test him to see if he could answer my question. He told me "your son is mad!" I wanted to know about this more and one day I asked Hasib again regarding Kabbah being built again. He showed me a particular paragraph in the book which I had read briefly a few days ago. I started reading it and understood the whole picture. In this chapter, the name of that person was mentioned, his nationality, and his body structure. He would be a very ugly person. He will travel from an African country and go to Saudi Arabia and the destruction of Kabbah would be his fate. References have been given in a few books about this and it is also one of our beloved Prophet Mohammed (pbuh) hadiths.

After reading and talking to Hasib, I contacted this molvi again and asked him the same question. He told me that he would consult his "Peer" and let me know soon, but he didn't. This molvi Sahib always started arguments with me because I was telling him off and tried to stop him from spreading the wrong message of Islam. Hasib was right. We cannot deny this is happening.

Another example happened when a friend of mine came to my house and complained that Hasib was reading Namaz (prayer) wrong. The way he told me, I was sure he didn't know himself. I asked Hasib about this and he said that "during Namaz I do Rafa-e-Yadian (lifting his hands and arms up in certain actions)." He told me he was just following the Prophet's actions to get more reward. I didn't say anything further to Hasib because I knew what he was doing. Some of our religious leaders always argue about this and spread mistrust among our Muslim brothers and sisters. Hasib knew a lot about Islam and Islamic teachings. I can say with certainty that by looking at his short life, he had a very good insight of Islam. The most important and fundamental thing is practice. In my opinion, he was a good Muslim practicing young man.

Hasib was now attending school regularly and after school he would come home, eat something and after getting fresh he would go to Islamic classes. He would come back and play with his friends and school mates. He would play alone if there was nobody to play with. He was very interested in making his own toys. He would take out a motor from an old toy and make something different and interesting with it. His interest suggested that he might be a mechanic or engineer. He was very well organised and disciplined. You could say he was a well organised perfectionist.

Hasib's other side was his religion and faith. He was a pious child. There were some unusual things he told his mother in his childhood and sometimes we were concerned. He would talk about things which happened a long time ago. Even a long time before his birth, he was telling us about things well before he was born; about the history of Holbeck and so forth, about things that were not in the history books. When some of our relatives found out about this they suggested that I take him to a Muslim priest. However I did not want him to become a person people would worship. I knew Hasib's splendour, kindness and dutifulness as a child. I often thought that he would become a very respectable and successful person as an adult.

When my specialist told me that I may be suffering from a brain tumour and it could be life threatening, I never said anything about my new illness to my wife or children. I thought about my children and asked my wife to consult with our daughters if this was the right time to get married. Both daughters were in college. Their wishes were very important to me. I would never force my decisions or opinions on my children. My duties and responsibilities were to teach them good things and become a good human being. I told my daughters they were free to choose their husbands. The only thing I stipulated was that their husbands must be Muslims and good human beings. I would not put their caste first. I would never do that. I am their father and adult enough to give them advice. I wouldn't force my daughters to do anything they did not want to do.

I was aware of the generation gap. It is very possible that the generations have different opinions about various issues but forcing my decision on them was not an option. I was also aware that at this age some children are bound to make very bad decisions and they would have to deal with the consequences for the rest of their lives. I believe if you talk to your children and communicate in a healthy way they are able to make the best choices. My daughters were old enough to make their own choices. I am a liberal and open-minded person. I'm not narrow minded and uneducated either. I am aware that some Pakistani and Kashmiri parents force their children to get married to someone who they do not like or are unsuitable to them because of other factors such as age gap, lack of education and so forth. It is also possible that parents choose their children's partners because they are very close relatives. But in our case, the choice was my daughters' and the partners were not mine or my wife's close relatives. Their partners to be were outside our family. My priority was always my daughters' happiness not close relatives who wanted to come to England.

In my experience it is a very delicate, dangerous and frightening situation. If you allow your children freedom, they can take advantage and bring shame on the family. It could affect other children in the family and disputes would start, such as if my brother or sister can do that, then why can't I? I had no objection if my daughters choose someone from a different caste as long as they were good, well-behaved Muslims. Our beloved Prophet (pbuh) told us to consider your daughter and ask her wishes before marrying her. A true Muslim woman and man are also required not to bring any shame on the parents. Marrying a man of her choice is not a shame; it is the fundamental Islamic right of a woman. I'm not a molvi but I have some knowledge of these issues. I strongly condemn parents who force their children to get married to a person who they deem unsuitable for them. No sound-minded parent will marry his well-educated daughter to a donkey herder. But in fact, I know one mother and father who did exactly that. There are a lot of other examples such as a 28 year-old girl being married off to a 70 year-old British pensioner! I do not think it is appropriate for me to tell you more about this unfairness. We all know it happens.

My eldest daughter married a man who she liked. My younger daughter married a man she chose herself. My wife and I were there for them for advice, help and provided all the financial help they needed. My elder daughter married a man who had been married before and I advised my daughter to make sure it was suitable for her to enter into a big commitment. I was not against it but I was concerned that she might not be thinking properly. Although she terrorised her mother and I, that was her life. She made her decision and she has to live with it. I asked my daughter to travel to Pakistan to see the other side of the coin. If they like anyone then it's okay for me and their mother. Otherwise she could stay until the younger sister got married and came back. I always showed them the straight path. It was up to them if they would act upon it or not.

Everybody knows most parents think about what is best for their children and guide them accordingly. Some children make their own choices and they are responsible for their actions. We are responsible until they reach adulthood. After that, the responsibility is theirs. As a loving and caring father, I did whatever I could. It was up to them as to what decision they make. They will be held responsible for their actions, not me. I can only guide them according to my experience.

My wife and I asked our daughters with full confidence, told them that they were free to make their decision about two boys who were not relatives. If they wanted to see them they could go to Pakistan and find out more about the family. With their full agreement I sent my wife, Hasib and both daughters to Pakistan – I planned to stay at home because I was now suffering from a brain tumour. This was Hasib's third visit to Pakistan.

The night before they left, I told my wife and children about my diagnosis and the reason for not travelling. I asked my daughters not to do anything which may cause problems for me. As soon as I informed my wife, she refused to travel. I begged her to go to because my daughter's might be put in jeopardy if she didn't. I told my daughters that they do not have to marry them, just see the boys. If they like them, I would travel to Pakistan and marry them, if not they should come home. They were always free to make their own decision. They all went to Pakistan the next day.

Sometimes it is not possible that everything goes smoothly. I think the set back was temporary but it may have been very good for us. My wife, Hasib and two daughters reached Pakistan. Although my wife sympathised with me, she did not fully co-operate with me. She may be confused but she also did something wrong against me later which was very upsetting for me. My eldest daughter returned to England and the younger one stayed and got married to a man of her choice and she stayed with him in Pakistan for more than seven months. My wife and I were very upset but there was nothing we could do. It was her choice. Two of my sisters in law were causing a lot of problems for us. They had some score to settle with the boy's family who arranged and asked for my daughter's hand. It was very upsetting. They didn't even care about their niece and sister. They were playing with my daughter's emotions as she wanted to marry. I had no objection whatsoever. When my younger daughter decided that she wanted to get married in Pakistan I asked my specialist if I could travel for a very short period. He agreed and I joined my wife and Hasib and my younger daughter got married. When I found out about my other daughter I left Pakistan, I was very upset. I was hardily functioning. I was already seriously ill. She and her aunties put another nail in my coffin. I was heartbroken, I was shattered and upset. Hasib was 12 years old and clearly upset too. A few days after my younger daughter's marriage, Hasib and ourselves tried to get back to normal but my eldest daughter was not there and we felt very lonely and humiliated but there was nothing we could do.

Hasib made a few friends and some boys started to come to our house to play and started learning English from him. It was also the season of mangoes. He would buy mangoes from the street hawkers and eat as many as he could. He loved them. We went to see our recently married daughter and she came to stay with us for a few days with her husband.

My elder daughter got married to a boy of her choice in England. I had no problem with it. The only thing was the boy who she married had already been married and he was already living with her. She got married without her mother and me. Most of her aunties and, strangely enough, her grandmother, supported her and they were present at her marriage. I was humiliated and scared in a sense that I was worried about her in case the married man might use her and then dump her. She had made her choice and had to live with it. Terrorising and humiliating a sick father, who was half buried in the grave, was her and her auntie's choice.

Hasib used to go to his grandmother's house and play with the other kids. He was very popular among the boys and they always wanted his company. He went to Pakistan because of his sister's marriage. One sister came back to England and the other was married and moved to Mirpur. Hasib felt a bit lonely and we tried hard to make sure he was fine but he was missing his sisters. It had a huge impact on him. I cannot control other human beings. My younger daughter was very happy and settled with her husband and the rest of the family. Her mother-in-law and her brothers-in-law were treating my daughter very well and she was happy there.

While he was there Hasib used to read the Qu'ran with his mother and read prayers 5 times a day and came with me to Friday prayer. He was revising and repeating the Qu'ranic verses by heart. He used to fly kites with the other boys in the late afternoon because during the day it was too hot. He loved flying kites and he had so many different colours and sizes. I also joined in the fun with him. When I was little I loved flying kites. I was very good at it but sometimes kite flying caused a lot of problems. I remember when I was about 12 and living near where our coaches used to park. The alley was very narrow and only one person could walk on it. On both sides were houses. I was flying a kite one day and another boy's kite tangled with mine. He went to the next door house and from the top of house he tried to jump onto our roof to snatch his kite from me but he fell down on to this narrow street from the third floor of this high house and broke both his legs. He was severely injured and stayed in hospital for many months. Although he survived, he became disabled for the rest of his life. He was causing so much trouble for the others in the household; people were somehow relieved that they had got rid of him! I was very aware of the danger of kite flying and told Hasib that he could only fly kites when I was around. He was allowed to fly kites on the ground but not on top of buildings. It was too risky.

I bought some kites for him to bring back to England. When we returned home I took him to Roundhay Park and we flew our kites together and one of them got wet and melted away in the rain. The other one was so high, we couldn't even see it. It was a very big kite and the wind made it heavy. Some people came to watch us and asked us how we made them. I told them that the kites came from Pakistan. Obviously, you can't fly paper kites in England because of the weather.

While I was in Pakistan arranging various things for my daughter's wedding, I saw so many unreasonable customs which have no place in our faith. I tried to stop these customs but my relatives wouldn't listen. I was not doing anything wrong, so I left them to it and paid the price later. I felt ashamed. These were not customs that belonged to Islam. They were customs imported from Hinduism and other cultures.

Hasib was only twelve and he didn't like it either. We immigrants from Pakistan have so many problems. We cannot cope with being part of two countries and two cultures. We have to be engaged with Pakistan because our families are there and our children's future somehow is also over there. I was concerned about Hasib and his elder brother's education. Although his elder brother has been looked after properly, I didn't want to leave him with his auntie for long. We had to come back.

We returned to England after the marriage. My youngest daughter wanted to stay in Pakistan for a while and I respected her wishes. Soon after returning to England, Hasib rejoined school.

7. HASIB'S UMRAH, JULY 1999

WHEN I REALISED that my eldest son wasn't interested in further education, I told him that I would take him to Pakistan and make arrangements for his marriage. I was concerned about him. I was already humiliated and torn apart following my eldest daughter's marriage and I didn't want more heartache.

After my parents passed away I felt very lonely and isolated. When my father was alive he was willing to do a lot for me but now I had no one apart from a brother who was only really interested in my money. He never bothered to ask if I needed anything. I was not in a position to help anyone financially because I was not working and the money I got was not even enough to care of my immediate family. I was sure that if my son got married outside our family, then a connection with our family would end. I talked to my wife, daughters and son-in-law and they gave me the go ahead to talk to my sister. I was very careful and I talked to everybody and asked their opinion and they all agreed. If my son wanted to marry to my sister's daughter, it was fine and a good thing but it turned out to be a huge mistake and because I was the head of household, I suffered the most. I tried to help and give what I could but it was very unfortunate, things turned upside down! My wife suffered the most. This marriage caused unforeseen damage to us. As soon as they got married our problems started.

I asked my sister for her daughter. She started messing around and was not prepared to give a straight answer. They knew what their daughter was like but we had no idea at all. I asked my daughter-in-law to be and she said she would be happy and she wanted to marry my son. Living in England and going to Pakistan for couple of weeks was not enough to check someone's behaviour and lifestyle. My sister did not give me straight answers because she knew about her daughter's disrespectful behaviour. I would never have asked for her if I knew what was going on in their household.

I returned to Pakistan and, as my sister was reluctant to answer, I stopped asking about this marriage. While I was there I never noticed anything to cause me concern. Cutting this story short, my son wanted to marry her and after the engagement I went to Pakistan for a short time. I noticed that in their household there was a lot of fighting, swearing and a lot going on. I didn't like that. The behaviour of the family members was disgraceful. I became very upset and asked my wife and children to call off the marriage. I always believed in consulting everyone in any decision but they made the wrong choice. By now my son was insisting on marrying her so we had to consider his wishes. I made my son aware about what I saw in Pakistan with the family, but they all said it would be alright later. I asked my son's prospective father-in-law and he agreed. He was living in the Middle East at the time and happy to give her daughter's hand to my son. I did not know if he knew what was going on in his family until later.

So the reason for Hasib's fourth visit to Pakistan was his brother's marriage. I told my sister that we were coming to Pakistan and that it would be a short visit as we'd be returning to England as quickly as possible after the wedding. I told her "we do not need anything from you so just prepare for a simple ceremony" but she was demanded everything and wanted to fulfil silly customs. I tried to make things better and reasonable, but I think too much Hinduism had been adopted by them.

While we were preparing for this marriage my brother-in-law phoned me from the Middle East and said he had started building another storey for his house and he asked if we would be demanding a dowry from them. I told him "we are ready to have a simple ceremony and we do not need your dowry". He wanted to spend the money on his house instead of giving a dowry to his daughter. I thought about the dowry as his wife was demanding a lot of things from us, but I ignored her because she was my sister, and I never thought that one day she would be so cruel to me and my family. My brother-in-law was begging me not to demand a dowry. I told him I wouldn't demand anything from him and told him not to worry and prepare a simple ceremony. I let him finish his building work. I always tried to make other people's lives easy, but not many people return the favour. Had I taken the dowry, he would have never built the second floor of his house.

I was not only her brother but also a practicing Muslim. I do not believe in a dowry and the other customs attached to it. You can give to your children whatever you can manage but to demand something is not my way of life. You can call me naive but I will never put a father and a mother who have a daughter or a son to marry in a difficult position because my Allah is not like that. I fear Allah because He is the Almighty and we have to answer Him one day about our good and bad deeds. May Allah Subhana Taa'la have mercy on me and save me from any calamities!

It's not fair for a Muslim to demand a dowry from another Muslim. If we carried on like this then that would pay dowry for young Muslim girls whose parents are very poor and cannot even afford food? This self made custom has no place in our culture, religion or society. This is completely shameful. What would she be feeling? We call ourselves Muslims but some of our actions are disgraceful. May Allah give us the ability to think about other people's needs too!

While we were making arrangements to go to Pakistan, I asked my wife if we could travel via Saudi Arabia and perform Umrah. As soon as I thought about it, the wish was granted and Allah gave us the chance to see Kabbah and Madina. It was a journey of a life time and we were all very happy.

I talked to my son-in-law as his wife also wanted to go to Pakistan for her brother's wedding. He was happy to send his little son and wife with us. Hasib was over the moon when I told him that we are going via Saudi Arabia to Pakistan, and his sister and her son would also travel with us. My wife started teaching all of them what we had to do when we reached Makkah and how to perform Umrah. Many times we sat down and learnt about Umrah and what was allowed and what was forbidden. Although my wife and I knew about it, Hasib and his brother and sister needed reminding. In a few days, everybody had been trained and well-educated on performing the Umrah. It was a very emotional, heartfelt and divine learning process.

I asked a friend who organises tours to Saudi Arabia and within a few weeks he had organised a group of 21 people. We had to have meningitis injections before travel. Then we handed over our passports to the travel agent with photos and our seats were booked on 17th July 1999. Hasib's school holidays were due. It was a good time for us to travel during the holidays. I was happy that my son was getting married and also that Hasib was going. I was a bit concerned about my grandson because he was only 12 months old and it would be very hot in Saudi Arabia and Pakistan. Our group leader soon informed me that all the arrangements had been made for travel.

We packed up our luggage and set off to Huddersfield and from there we travelled to London Heathrow. My son-in-law took take care of our house while we were away. Our flight was through the night and the group leader had arranged two coaches, one for passengers and the other for luggage. We set off from Huddersfield at about 11am and we had no idea that there were road works on the M1.

All the passengers were happy and greeting each other as we were going to Makkah and Madina, the most holy cities for a Muslim. We were sitting at the front of the minibus and the driver and his wife were talking to us and asking questions about our journey. Unfortunately the traffic near London was a nightmare so we were cutting it fine to get to our flights on time. We were all praying and we reached the airport just 35 minutes before the flight was due. Despite the driver's effort, we were late. As soon as we reached check out, a lady told us to leave our luggage and take our hand luggage with us and run to the gate. As soon as we boarded the plane, we became scattered and we had to sit wherever we could. As soon as the plane took off, I started to look for my family. Hasib and I were sitting together and the others were far from us.

I asked the air hostess but she could not do anything as all the seats were occupied. Most Saudi Arabian airlines have a special space on their aircraft for praying. I asked Hasib and Imran to wear their Ihram and I did so too. I kept going to see my wife, daughter and grandchild to check if they were okay.

Imran is hot blooded and loses his temper quickly while Hasib was very quiet and patient. I had to make sure that they wore their Ihram on time. Imran was taking his time. Our grandchild was only little. I tried to put the Ihram around him but he started to cry so I left it. I told the family to have some rest during the flight, if they could, because we would be very busy when we landed and we might have no time for rest later. It was the first visit for my sons. I was proud that both my sons were with me and they were travelling with me to see the holiest place on earth.

We reached Jeddah airport early on the morning of 18th July and it was very hot. From there we had to travel by bus to Makkah. When we got there a big room was allocated for us. The hotel was a bit far for my children but I told them not to worry, we would be alright when we settled down. After we checked in we got ready. We had some food, showered and then walked to Haram. We carried our grandchild in turn and reached Haram. It was the most beautiful view and one of the most emotional moments of our lives when we saw Kabbah. We all prayed and asked for forgiveness. We were all very happy. We did Tawaf and then we went to Safa and Marwa for Sa'i. Hasib, his brother and our grandchild were with me, and my daughter and wife were both together. I think it was during the Sa'i when my daughter had a panic attack. She was getting claustrophobic with so many people there. When we completed our Sa'i my eldest son started having stomach pains. He had eaten something which made his stomach upset. I was worried about my wife and daughter but I was sure that they would find their way back to the hotel. We completed our Umrah before going back to the main gate, I had decided to go to Hajr-e-Aswad and tried to kiss it. We joined a queue and soon we were able to kiss the Black Stone. I kissed it first and then I put my grandchild's head gently on the Stone but he started to cry. Then Hasib kissed it and then Imran. As soon as we had done this we were over the moon. I was very happy. I could clearly see Hasib's emotions. He was very happy and smiling.

We read our Zohar prayer and went back to the main gate and waited there for some time. Then my wife and daughter joined us. They told us what happened and my daughter was not feeling well. I was not aware of her condition. We all returned to the hotel. We all were very tired and thirsty. We slept until Asr prayer.

The next day it was 54 degrees. We settled down quickly and we all went to Haram together, and sometimes my sons and I went together for prayers. The climate affected us all. Most times we slept between prayer times. Hasib loved to shower and he used to cool himself many times a day. I brought food from a nearby Pakistani hotel three times a day and my children were drinking all kinds of drinks and Zamzam water. Our grandchild Saif settled down. We all carried Saif each time we went to Haram. My wife, Saif, Hasib and Imran used to go shopping in the evening. I stayed in the hotel or went to do Tawaf. I was very happy and satisfied that my son was able to do Umrah before his marriage. I phoned Pakistan and talked to my sister and she demanded more gold bangles for her daughter, she also warned me not to allow my son to shave his head after Umrah because it will not look good on his wedding day. I almost shouted at her for saying that! She should be grateful and happy that her son-in-law has performed Umrah, but instead she was saying silly things.

On 19th July, we did Tawaf together before travelling to Madina. As we were doing Tawaf-e-Kabbah, where the Zamzam water well is, and also where the Imam stands to lead the Salat (prayer), I saw the Pakistani Prime Minster sitting there with his colleagues reading the Qu'ran. I pointed this out to my wife and children. Mr. Nawaz Sharif had some bodyguards beside him. We were doing Tawaf and we saw him many times. I saw many Pakistani people shaking hands with him. He stayed there until Maghrib Salat.

It was obviously my duty to buy food for the family. My sons were drinking a lot of fizzy drinks and other fruit juices. The fridge was always full with drinks. Despite that, Hasib and his brother were still buying drinks from the nearby shop. I gave Hasib and his brother money to buy anything they liked and they returned with a Seiko watch apiece for about £90 each. Imran has still got his watch but I'm not sure whether Hasib took his watch with him on 7/7 or whether he left it home. There is a watch in his room and its looks like that watch, but I am not certain if it is the same one. Most of the other things Hasib bought during this journey are still in his room. Some Zamzam water is also in his room. I was with them when they bought the watches from the shop. The shopkeeper was a very nice humble man. I still remember that he told Hasib and my other son Imran that "you will remember me as I am giving you the best Seiko watches". I do not know whether Imran remembers him, but I do. This man looked like a Saudi but in fact he was Indian. He was very white and his beard was a beautiful example of piety. These shops and hotels have long since been demolished and new hotels have been built.

I tried my utmost to make sure my guests, and above all Allah's guests, were happy with me. Unfortunately my daughter was not happy. It may be because she was away from her husband, it may have been the hot weather but I did my best to please her. She might be angry with me because I told her to cover herself.

During our stay in Makkah we went to see holy places like Ghar-e-Saur, Masjid Jin, Arafat, Jamarat, Mina and some other places. Our guide was an experienced man. Hasib performed 2 Umrahs and he kissed the Black Stone 4 times and performed a lot of Tawaf. He would pray 5 times a day in Haram. Most times he was with his brother and I. His mother, sister and Saif were at the women's side and we always got together at the main gate after each prayer. Hasib went shopping many times with his mother and sister. I worried about my illness, but apart from one incident when Imran had stomach ache, nobody had any trouble at all. I was worried about little Saif but he was alright. I kept telling him that I will show him some camels in the desert and he would smile. Saif was spending a lot of time with me. One evening I sent my daughter and wife to the jewellers and asked them to buy 6 bangles for their future daughter-in-law and they spent £410 for 6 of them. Of course, in those days gold was very cheap compared to the present day. It was soon time to go to Madina.

Madina is approximately 406 km from Makkah. Hasib was

very happy and patient. He never complained about anything. Saif was also fine. It was a long journey by bus and it was also very hot. I kept Saif with me because I wanted to give his mum a break and wanted to show him some animals while we were travelling. It is a bit cooler there than in Makkah and very peaceful in comparison. Makkah people are renowned for being hot blooded while the citizens of Madina are regarded as caring and welcoming. We set off in an air conditioned bus. Saif was not feeling well with the heat. He would not sleep either. I kept showing him camels, sheep and goats grazing by the road side. He was very happy but as soon as the animals disappeared, he would cry and not sit still. His mother gave him milk and then he went to sleep for 2 hours. We all had a good rest and slept during the journey.

We were going to a sacred city where our beloved Prophet emigrated because of the harshness of Makkah's inhabitants to our Prophet (pbuh). When we reached Madina, we went to offer our salaam to our Prophet (pbuh) and his Companions (May Allah be pleased with them all). We went to offer our salaam after each salat. Hasib was very keen to see our Prophet's (pbuh) grave and that of his Companions. He asked some questions but I was surprised how much he knew about the Prophet and Masjid Nabavi. Our hotel was very near to the masjid and it was a very straightforward road. Our hotel was on the way to the ladies main gate and my wife, daughter and Saif would go there and we would go in to the men's section. On the way to the hotel we waited for our ladies to come out to get together and return to our hotel. The hotel was Lolo-Assnabal and it was clean and very near to Haram.

We had rest whenever we could and looked after each other very well. Hasib and Saif would play and have fun and games. There was a Pakistani hotel opposite where we were staying and it was very easy to buy food. We sat together and ate in our hotel room. It was a big room and enough for us all. We went to see the holy places and a guide was in the bus. Our whole group went with us. We went to see a lot of holy places and enjoyed it very much. Hasib and the others also bought a few things during our visits to the holy sites.

Hasib used to have a shower 3 or 4 times a day because it was also too hot in Madina. Hasib bought a gold embroidery cap. It suited him. I think it was made in India. Many times Hasib went alone to offer his salaam to our Prophet and his Companions. Each time he came back, he seemed very excited. Sometimes there were too many people and it took him a long time to get there.

Soon we had to return to Makkah again to perform another Umrah and we were just waiting for the group leader's instructions. We bought some dates from Madina and my daughter did some shopping. We returned to Makkah again on 28th July 1999 to perform one more Umrah. Many times Hasib and Imran went alone to Haram and they kissed the Black Stone and touched Bab-e-Multizam and stood there for a short time. There were hundreds of thousands of people but I let them go and explore.

While staying in Makkah and Madina, Hasib would ask his mother a lot of questions. When he went to Madina to the holy site of the Uhad Mountain, he visited the graves of the Martyrs of Uhad nearby. He started questioning us about them. He was very interested in finding out how these Companions gave their lives for Islam and suffered at the hands of the non–believers. This was our history and I let him ask questions, and we both gave him appropriate answers according to our own knowledge.

When he visited Baqeeh in Madina, he showed a lot of interest and wanted to know who was buried there. He went down to one grave and picked some dust and a piece of old pottery. Although it is not allowed, nobody stopped him and he took those items back to England with him. I did not think anything of him taking dust from a Martyr's grave, and why he was interested in them. He would stand beside the graves and pray for them. We had to tell him that we were going by bus to another holy site. The same dust was scattered on Hasib's grave when he was buried. I don't think this is a coincidence!

We were soon at the end of our holy journey and getting ready to fly to Pakistan. We had stayed in Makkah and Madina for 2 weeks and then we flew to Islamabad in the first week of August 1999. This stay was very emotional and my children had learnt a lot and enjoyed every minute of it. I still do not know why Hasib was interested in Baqeeh and the Martyrs of Uhad. Hasib was only 12 at the time yet his interest was extraordinary and he never stopped asking questions about them. I am sure people will make a lot more of it given what happened to him but at the time I saw it as a healthy interest in Islamic history.

We reached Islamabad in late afternoon. As soon as we reached home, we started cleaning and dusting our house. My brother was there but not to look after our house, he was there for money. He never held a brush in his hands or even cleaned his own room. Our house was a mess. I told everybody not to panic. My wife took all the bedding downstairs from the upper rooms and my sons helped to bring some furniture from upstairs. It was very hot and we were very tired, but we carried on sorting things until late in the night. We went to bed about 2am and some of us could not sleep because of the heat, and of course the flies and the mosquito bombardment. My back and whole body was hurting. I was responsible for everybody and I had a very difficult time there. My sister had an army of helpers from Jhelum but nobody was preparing to help me. I was virtually alone and I tell you one thing, I have never ever seen such greedy, selfish, argumentative and hungry people in the whole of my entire life. They were from a town near Jhelum city. There may be some good people but they fought and argued for hours and hours with each other. I found no morality whatsoever and as we say money is not everything but it was everything for them. I could not change anything, so I just carried on preparing for my son's wedding.

After sorting out our house and preparing ourselves a place to sleep, I was told by my sister and her daughters that they do not like my son's shaved head. I lost my temper and told them "to get a boy who had a lot of hair on his head then!". My sister told me that people come to Pakistan with a lot of gold and money and you brought your son without hair on his head. I was furious. I tried to calm down. At one point I decided to call off the marriage. Now I feel this is exactly what I should have done, I regret backing down. I asked my wife, daughter and son about it but they wanted to keep their promise. To be honest, although the decision for my son's marriage was a collective one, I asked everybody concerned their opinion and they all agreed but there remained a doubt about this part of my family.

I was keeping my son, wife and daughter informed of what was going on but they never encouraged me otherwise I'm sure I would have called off the marriage. These people were begging from us as soon as we got there. They didn't have any food or clothes, but as soon as some money came, they lost their heads and demanded more from me. I am her brother but there was no respite. I was in a very tricky situation and tried the best I could.

The other disturbing thing was that it was democracy in Pakistan then, and Mr. Nawaz Sharif was the Prime Minister at the time. What happens when a country is democratic? You have the freedom of speech and as long as you don't break the law, you are able to do certain things freely. But in Pakistan back then you were not allowed to cook and offer food to your guests at weddings. It was the most idiotic rule! We were only allowed to provide tea and biscuits, not traditional food. I was hoping that there was a way out of this but I didn't want to fall foul of the law. I had heard that you could just pay a bribe to the local police and nobody would bother you but this is not my way and I always feared Allah. It is really not my style. The tea and biscuits were not popular among the wedding guests – then again, even if you invite them they probably wouldn't turn up and the food would be wasted. I was ashamed as I saw the Pakistani Prime Minister in Kabbah reading the Qu'ran and had no idea that he had determined what a Muslim is allowed to provide at his son's wedding. Our religion, Allah and our beloved Prophet (pbuh) never restricted what you could cook and eat at your son's wedding. Our Prophet (pbuh) said, "If you have capability to offer food to your guests, you can do so. It all depends on your affordability". Our Prophet never proscribed against it. He (pbuh) was happy to serve food to wedding guests and he was happy to care and give food to poor people too. The things he stopped were not to engage in non-Islamic way of teachings. There are no restrictions for offering food to your wedding guests in Islam. I don't understand why they call themselves Muslims and don't act according to Islamic teachings. Allah's Prophet Mohammed (pbuh) gives permission to celebrate and offer food as much as you can but an Islamic Government banned it! They were clearly going against the Prophet's (pbuh) teachings.

Walimah (serving food to your guests the day after a son's marriage) is banned but you can pay a bribe or send a big container of food to the local police station then nobody will bother you yet in Pakistan we have a lot of processions which have no basis in Islam. They are permitted to spend a lot of money and, of course, you can waste as much electricity as you like because the electric can be attached to the grid. All you have to do is to join a wire illegally. Hospitals are without electric and people are dying, but the so called Islamic processions are going on and birthday parties are going on. We do not obey our Prophet's teachings but we celebrate his birthdays. I have seen it all!

It was permitted to prepare a food package of various types of food and hand them over to each quest. Tea, drinks and biscuits were permitted but nobody wanted to come to that sort of wedding. I called a few neighbours and some relatives. I had ordered food boxes according to the invitation. Not many people turned up. I also called a few neighbours who unfortunately were very poor. They didn't turn up either. After the wedding, whatever was left over, I took all the boxes and gave them to our poor neighbours. They were grateful and thanked me and I felt a strange happiness, as they had probably never have had this kind of food in their lives before. I am not attacking anybody, I am just telling the truth as everybody knows what happens at weddings in Pakistan. Anything which is against Islamic teachings should be banned but not food. I do not have to go in to great details but everybody knows what kind of Shariah (Islamic Law) we act upon for Pakistani weddings.

My children thought it was strange that Pakistan called itself an Islamic country. They had never seen anything like it. They were confused at what was going on. Hasib would talk to his mother about the subject and each time he returned from the local Bazaar his reaction was different and upsetting. Most shopkeepers were looting their customers and as his feet were very big, he could not find his shoe size. He had to order them to be made by hand. He wanted a sandal with gold embroidery on. We say in our language 'Kohati Chappal'. He had to pay more than the going rate because he was from England.

Some of our wedding guests, who were closer to my sister, started asking silly questions about my children, especially one man who was causing me a headache. He told me he worked in a bank as a Regional Officer and that his wages were very good. He also made a lot of money on top by doing "customer's jobs". His children went to Islamabad English Medium schools and he pays a lot of monthly fees to schools and colleges. He complained that my children spoke English and that they should "speak their own language". I asked him to tell me in which language he had passed his bank test. He told me it was in English. I asked him how much he had to bribe someone to get his bank job! He was sending his children to English medium schools to learn English and he paid monthly fees. Our children in England go to school and they do not have to pay any fees and they learn in English. I asked him "if he was living in any Middle Eastern country, which language his children should speak" and he replied that it may be Arabic. I told him "my children live in England and the language in England is English and that's why they speak English". He soon shut up.

Hasib was very happy for his "Bahia's" (older brother) wedding and he always stayed with him. We took a lot of wedding photos and Hasib always wanted to be with his brother. Hasib was a very well respected child. Everybody liked him. He used to play with his two friends. He never went outside in the street to play. His friends came over to our home to play with Hasib. He used to make fresh cold drinks for them. He would often call them to come to our house to play with them. Hasib never played with boys who would mess around.

After the ceremony Hasib wanted to stay in Pakistan but I was concerned about his education as he had to go back to school. I was ill and my son's wedding put more pressure on me. I became more ill and I was unable to do anything for a period of time. As soon as the wedding ended Saif became ill. I took him to a local doctor but he was not getting better. He lost a lot of weight due to dysentery and a high temperature. I was very concerned about him. His mother was giving him mango juice a lot and I asked her to stop it because it was making Saif's stomach upset. Saif became very weak and dehydrated.

I went to the Saudi Airline office for an earlier return flight so we could send Saif back home to England. They said you can buy new return tickets but there is no earlier flight available on your existing tickets. I told my wife and daughter but they wouldn't believe me. They both went to the Saudi Airline office and got the same reply. I was under huge pressure and worried sick about Saif. I asked my sister and her husband but they weren't helping. As I was thinking of taking Saif to the local hospital, Saif's grandmother came from Mirpur and took Saif and his mother with her. Saif stayed in hospital for 3 days and got better. When he returned to Rawalpindi, Saif told us that he didn't like the doctor because he put a needle in his arm. The poor child was frightened. He told us that he didn't want to go to Mirpur. As I remember, Saif and his mother returned to England before us. Hasib and I came after and then Imran and his mother after that.

Hasib always seemed to visit Pakistan when the weather was boiling hot. He was used to that kind of weather. He was always patient and never complained about the heat, although his cheeks were always red and flaky because of the blazing heat. He would read his prayers regularly and read the Qu'ran too. He had chosen his own clothes and sandals for his brother's wedding. His gold embroidery sandals, clothes, silk jacket and laser lights are still in his room. I hope someone looks after his belongings after I die.

On his return Hasib rejoined Matthew Murray High School. I made an extra set of keys for him so if I was out, he could get into the house. Although I am not a good cook and we were alone at home, I had to make something to eat. Hasib never complained about the food. I was ill and taking a lot of medicines. I was also suffering from high blood pressure and during the day, for no obvious reason, I would go to bed and sleep. It may be because I was tired or my blood sugar levels were high. Hasib would come home from school, eat a little and have some rest then go to Islamic class. He would watch television which he had in his room and then he went to play with his school mates. He always told me where he was going and with whom.

Hasib was very quiet and he would always talk to me with great respect and humility. He was a very dignified boy and it was a good chance for me to get to know him better as we were alone together living in the house. To keep myself busy and away from my phobia, I started to take off the ceiling paper in our bedroom. I wanted to put some wallpaper on. It was a very difficult job as I was ill and had a big cut to my stomach. I made a mistake doing that but I had to finish it somehow. I asked Hasib if he could help me out of this mess. He made some wood designs and put wallpaper up with me. One day, he might be tired and not so keen to help but I gently told him off and I never lost his respect. I just asked him why he wasn't taking any interest. I think this was the only one time in my life I said anything to him with a little anger. I am sure and I'm honoured that I am the father of Hasib because to me he was a pious person and a true friend of Allah.

When I remember this part of Hasib's life, I always cry. I cried a lot when I was writing the last page. That one page took me more than two hours to write. I am crying now. I have lost everything. I have lost my beloved son. I have lost my best friend. I have lost my future and I have lost the most precious respectable human being in my life. I have not lost my hope. I am very hopeful that one day we will meet again. He will embrace me and let me know what happened. I do not care what people say about Hasib as I know how Hasib was. I am his father and I knew him well. He was the most respectable, dignified, humble and pious person I have ever known. Ask anybody who met Hasib and they would tell you how Hasib was. May our Creator have mercy on him and give him the most beautiful place in paradise.

I always feel him around me. We talk every day and we hug every day. One day we will embrace each other in paradise. Hasib never gave me any trouble in his life. He always listened to me and respected me a lot. I wish I knew what was coming. If I knew then what I know now, I would have stopped him from going to London but I couldn't predict anything and I did not know what was in the future. There was nothing I could do. Our Almighty only knows about these things. I cannot do anything against His wishes. He gave me Hasib and He took Hasib away from me. I am weak and powerless.

So, Hasib was going to school every day and would read his prayers five times a day and I was very pleased with him. I tried my best to provide him with what he needed in his mother's absence. He loved Burton's clothes and his mother would buy them for him regularly. This shop is a little expensive for us but she would go when the sales were on. He never demanded these clothes but he would wear them. He was a person who could take and give graciously in his life. He was not a worldly human being. He was always satisfied with less. His clothes fit me too but I never wore his clothes except on one occasion when he was giving away two jackets, I asked him if I could take them. Once I used his dark jackets and it felt very strange, as if somebody was not happy for me to wear this jacket. I felt as though somebody had control over me. I put it back in a suitcase and it's still there.

Hasib was not a stubborn young man. He was very polite, considerate and an easy going young boy. He was very easy to talk to. I washed his clothes, cooked for him, took him to school and took care of him whilst his mother was in Pakistan for a short time. I used to give him pocket money and he was very careful with it. He never demanded more.

Once his Islamic teacher came to our house and asked me tell Hasib not to play with a particular boy and his friend. He was complaining that those boys do not come to Islamic class and they are bad. I knew those teenagers and I had never heard any complaints about them. They would walk with Hasib and play, but not attending Islamic class does not mean that they are bad. I had seen Hasib walking with them around Holbeck. They were alright. One boy was having a difficult time because his mother and father had separated and his mother had returned to Pakistan. I do not think that this made him bad. However I asked Hasib and told him what his teacher had said. Hasib told me "they are my friends and they just play and we walk around Holbeck. Their parents do not let them go to Islamic class." I told him what had been said and advised him to be careful. Hasib was not doing anything wrong so I let him stay with his friends.

I think the reason was that the boy had stopped attending Islamic class and the teacher was not happy. Instead of talking to his father, he came to me as he was losing children in his class and, of course, money too. But I never understood why he came to me to try to stop Hasib playing with his friends. I saw Hasib and his friends walking around Holbeck. They never caused any trouble for anyone. When his mother and brother returned to England, Hasib was very happy to see them. I often asked Hasib about his education and progress and he told me that he was happy with his school work. He was also happy that his school teachers were satisfied with his school work.

I used to remind Hasib that he was very lucky to visit Saudi Arabia and to see the Kabbah. He was very honoured to do Umrah at the age of 12. He used to talk about going to Makkah and seeing the Prophet's Masjid and His (pbuh) holy grave. He unintentionally brought back the key of our hotel room from Madina. He did not realise that it was in his bag. The key is still with us and I think my wife kept it in a safe place. All those hotels were demolished soon after we went to Pakistan after our Umrah anyway and a lot of new hotels were built.

It was Hasib's habit and splendour; he would talk to me with great respect and love. A lot of other people told me that he is a very respectful young boy. He would always keep his voice low and always come near me if he had to say something. I never had any complaints about him from any relatives, friends or his brothers and sisters. He treated all of us with great respect but some people were not aware of him, or maybe they were ignorant.

Not long afterwards, my eldest son's wife arrived for the first time in England. Hasib used to go to his brother's room to play with games. Once he did not know and he started to play his

Nintendo game. This newcomer shouted at Hasib and he told his mother and brother. He never talked to her again.

Hasib told his mother many times and she also started shouting at Imran. She was disrespectful and my eldest son didn't deserve this treatment. Hasib also told his mother what his brother should do according to Shariah Law when his wife treats him in this way. Some Pakistani women and men, when they come to this country, they change in a way that they forget who they were in the first place. Soon after they get the right to stay in this country, they change and this change is selfishness and ignorance. This was exactly what happened in our case. I think people forget their roots and sometimes they bring a lot of shame on themselves.

My son Hasib was right when he complained about this newcomer. Whatever he said he was completely right and whatever he told me and his mother about his brother's future was also, as it turned out, right.

8. HASIB'S HAJJ

"My Lord! Grant me the power and ability that I may be grateful for your favours which you have bestowed on me and on my parents, and that I May do righteous good deeds that will please you, and admit me by Your Mercy among Your righteous slaves".

(Al Qu'ran 27: 19).

MY BELOVED SON Hasib (May Allah shower His mercy on him), my wife and I embarked on a most sacred and most emotional journey to perform Hajj in 2002. It was a once in a life time pilgrimage to Makkah for Hasib. It was my third which I was performing for my late father. May Allah accept our journey and May Allah forgive my father?

It was December 2001 when we made our intention to travel to Saudi Arabia for Hajj. I talked to my wife and discussed whether we could take Hasib with us. She was very happy to hear my intention and I prepared myself to give Hasib the very good news. One evening, I went to Hasib's room and asked him if he was prepared to come with us for the pilgrimage. Hasib was doing something, perhaps school work. I told Hasib the good news, but suddenly without any thought he refused. I told him the benefits of this sacred journey and that he would be very lucky as he was only 16 and this was a very privileged opportunity as not many young men of his age went for Hajj. I told him if he is happy and willing then good, but I would never put pressure on him to come with us. His mother also asked him if he wanted to go. We told him there was no rush and to take his time. "If you decide just let me know, I will make all the arrangements". I was satisfied that if this journey was his fate then nobody could stop him travelling for Hajj.

Next day, Hasib told his mother that he was concerned about his school work and that this was the only reason he was hesitant but then he said after thinking on it, if he could get time off school then it would be okay. His mother told him not to worry about his school work, we would see his teacher and find out if he is allowed to go for Hajj without losing his lessons, or perhaps they could be done when he returned. As soon as we assured him, he was full of joy. I suggested to him that we could go to school and tell his teacher now. I went to his school and asked his teacher and he would let Hasib know what lessons he will miss and would be given some extra lessons before he goes. His teacher advised me to fill in a form in which I returned to him. The head teacher was also very happy for him and he provided all the information and help for Hasib's school lessons. Now everything was running smoothly and Hasib made his intention to go for Hajj was very happy and I told my tour operator that Hasib was also coming. The teacher had given Hasib his signed application form back and he was allowed to go for 4 weeks. Many times Hasib told me that he was very surprised and shocked when he heard about going to Makkah. He was told by his teacher that he could complete his school work when he returned home.

Following the events of 7/7 there was a lot of discussion regarding the radicalisation of Hasib and many 'experts' pointed to this trip we made to perform Hajj which is why this section of the book is very detailed. No one else has actually written about took place during our stay there so by detailing his whereabouts it might shed some light on Hasib's state of mind just a few years before the event.

The Yemeni Airline we went on was poor. We didn't choose to fly with this airline, it was our tour operator who was making money from the Hajjis. The aeroplane was filthy - it was a cargo plane converted to take passengers. We were all shocked. It was pure selfishness and greed by the tour operator. He must have made a lot of money. When we reached Makkah we performed our first Umrah on 28th January 2002. It was Monday and a very hot day and after the completion of Umrah, Hasib and I kissed the Black Stone (Hajr-e-Aswad). I was very aware of the rush around the

Kabbah and some pushing too, that's why I had decided to kiss the Black Stone after the Umrah during which the wearing of perfume is not allowed.

According to the programme, we only had to stay in Makkah for a few days then travel to Madina. Therefore, we travelled to Madina on 29th January at night time. The first day we stayed in Makkah at the hotel Dar-ul-Ghazi. It was a very old and dirty hotel. We had no beds and 8 people slept on the floor of one room. I am sorry I cannot describe the hotel's condition any more. However we were there for a reason and despite difficulties and restlessness, we had to be patient. I remember some Hajjis did complain to the group leader but he didn't listen. One couple complained to the Saudi Authorities and then the group leader had a good grilling from them. I was told that he paid some money back to the couple and apologised. Some Hajjis complained about the quantity of Hajjis in one room. There was not enough space for Hajjis in the allocated rooms. Hasib was concerned but I told him not to worry and he should leave it to me, I would sort it out. Anyway, we went to Madina according to the tour operator's programme. It is sometimes very difficult staying with other people in one room. It is very unfortunate that a lot of Hajjis don't care about their room-mates. I have a long list of what they do. There may be some travel comforts now but it was very difficult travelling to Makkah in those days. We reached Madina on 30th January 2002. It had taken us 16 hours to reach there. It usually take 6-7 hours but again, unfortunately, the Saudi Mu'allam arrangements were not up to scratch, and unnecessary coach stoppages make Hajjis lives miserable. Of course, we had to be patient but a tour operator is supposed to make Hajjis lives easy!

Hasib was 16 years old but a tall man. The bus seats were very small and there wasn't enough leg room for 16 hours travel. You could imagine yourself how difficult it was. I told Hasib to have some rest during the coach travel. His mother was very tired and she slept on and off during the travel to Madina. Hasib was very patient and I tried everything to make him comfortable. I told him to come out of the bus and stretch his legs instead of sitting inside when it stopped. We both did just that and made our journey as comfortable as we could.

We were about 7 km from Madina City when our coaches stopped at the welcome centre for Hajjis who came from Makkah. We stayed there for almost 6 hours to clear our coaches. This is a Ministry of Hajj office and again red tape, laziness, unhappy Saudi workers who do not want to work made our lives more difficult, but we were patient. Many workers came and went after counting us. We had to comply with the Saudi rules. This was not a welcome gesture or even near to it as we have to wait 6 hours for clearing. Many people were fed up and complained but there was nothing we or our tour operator could do to make them work quickly. These young workers had no worries about Hajjis. They were just 17 year-old boys who had no idea about our feelings. This wasn't my first experience of Saudi Arabia and this sort of experience is a part of the journey. Some travellers can take it but some get fed up very quickly. I am not saying all of these workers are lazy but there are some who don't bother at all. The poor coach drivers had no rest at all and if they got chance to sleep, they slept under the stationary bus or on a steering wheel.

We reached Madina on the 30th at Asr time and we both offered our humble Salam to our beloved Prophet Mohammed (pbuh) and his Companions (RA) after Asr Salat. It was the most gracious, emotional and humble moment of our lives when we offered our Salam to our Prophet and Companions. I had never seen such a divine light on Hasib's face before. Many Muslims depart from this world without having this most emotional experience, and here was my Hasib about to perform his first Hajj at just 16. This young man was not Hasib; he was somebody else. I was scared to see him. I have to say, it doesn't matter how many pages I write about him, when he was standing before our prophet's grave, I observed Hasib offering his Salam to his beloved Prophet (pbuh) and Companions. It was also my first experience of witnessing Hasib before in Madina, but it was different this time. Hasib and I stood humbly in front of the holy graves and kept reciting Darood Sharif. The Caretakers of the holy graves never said anything to

Hasib for example to move or walk. They were so kind to this young man, I can't imagine why?

> *"May Allah Subhana Taa'la shower His blessings and*
> *Peace upon our Prophet Mohammed, and on his family*
> *and all his Companions. By Your mercy O Merciful*
> *of all those who show mercy."*

A young man, only 16, stood before his beloved Prophet (pbuh) and offered his Salam. Not only were the humble servants of graves smiling at him, but above all, our Prophet and his Companions were saying to him, "Hasib, we accept your Salaam and one day, we will grant you the most precious covering of our graves and also present from our Burial Chambers." Hasib has gone to heaven now but I got the most precious green and red covering of holy graves and a Tasbeeh from the gracious chambers. "O, Allah shower Your mercy on Hasib."

Our hotel in Madina was clean and very near to the masjid. The manager of Dar Bin Mazi hotel was a young Pakistani man and a very nice person. Our tour operator allocated a separate room for us. Hasib, his mother and I slept in the same room. Some of the hotel workers would come to our room and provide us with food and tea three times a day. This hotel was near the main entrance of the ladies gate and the gates number was 28, 29 and 30. These hotels were demolished in 2007/08 and some of them rebuilt. They all have modern facilities now. A Pakistani hotel was also opposite our hotel where we stayed. If Hasib needed some more food or he wanted to have different food, than we always bought from that Pakistani hotel. The food was very tasty. Many times I bought food which Hasib liked particularly roast chicken and kebabs. I asked him if he wanted to eat from that hotel regularly then we could go there and eat, but he said he would also eat food provided by our tour operator. The men who supplied food to our rooms were very polite young men. They loved Hasib and used to talk to him. They asked many times how Hasib was and they liked his quietness.

It is not compulsory but we read our 40 prayers from 30.1.02

to 5.2.02 in the Madina Masjid Nabavi. Many Hajjis make this an issue and just blame each other. I have no idea why they sometimes argue among themselves regarding this issue. Hajj is in Makkah not in Madina. Offering 40 prayers in Madina is not necessarily part of the Hajj. I have heard strong arguments against and also in favour, but to me, this is certainly not compulsory.

I got a plan which showed who was buried in the nearby Baqeeh graveyard. I took Hasib with me and we spent a lot of time finding out the names on the graves. There were also freshly dug graves and Hasib jumped in to one of them. He was very interested in finding out who they were. He would stand on the head side of graves and read Dua (prayer) for them. Some of the officials were also guiding the Hajjis but they were not giving any information about them. I had a map with me but surprisingly, Hasib took me to the grave where Dai Halima (RA) is buried. I was shocked he knew about her. He also took me to some other graves who were Martyrs and he told me who they were. Whilst this was going on, I started to walk behind him and he told me who is who. I was astonished by his knowledge.

We went to Baqeeh four times to pay our respects and read our Duas. Hasib was very interested to see freshly dug graves. When he stood there, I could see his great interest in the graves. I felt he was a noble young man and very near to his Creator. I saw many times as he walked in the streets of Madina, his face was lit with a divine light. To be honest with you, I was taken aback sometimes when I saw this very young man who was showing me the graves of the Martyred in Baqeeh. I was astonished at his nobility, dignity and of his insight into places. I told his mother each time we went to Baqeeh and she just smiled. She knew Hasib was a special son but I was frightened at times.

We always set off from the hotel to the masjid at least an hour before each salat. Hasib's mother would go to the ladies side and we read our salats in the men's side. We always read our salat very near to where our Prophet (pbuh) is buried.

I would like to discuss here a very dignifying experience. Hasib would wear Arabic dress and he was well built, tall and the clothes suited him very well. He would wear different coloured dresses but he would usually wear white. He would put a red striped scarf on his head and he looked like an Arab. He loved Arabic white musk perfume and people often looked at him. He was the centre of attention. It is very difficult for me to explain my emotions because it tears me apart.

There were a lot of shops around our hotel and most workers were Pakistani, Afghani and other nationalities. I hardly saw an Arabic person serving in a shop. Each time we went for prayers, we had to walk through a street and at the end of the street there was a bend, on that bend was a clothes shop. We could see two young men and an old man serving or sitting in their shop. One young man always looked at us as we passed near his shop and then he would whisper to the others and then to the old man. The old man had a long white beard. After whispering, they would all look at us and talk to each other while smiling. Many times I asked my wife to make sure she was properly covered as I thought they may be staring at her, even though I was sure that my wife was fully covered, her dress was long and she was covered from head to toe, but then I thought I might be doing the men a disservice. Perhaps they weren't looking at her. I became very edgy and upset and asked myself were they looking at Hasib, me or my wife? I dare not go near them and say something. I thought if I say something to them or ask them why they are looking at us I could make a fool of myself. It wasn't possible to change our route as it was the only quick way to the masjid.

Each time we passed I tried to work out whether they were looking at my wife but they were actually looking at Hasib. Eventually I decided we would change our way to the masjid but before I did I thought I should talk to the shopkeepers and ask them why they were staring at us each time we passed. My problem was that Pakistani people are aware that when we go to Pakistan, local people sometimes look at us but especially our women. This is a very bad and humiliating habit. Here I was thinking in Madina maybe these young men were looking at my wife, as some Pakistanis regrettably do.

One day, bearing in mind that we were going to change our route to the masjid, we set off early. We went straight to their shop. No customers were there, so I asked them if they could explain why they looked at us and smiled when we passed the shop? A young man replied "when I see a tall boy with you, I think he is Arab, but when I see you wearing Pakistani clothes, then I guess he is Pakistani." He told us that "this young boy is very smart and I always thought he was Saudi Arabian. We just guessed and looked at you all and talked about this young boy. He is very good looking."

The old man asked me if Hasib was my brother. I told him he was my son. He then pointed to one of his young men there, "I told you this young boy was not his brother." The other two men started to argue with each other about Hasib's nationality or ethnicity. I told them that our son wasn't Pakistani but he was born in England and he is British and he is our son. I told them that Hasib was here to do his Hajj. The old man and the other two praised me and my wife and told Hasib in their language that he's very lucky and fortunate to come here for Hajj at his age. Hasib smiled at them and said something in English and we went towards the masjid.

I really felt bad about myself because I had done them a disservice. I apologised and shook their hands. They greeted Hasib with a very respectful hug. We passed this shop many times after and we always greeted them and smiled. I have been there many times since but I was unable to meet them because that area has been demolished and new hotels and shops have been built. The old man always carried a bamboo stick in his hands. I was not sure why he carried this but I found out later that it was a fabric measuring stick which was a yard long. He was an old man then, may Allah have mercy on him, wherever he is now. I always pray for those two boys. It was a very good experience. It is worth remembering that the Saudi Kingdom paid 2 million SR for each meter they took from the shopkeepers, hotels and other businesses (about £200,000 per sq meter). The Saudi Kingdom spent huge amounts of money to extend and refurbish Masjid Nabavi. This is one of the greatest and the most beautiful places in the whole world for Muslims.

On 31.1.2002, Hasib and I read 12 Nafals in Riaz-ul-Jannah. Hasib already knew most of the holy sites in the masjid. If he was unsure he always asked or I would inform him according to my little knowledge. We read our Friday prayer on 1.2.2002 on the roof of the masjid. It was very busy on Friday. We also wanted to see the roof. It was huge and full of people. We both offered our Salam to Prophet Mohammed (pbuh) 18 times and each time it was more emotional and a more extraordinary experience than the last. We went to see some of the most historic and holy places in Madina on 3.2.2002. Hasib was glad to see so many historic places.

Hasib was very unsettled and agitated somehow when he stood before Shohada-e-Ohd (The Martyrs of Ohd). He looked at the graves and read Duas for them all. I had no idea why he was so upset or concerned about them. Our guide was very experienced and Qari Khalil Ahmed took our group to some new historic places. Hasib walked over the mountain where the holy war took place. I cried many times when he was telling us about what non-believers did to our Prophet (pbuh) and his Companions. It was a very emotional visit.

Qari Khalil Ahmed, our guide, was also crying when he told us about two boys (May Allah be pleased with them) when they were little and wanted to participate in the fight. Our Prophet (pbuh) refused to allow one of them to fight because of his age. The story of the two boys is exceptionally emotional. The little boy was disheartened because he could not participate in the Uhad war and Prophet Mohammed (pbuh) told him not to because he was not capable for war. But after seeing his great interest and a type of wrestling with the older boy, he was allowed to participate. It was a fixed match with the older boy as the younger asked him, "when we wrestle, you pretend to be the loser and then I can tell Prophet (pbuh) that I have won and I am also strong enough to go to war." Looking at his young boy's determination the Prophet (pbuh) was happy to let him go.

2nd February 2002 was my 47th birthday. I was lucky that my

birthday occurred when I was in the holy city of Madina. Although we do not celebrate our birthdays, I asked my wife where my present was. She told me that Madina was enough for me. Hasib was totally against celebrating birthdays and instead he suggested that we should give money to poor people and look after the needy.

On my birthday it rained very heavily in Madina. When we were out we got soaked. The ladies side of the masjid was full inside and out but there was still enough space at the men's side.

As I mentioned, Hasib was wearing Arabic dress and he looked like a very dignified young man. I wore my own Pakistani clothes. The Saudis were thinking that Hasib was Arabic. Each time we went to offer our Salam to Prophet Mohammed (pbuh), Hasib always walked in front of me and I kept myself close to his right side. I saw some Saudis put their arm around Hasib's back and they would take him to the right side of the grave. Hasib would stand there and offer his Salam without any problem. He was not asked a single time to move and neither did any policeman ever say anything to him. They thought he was Arabic too. Although there are no favours in that place for anybody, Hasib was like an Arab and so all Arabs treated him with respect. Hasib smiled at policemen and others who were responsible for keeping a straight queue and they smiled back. Hasib stood there for a long time and because of this, I was able to stay with him.

A few times, I commented to Hasib that he gets special treatment from the police and others because of his dress. Hasib always smiled and suggested I wear Arabic clothes but he knew I wouldn't do that because although I like Arabic dress, I do not feel comfortable in it. I have worn it once in my life but that was after Hasib passed away. I have been to Madina many times since with the gracious permission of my Prophet (pbuh) and my Allah. I always wished that Hasib was with me. My heart melts and my eyes weep when I am unable to see him around. I cannot describe my feelings when I saw him standing before our Prophet Mohammed (pbuh) and his Companion Hazrat Abu Bakr Siddique and Hazrat Omar Din Khattab (May Allah be pleased with them).

I am very happy to say that the Saudi people loved Hasib. A lot of people wanted to come near him and adored him. I am witness to the divine light on Hasib's face, each time he went to offer his Salam to his Prophet Mohammed (pbuh) and his Companions (RA).

My wife and I were very happy that Hasib was enjoying his Hajj journey and learning a lot of things about Islam. Hasib bought some silver rings for himself. The shopkeeper was very surprised when Hasib started speaking English. He thought Hasib was an Arab. I told the shopkeeper my son is from England and a Pakistani. Hasib bought some perfumes and a full set of Imam Kabbah Abdul Rehman Sudais CDs. He also bought some books and brought them home. The shopkeeper would give him extra attention and he loved it. Hasib had a magical personality and as soon as someone talked to him, they would feel his humble, respectful and divine personality. Hasib also bought some pictures of Kabbah and Masjid Nabavi and they are hung on our walls. We are allowed to clean them but not to take them down. As long as I live, nobody is allowed to take those pictures down.

As many people may know, during Hajj there are too many people and not enough space, and it's very difficult to get space inside Haram. But when Hasib and I were looking for a space to sit, they would offer Hasib a place beside them and I would also find seating near him. Sometimes they would squeeze themselves together to make room for him to sit beside them. You may say that I shouldn't be doing this but I always tried to sit behind him. I respected Hasib so much and I always thought and I was sure that he was a divine person and very close to his Creator. I always followed him and it made me very proud when Hajjis were giving him so much respect, honour and a space to sit beside them. Many times, Hasib went with his mother shopping. He was very keen to buy alcohol free oils and perfumes. He loved white Arabic musk and he would go to a special shop called "Hamel-e-musk". He also bought some Oud musk which is very expensive. He bought a lot of caps, Tasbeeh, Zamzam water and other things for his friends.

The Hajj journey is very tiring and having to share rooms with other people made it worse. Sometimes groups of incompatible people find it hard to pass time easily. Some smoked, some stayed out late at night, and some would spend more time in the shops than in Masjid. Hasib had borrowed a movie camera from his auntie and took it with him. It was faulty but somehow Hasib managed to make a movie. Although all that he recorded is still with us, I have not seen it since Hasib left us. We stayed in Madina for 8 days and then came back to Makkah on the 8th February 2002 with the group. It was Friday when we came back from Madina and we had to do our Umrah and Friday prayers. Hasib did his second Umrah for himself and I do not know about my wife. Although there were too many Hajjis, we still managed to perform our Umrah very easily. We had to go to the second floor for our Sa'i because the first floor was full.

It took us 12 hours to come back to Makkah. The coach driver was a good person and he drove the bus very quickly. Most Hajjis were aware that the coach driver always asks for Baksheesh and we understood it is their working season. We collected some money and gave it to him. He was very happy as Hajjis filled his hat with Saudi Riyals.

After arriving at Makkah, we stayed at a different hotel. Apart from us, there was another family in our hotel from our group. We had a big room but there were extra men in our room. These two young men were older than Hasib but they were like our sons. One of them was a Qu'ran Hafiz and Imam of the masjid. These two men were sleeping on a hotel reception sofa and our group leader asked me if they could use our room at night time. I asked my wife and Hasib and they reluctantly agreed. What actually happened was that this family had no space in the other hotel and so were transferred to this hotel. An old man and all his family including Hafiz's wife were in a large room but there was not enough room for them. So we were told to give some space to these two young men. They would return late at night and sleep for 2/3 hours then go back to the masjid. They only used a little space and never disturbed us. We were fine and they were happy. We hardly saw them for more than 2 hours at night.

Hafiz was a newly married man from Glasgow and he stayed

with us in Mina, Arafat and Muzdilfah. He also led our prayers five times a day in Mina. The other young man was with his mother and his luggage was in another hotel. The arrangement suited all of us and we got on well with each other. I used to bring all the food from the other hotel because it was prepared there, so it was my duty to bring the food for my family. I was very shocked and angry when I saw so much food outside the hotel rooms, and many Hajjis were ignorant and ungrateful for what they were getting. It was really bad. There was chapattis and curry all over. I feel bad that they were just wasting food. I ate some of that food but I couldn't eat all of it. I hardly saw any meat or chicken there but when it was vegetables or lentils, then nobody would eat them and leave outside their room door. Hajjis shouldn't be doing this at all.

While I was doing Tawaf Kabbah, I saw two young girls carrying their mother on their back and circling the Kabbah. The old woman was very thin and weak and her daughters carried her turn by turn. The other Hajjis were saying something to her daughters, and of course it was emotional for me. I heard and read in books that a long time ago sons used to carry their parents and do Kabbah's Tawaf but I had never seen this before. Tears came to my eyes and I pointed out to Hasib that this is how children should be when their parents are weak and you should look after me when I get older. He just smiled and told me not to worry.

Hasib and his mother used to go upstairs on the third floor and do Tawaf after Isha prayers. It is very long and takes at least one and a half hours to complete. They have to walk 7 times around the Kabbah and one round is about 1 km from start to finish. Hasib and his mother would like to walk and avoid the rush. I, on other hand, would do my Tawaf on the first floor, although it takes time and there are too many Hajjis there, I didn't have to walk so far. It was easier for me on the first floor. I told Hasib a few times that he should come down with me and do Tawaf on the first floor but he disagreed as he didn't want to do that as there were a lot of women on the first floor, and he didn't want to touch or push them, even accidentally. Hasib was right and it is advisable to avoid this pushing and unnecessary cause of suffering to other Hajjis, but it is still not always avoidable. Hasib did Tawaf on 10/2/02, 11/02/02, 12/02/02 and 13/02/02 on the third floor. Hasib and his mother went touring holy and historic places while I stayed back at the hotel and completed my Tawaf because I had been to those places before. We read our Friday prayers right in front of the main gate called Bab-e-Abdul Aziz. We couldn't even enter on the first floor as it was packed with Hajjis and the police blocked our way. Hasib and I found a place together and my wife sat down nearby with the ladies. It was very hot but we used to it now. We, most times, read our Maghrib and Isha prayers on the third floor together. The view of Kabbah from the third floor is beautiful and raises emotions. This is the best view your eyes could see on this planet.

I saw Imam Kabbah Abdul Rehman Sudais entering Hateem (Part of Kabbah), minutes before Maghrib prayer. I saw him on 12/2, 13/2, 15/2 and 16/2/02, continuously 4 days. I was lucky to recognise him from the third floor as many Hajjis didn't know who our Imam was. This Imam is very popular and his voice is beautiful and when he reads the Qu'ran, he brings tears to your eyes. Once I saw a cleaner who was in Hateem kissing the Imam's forehead and he offered a glass of Zamzam water to the Imam. He may be the security officer as well because nobody is allowed to go near the Imam. I have met him many times during my Umrah and Hajj. His beautiful electric voice makes everybody tearful. Hasib was very happy to see him from the top of the third floor. He loved this adored scholar.

After the Maghrib prayers, I would read some voluntary prayers and Hasib would also sometimes do Tawaf with his mother until Isha prayer. As I mentioned before, it was very lengthy and hard and also time consuming. Being a diabetic, it is not easy as I had to go to the toilet often. I have only one kidney and I have to empty my bladder regularly. I cannot hold myself in until Isha prayer. Imagine millions of people were all over, then I had to walk outside to the toilets and they wouldn't be vacant either. I would go down from the third floor to the toilets outside and come back upstairs the same way. It took about 45 minutes both ways. It was very tiring, I didn't like it but I had no other choice.

If you enter through the main gate of Bab-e-Abdul Aziz by the escalator you arrive on the third floor through gate No 92. When you come out of gate 92 on the third floor you reach an open space, and you can see a dome on your right side. On your left, there are 3 golden domes called the Bab-e-Fahd domes. Hasib and his mother would sit under that dome on the round edges. As we always sat in front near the wall fence, I would ask my wife to keep our prayer mats there and when I returned, we would read our Isha prayer together on our mats. In the meantime, she would sit under the dome and read the Qu'ran and wait for me. I always found them when I came back from the toilets. I remember, as soon as I come back and they saw me, they would both get up and we would all go back to our prayer mats. We read our Isha prayers and return to our hotel for the night.

Now this place is like a shrine to me and my wife. It is very hard to write about this. It makes me very upset and tearful. It may not be of interest for some people but this place is very important to us. Each time we have returned to Makkah since Hasib's death it is emotional. My wife would not want to go to that particular spot but I did although it was very hard. I would sit and read some prayers for Hasib and stay with him for a bit. As I say, it is not so interesting for other people but this place is like a shrine for us.

During Ramadan 2007, we went to Makkah for Umrah. On 16th September 2007, it was Hasib's birthday and we performed our Umrah on that day in the morning. This was the best present we could give our beloved son. He would have been 21 years old. One day my wife and I went to the third floor. We had no idea that it was allocated for men only. A Saudi official told us to leave this floor as some Saudis couples were sitting there talking to each other. I told him we will leave soon and he agreed. We went towards that particular dome. My wife would not go near it. As we were passing the dome, we saw a couple with a little child. My wife shouted at me and said, "Look Hasib!" I asked her, "Where", and she pointed out a couple and said, "He is Hasib." He looked like Hasib. I said "yes, he is". Then she started crying. It is worth remembering that I rarely see my wife cry. She is a very patient woman. She asked me if I could go near to him. There wasn't much difference between Hasib and this guy. My wife was crying and walking a few steps towards him and before walking back. She asked me again to go and talk to him. My wife was hysterical and kept crying. That's the first time I had seen my wife in that state and I will never forget those moments.

We have been through a lot of pain and heartache but looking at this man, the resemblance was mind blowing. I was afraid that talking to a stranger when his wife was with him wouldn't be easy. I went near to them as they were sitting on the steps of the dome. I greeted them and asked if he could speak English. He was an Arabic young man. He couldn't understand English and I was not able to convey my message in Arabic. My Arabic language skills are limited. I shook his hand and kept it tight. I used some sign language but he still did not understand me. I daren't look at his wife. I put my hand around his child's face and stroked him but I kept away from his wife. I started crying too and he became a bit concerned when he saw my tears. Despite all my efforts, he couldn't understand what I was saying to him. I could see my wife about 10 yards away, wiping tears away and she asked me to leave as we both were very upset. I hugged the "Hasib" look alike and walked away. As soon as we reached near gate No. 92, there were some Pakistani men filling up the coolers with Zamzam water. I asked one of them if he could translate and help me to tell this young man of our plight, but he started swearing at the Saudis. I found this shocking. I was only asking for help but he became abusive and used bad language towards the Saudis. He also said they are all the same and bad people. That particular day was very upsetting for us. After that we hardly spoke to each other and didn't talk about Hasib. This young man was about 20 years old, with the same colour and complexion as Hasib. I have seen that particular dome on the television many times during the Ramadan prayers. I do not know why the camera always goes on to this dome again and again. It brings a lot of memories back but it is very upsetting.

Now I want to take you back to 2002 and Hasib's journey for Hajj. Hasib, my wife and I would go to Haram for least an hour before each prayer. If we got the chance, we would do Tawaf (7 circuits of the Kabbah). It all depended on the rush. We did as many Tawaf as we could. Now, as the Hajj days were approaching, the rush was getting bigger and bigger. Each day we found it hard to go inside the Haram and all the floors were packed every day.

We went to Mina on 20.2.2002 and before that we wore our Ihram (two white cloth sheets) before we travelled. It was our intention to go to Haram but due to the rush we couldn't. Instead we did it in our hotel. It is allowed and many Hajjis prefer this to avoid unnecessary discomfort to other people in Haram. We had been asked to get ready after Isha and the buses could come any time. We waited all night but there were no signs of the buses. We were unable to sleep in case we missed our bus. They arrived at about 6am and we reached Mina at about 7am. It was nothing to do with our management as Saudi Authorities were make the travel arrangements. Just imagine millions of Hajjis travelling by bus on this particular day and it is likely to have delays. Hasib and I stayed in our allocated tent with the other Hajjis and Hasib's mother was with the women in a different tent. Our air-conditioned tents were joined together and if we needed to see each other, we were able to communicate easily.

On that day, after a short rest, the three of us walked to see Jamarat (where we threw stones on Shaitan). It was a very hot day but we were in good shape and looking forward to completing our Hajj. We checked all our directions and showed Hasib what to do in case we got lost during the travelling to and from Jamarat. We came back to our tents after 4 hours. We always found it very easy as we knew our route and checked where we should go to come back safely. As it's very easy to get lost, it is advisable to go on a test journey so one is used to the route. We chose an electric pole No.19 and that pole was attached to one of the buildings of the Al-Baik hotel. On the way back from Jamarat, we had to turn from that particular pole and restaurant. It's possible if anyone forgot or lost their direction, it might take a day or two to find your way back to your tent. All the tents are white and the roads look similar too. It is very easy to get lost there. If you lose your way back to the tents that means sometimes you miss your stay in Arafat and that means you have missed your Hajj. Although there are many boy scouts and policemen, they sometimes give you the wrong directions and you would be all over in Mina and still unable to find your tent. I have seen many Hajjis asking about their tent when they were lost.

We spent our first night in Mina and the young man who was in our room in Makkah led us for the prayers. He was a young Imam but very experienced. Some Hajjis objected because he was young but when he asked them "if anyone wishes to lead the prayer, they are most welcome," nobody came forward. The women's tent next door was noisy, they never stopped talking, even at times during our prayers – it was really very embarrassing. Our Imam told them from his tent that they should consider quietness at least during prayer time but there was no change. We were unable to sleep during the night as they kept telling stories to each other all night. I can only ask Allah for His guidance for them. Next day, we got to Arafat and it was our main Hajj day. On 21.2.2002, we got ready and packed our handbags and took only necessary items with us. We reached Arafat at 11am.

We spent our time reading Qu'ran, Duas and asking Allah to forgive our sins. We read our Zohar and Asr prayer behind our young Imam. It was hot but it was the most important day of Hajj. Most Hajis came out of their tents just before Maghrib prayer and keep reading, asking for forgiveness. Hasib, his mother and myself were very happy as we had completed a part of the Hajj today. We greeted each other and I embraced Hasib. I took some memorable photos. Hasib was really very happy.

We had to go to Muzdilfah that night and I asked Hasib and his mother to have some rest. We had to travel by bus and again millions of people were going to Muzdilfah and we saw thousands of buses travelling towards Muzdilfah just after dark. It was a very heartfelt time for everybody. We had our evening meal and just laid down. Our buses arrived and we reached Muzdilfah at about 11 pm. My God, this open place was full of people, at least 5 million of us. What a great gathering! What a place where all Muslims were together for just one reason. We manage to find an open space and spread our mats. We found it difficult to spread our mats because the space was like a ditch. We read our Maghrib and Isha prayers turn by turn. We then had a bit of food and lay down and kept reading. I went to sleep and woke up about 3.30 am and saw Hasib talking to a young boy from London. He was telling Hasib that it was permissible to go back to Mina early in the morning, but I informed him that only children, mothers, old and ill people are allowed to go to Mina *before* Fajr prayers. Anyone who is healthy and able to travel must returned to Mina *after* Fajr prayers. Hasib wanted to go earlier but I told him that we would follow our Prophet (pbuh) and stay until we had read Fajr prayer, wait a bit and then go. We read our Fajr prayers and then come out of our designated ground to our numbered buses. Outside the metal fence Hajjis were waiting for the buses. We boarded a bus which was going very near to our Mina tent and which was full of our Bengali brothers. Their tent was very near to us and we got off in Mina and walked a little to our tent. It was a very tiring journey but this is Hajj and we were bound to have some difficulties.

The arrangements in Mina were a lot better than last time. There was more space created for extra Hajjis and better toilet arrangements. There were still long queues for the toilets. I saw people shouting at each other just to go to the toilet first because they were desperate. I saw some Bengali men selling tea on make shift stalls. They were charging very high prices but that didn't stop long queues around the stalls.

We went back to Mina about 6.30 am. It was the morning of 22.2.2002; we quickly got in the empty tent. We were very early and had plenty of time to freshen up and get ready to walk to Jamarat because it was our first day to throw stones at Shaitan. Although we could do this the following morning, we didn't want to waste precious time, otherwise there would be millions of people at Jamarat and sometimes it is possible that Hajjis can lose their lives. We walked to Jamarat and obliviously it was very hot and we were not allowed to have direct shade on our heads. I had difficulty walking and I asked my wife and son to walk slowly. I had to stop a lot of times during this walk. We had no problem going to and coming back from Jamarat as we had already checked our route. There were hundreds of thousands of Hajjis, but we managed to throw our stones at big Shaitan easily and return to our tents, by which time many of our group Hajjis were also returning from Muzdilfah. They were surprised that we had already been to Jamarat. On the way back to Mina from Jamarat, we were given water, juices and other food from the government and the Saudi King. You could read these messages on huge Saudi trucks.

Today it was Friday and a momentous and very busy day for everybody. I don't want to go in to great detail but we took our Ihrams off today and went back to our usual clothes after various restrictions. Hasib had his head shaved and so did I. This was a very memorable and happy day for us. It was also a good day for the barbers who worked very hard and made good money, although most were overcharging. I tried to cut Hasib's hair but the machine was not cutting properly, then I asked the barber to finish the job. I congratulated Hasib and his mother on completing another part of the Hajj. I hugged Hasib and kissed his forehead and at that point I was very happy as my son was doing Hajj with us. I was very emotional. I asked Hasib if he would like to have a little walk with me. We came out of our tents and had a little walk around the place where millions of Hajjis stay for a few days. This is a place to die for. After a while Hasib's thigh was hurting so we returned to our tents. Hasib was always with me, day and night, and I kept asking him if he was alright. He would say "yes." I know it's hard for old people but it's hard for the young too, but we get extra strength from our Creator.

I advised Hasib and his mother to have as much rest as they could because we had to travel back to Makkah that night for our compulsory Tawaf-e-Ziarat. Without this, our Hajj would be incomplete and we had to do it. This is the main pillar of Hajj. I also went to sleep after Isha not forgetting to put the alarm clock on. Hasib, myself and his mother always consulted each other and then they left me to make the final decision.

We got up about midnight. We had quick showers and performed ablution. We had left our travel bag so we only carried what we needed and the necessary items in the tent as we had to come back to Mina. We travelled from Mina to Makkah in a taxi. I paid 50 SR to the taxi driver. He dropped us off very near to Haram. We went straight to our hotel and put away our spare luggage. It was 3.30 in the morning and we started our Tawaf and then performed our Sa'i. It took us only 2 hours and 20 minutes to complete our full Tawaf-e-Ziarat. We finished this at 5.40 in the morning and finished by reading our Fajr prayer as well. It was Saturday 23rd February 2002. I congratulated Hasib and his mother for completing another compulsory pillar of the Hajj. I hugged Hasib and kissed him again and his mother was also over the moon. She kissed Hasib and hugged him. What else did she need in this world? Our 16 year old son had completed his Hajj! This young man was very lucky. We walked to the third floor and watched the Hajjis around the Kabbah. It was a scene to remember for a lifetime. I was crying. Not only had we completed the hardest part of our Hajj, but also Hajjis were doing Tawaf, and millions of people longed to complete the most important part of their journey of this lifetime. Haram was full and Hajjis were flowing around the Kabbah like water running slowly around it. The Hajjis were touching the outer walls. Allah o Akbar! How lucky your eyes are when you see this remarkable scene. We stayed on the third floor for some time and came down after watching the scene of a life time.

We came back to our hotel and had a little rest. It is permissible to spend some time in Mina, and then come to Makkah for Tawaf, but you are not allowed to stay in the hotel all day or night. You must return to Mina after Tawaf-e-Ziarat. The second day stone throwing starts after midday. We got up after a little rest at about 10am. We came out of the hotel and looked for a taxi. I always liked this arrangement as it was very easy, and somehow less time consuming.

When we came out of the hotel we were tired but we had to throw our stones today and tomorrow. We had to do this. I told Hasib not to worry, as we had all the time in the world on our hands, and we would do it all in our own time. His thighs were hurting and there was a lot of walking ahead of us, but Hasib was determined and ready to do what he had to do. He was an obedient son, of whom I am very proud and I am very humble to have had a son like Hasib.

A taxi stopped right in front of us. I thought the passengers would finish their journey and get out but there were two men already sitting in the taxi. The driver asked us where we wanted to go. I told him to drop us near Jamarat at Daud Bin Shisha. These two passengers were in Saudi dress and I thought they were Saudis. Now Hasib was also in Saudi dress. The taxi driver hand signalled to me 10 SR each. I agreed but where were we all going to sit? I sat in the rear with the others and Hasib and his mother were on the front passenger seat. Hasib sat first with his mother on his lap. She looked like a child was sitting in his lap. Even the taxi driver smiled.

It was very dangerous but there was too many people so whichever transport we managed to get, we would have had to use it. The next two days would be very busy because Hajjis would travelling to Makkah and returning to Mina day and night.

After an eventful taxi journey we arrived at Mina and walked to a garden to sit down for an hour to have some food. It is worth remembering that I always found it very easy to come back to Jamarat after our Tawaf-e-Ziarat. It was very hot at midday and Hasib was very thirsty. It's daunting when you are in a different country and you lose your way to a destination. I was very happy so far that we were on the right track and the right place despite a little hiccup. By now Hasib's legs were causing him pain and he was not feeling well either. I encouraged him and sat down a few times so he could rest. We walked to small Shaitan. It was stone throwing time and Jamarat was full of Hajjis. This is a very scary place and it is very easy to lose your life or get seriously injured if you are not careful. I have seen many dead Hajis on the first day of stone throwing. I was holding Hasib's hand and he was holding his mother's hand. We had stones in our other hands in a cloth pouch. We took our stones and threw them on the round wall of small Shaitan (Devil). This place was packed with Hajjis and their luggage was everywhere. Big groups were coming and going. Nobody was stopping. Large groups were not stopping and there were thousands in each group.

Then we went to the middle Shaitan and without a problem we managed to throw our stones but when we came near the big Shaitan, it was different situation there. While we were throwing stones a huge group of Hajjis, perhaps Turkish, pushed us and before they crushed us, I pulled Hasib and his mother out of the way. It wasn't a good experience and I was very scared and started shaking. Hasib was trying to hold on to his mother. It was very dusty. We felt dust in our eyes and noses. Anyway, we managed to throw our stones on the last Shaitan. As soon as we recovered, Hasib told us that someone had cut his pocket. His Hajj badge was missing and there was a sharp cut on his pocket. I told him not to worry about it. The most important thing is that we were safe and well. I am unable to describe how I managed to save both Hasib and his mother from being crushed under the Hajjis. I am very sorry but I would like to stress that many Hajjis never bother about other Hajji's safety or well being, when it comes to stone throwing, especially from the large groups like the Turks. I have seen many women crushed to death like this. I have seen bodies and opened stomachs. I have seen Hajjis jumping to their death from the top floor.

After this we walked towards Mina and, of course, we were on the right track as we had marked our route a few days earlier. It was very hot and the Hajjis were walking to Jamarat in their thousands, and the opposite road was packed with Hajjis but we could easily walk as not many Hajjis were returning to their tents. We walked slowly and on the way we had fresh drinks and water which was supplied by the Saudis and the well wishers. As soon as we reached our tents, our group of Hajjis asked us when we were going back for Tawaf-e-Ziarat and I told them that we already been last night and we just came back after throwing stones. They were very surprised and some of them said they are still waiting for their group leader to take them there.

I always did my best to protect Hasib and his mother during the journey. I always stood guard for Hasib and his mother. Although I was ill myself, I never let them out of my sight. Nobody knows about the future other than our Creator Allah. I didn't know that one day I would lose Hasib, and my life would be in darkness, and without any meaning or purpose.

We read our prayers in the tent. All the other Hajjis were very pleased that Hasib had done his Tawaf-e-Ziarat and congratulated him for doing his Hajj at such a young age. Hasib smiled and seemed very pleased. We had plenty of rest and then we went shopping. The place was heaving with Hajjis buying and selling. Hasib bought a few things he liked. He bought some small and large knives and some knives with sheep horns attached. They were very decorative and beautiful and came from Islamic countries. He loved those types of things.

The next day was our last day in Mina and the last day for stone throwing too. It's not permitted before midday. We had our breakfast and got ready. We bought some delicious cakes and nuts to take home from Mina. We read our Zohar prayer before we set off to Jamarat for the last time. We prayed to Allah for forgiveness and asked for another opportunity to come back again to this holy place. Our group leader arranged for some very ill people to travel by bus, and they had already left that morning. It's allowed to throw stones on behalf of a genuinely ill Hajji, but sometimes women take advantage of that and leave Mina without throwing stones. That's wrong. Although they can manage to shop all day but when it comes to stone throwing and walking they become ill. It's not a good practice. Many workers love to do this duty on their behalf and of course they get paid. We always did our stone throwing ourselves. It is hard to walk in very hot weather but it is possible to walk slowly and have some rest during your travel to Jamarat.

We reached Jamarat just before Asr prayer and we read our

prayer before stone throwing. I was very frightened and hoping not to have any more crushing experiences like the day before. We stoned all the Shaitans turn by turn and came out of Jamarat and walked towards Makkah. The rush started to build. We went to a place where the taxi driver dropped us and we hired a taxi for 50 SR. I immediately asked Hasib and his mother to jump into the taxi before someone else got inside. The taxi driver was a very good and decent young man and I asked him to drop us very near to Haram. He dropped us very near to the other side of Bab-e-Fahd. We read our Maghrib prayer in Haram and came back to our hotel. There was a huge flow of Hajjis coming back from Mina and everybody was in a hurry. A lot of Hajjis were carrying big bags. Other group members started to return to the hotel and told us that they got lost and it took them 6-8 hours to reach Haram. We read our Isha prayer and went to bed after our evening meal. We were very tired and slept very well. We got up early the next day and read our Fajr prayer. All our Hajjis were in the hotel and had reached Makkah safely. A few times Hasib went to Haram by himself and stayed there for a long time. We also let Hasib do things on his own so he could find out about different places. We did our last Tawaf on Monday 25.2.2002 at 10.30 am. We had to come back to England, so we bought some dates, Zamzam water and Hasib also got some Zamzam and a lot of gifts for his friends.

Our return journey was a nightmare. We had to wait 28 hours at the Saudi airport and then when the plane came we were flown to Yemen and had to sit on the tarmac for hours because the pilots needed a rest! Meanwhile our fellow passengers stuffed their faces so needed the toilet. As you can imagine being stuck in a tin can filled with people in the middle of an Arabian desert for hours the place was fairly pungent. We were very grateful to get back to England.

After Hajj, I saw some changes in Hasib. They were not major changes. I think some changes were unavoidable. Hasib would wear

Above: Hasib aged 9 months with a spotted baby goat at his grandma's house.

Left: Hasib and his grandfather during the same trip

Images: ©Empire Publications

Hasib in Azad Kashmir at his grandmother's house holding his uncle's rifle.

Hasib and I with famous Pakistani actor Nadeem on the same trip

Images: ©Empire Publications

Hasib on his Hajj in Saudi Arabia in 2003. A lot of the locals thought he was Arabic!

Hasib posing as a model for his cousin's fashion show.

Images: ©Empire Publications

The timeline leading up to the bombing. Above: Hasib, Shehzad Tanweer, Siddique Khan and Jermaine Lindsey at Luton station Left: Hasib entering and exiting a branch of WHSmiths in Kings Cross station having failed to detonate his bomb on the tube.

Hasib detonated his bomb on the no. 30 bus in Tavistock Square at 9.25 am on 7th July 2005. In total the attacks killed 48 innocent people.

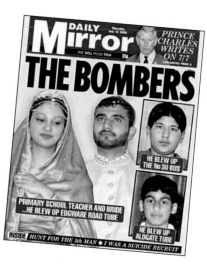

The press reaction following the bombing focussed on the Tavistock Square attack. However it went unreported that the police would not have known about the terror cell without my detective work on the Friday after it happened.

The anniversary of the attacks always brings press attention.
Here I am praying for Hasib at his grave side in 2010.

Father's tribute to his 7/7 terrorist son: Family of bus bomber Hasib Hussain are seen at teenage killer's grave on 10th anniversary of London attacks

- The parents of bus bomber Hasib Hussain visited son's grave yesterday
- Hussain was the youngest of the four suicide bombers responsible for 7/7
- Fresh flowers are regularly left at the grave and the family home in Leeds

BY CHRIS BROOKE and NARZIA PARVEEN FOR THE DAILY MAIL
PUBLISHED: 01:12, 8 July 2015 | UPDATED: 07:58, 8 July 2015

2.3k shares **756** View comments

Deep in thought, the parents of 7/7 bus bomber Hasib Hussain stood by their son's grave yesterday to remember the boy they still love.

To the outside world the 18-year-old will always be an evil suicide bomber responsible for murdering 13 innocent people on a double-decker bus in London's Tavistock Square.

But his family appear to have ignored the terrible circumstances of his death ten years ago by mourning his passing as if he were a victim himself.

Scroll down for video

And again in 2015 which led to an article in the Daily Mail and a mixed reaction.

FATHER OF SUICIDE TERRORIST MEETS BOMBING SURVIVOR

MEETING

HORROR

I forgive your bus bomb son

Mail Online   News

7/7 survivor, 44, says she FORGIVES bus suicide bomber as she comes face to face with the killer's 'broken-hearted' father in an incredible meeting

- Lisa French, 44, told Mahmood Hussain she 'felt sorry' for his terrorist son, Hasib
- Hasib's bomb killed 13 people on the number 30 bus in London on July 7, 2005
- Father Mahmood said: 'My heart is broken. I just walk around like a skeleton'

By ISABELLA NIKOLIC FOR MAILONLINE
PUBLISHED: 13:02, 16 June 2019 | UPDATED: 17:07, 16 June 2019

24

A survivor of the 7/7 terror attacks that killed 52 people and injured 700 has told the father of one suicide bomber that she forgives his son.

Lisa French, 44, sat opposite Mahmood Hussain and said she 'felt sorry' for suicide bomber Hasib Hussain who blew up the bus she was on.

The 19-year-old's bomb killed 13 people on the number 30 bus on July 7, 2005.

7/7 survivor Lisa French says she forgives bus suicide bomber

DON'T MISS

A couple of articles following the launch of this book and my meeting with Lisa France who survived the attack on the bus. It was an emotional meeting which hopefully will start to bring a bit of closure for both of us.

Islamic dress instead of western clothes. He would wear Arabic dress to college. He loved Islamic dress and had started wearing it during our Hajj journey. He was free to wear what he wanted, it really suited him.

Hasib started reading prayers in the masjid and many of his classmates and friends started to follow his lead. I can only describe what I saw. His Muslim teachers and classmates started going to a local masjid for Friday prayers. Prior to this, they would read their Friday prayer in Matthew Murray High school in a designated hall but after his Hajj, Hasib started to go to the masjid. An Imam from Bradford also used to come to school on Fridays to lead the Friday prayer. Hasib would come back home early from school on Fridays and, while he was changing, his school friends and two teachers would wait for him outside our house. In two taxis they used to go to Abu-Hurirah Masjid, Beeston. I saw his Muslim teachers and school mates outside our house many times. They may deny this now but one teacher told me Hasib had made a huge impact on them and because of him they also started reading their prayers regularly and on Fridays they would go to the masjid.

I am very sorry and somehow ashamed to write about this, but I will write about my feelings and experiences. The Muslim school teachers who used to go with Hasib to a masjid for Friday prayer told me they always avoided me and kept themselves away from me. His three teachers from Matthew Murray High school never came to me and said anything about Hasib, although they knew I was there and they could see me. One of Hasib's Muslim teachers met me by accident. He was alone and told me almost three years after 7/7 that he was very sorry. I said to him, "I'm sorry too". This religious teacher's behaviour was unfortunately sickening and shameful. He always tried to avoid me. I was thinking "my God, have I done anything wrong?" This is the Islamic freelance teacher who taught Hasib the Qu'ran and other teachings. I was very shocked at their double standards and hypocrisy. Hasib made them to go to the masjid for Friday prayer and they started reading regular prayers. Those teachers, who used to see me at home regularly praising Hasib, never came to my doorstep after 7/7 to say "We are sorry to hear about your son." I have never experienced such shameful hypocrisy before!

Although in this country we have the freedom and choice to wear our own dress and any style which we like, I am also aware that maybe some people would not like to see people in Arabic dress. Meanwhile, some women in this country are allowed to bare their chests and legs and wear whatever they. I have no problem with women dressing as they please, this is a free society, I respect their choice. Yet some of our elected Members of Parliament have problems with female Muslim dress. They must think 'what is modest and what is not?' Saying something in the press, which makes other people angry, is not freedom of speech and neither is attacking religion. I believe in freedom of speech to some extent as long as it's inside the boundaries of the law and doesn't harm others.

Although schools are here to teach and make children good citizens for this country, I am also aware of the fact that some teachers may not like some students to turn up to school in Arabic dress. I have no problem with that. They are free to say and think what they want. They might not like women wearing a Burqa, Veil or head scarf. This is also their problem if they are against it, but if they are free to think and make choices, but they should also think about other people's reactions. I believe in modesty and freedom. This is our basic human right. If our country is not allowing our basic human rights then this is certainly not a free country and those who are narrow-minded are those telling the British public what they can wear and what they can not wear. I was very much aware that some teachers and school kids did not like Hasib's Arabic dress.

After his Hajj, I was never made aware of any complaints about Hasib from our street, area, school or college. Once an Islamic teacher told me to keep Hasib away from one particular boy. I felt it was unfair for me to stop Hasib associating with that boy, he was a good lad and not a problem. In fact, one Islamic teacher was a problem and had his own agenda. I mentioned this to Hasib and asked him to be careful but suddenly one day I received a long letter from Matthew Murray High School about Hasib. It said he was emptying wheelie bins on the road and school grounds and he had also picked up wheelie bins from other people's yards and gardens and they had complained about Hasib. The next complaint was that Hasib was rude to a particular teacher. The third complaint was that he was getting more religious. The most serious complaint was that he had written on his book "Osama Bin Laden Power". I was told that school would not tolerate this kind of behaviour and Hasib would be excluded. When I read this letter, I became very upset and concerned about Hasib and thought my child would suffer if he was expelled. I was advised to make an urgent appointment with the school head to discuss the issue. I immediately made an appointment but before attending I did my homework.

I knew that Hasib wouldn't lie, even if it would cause trouble. He was never scared of anybody. Hasib was a brave and determined person and he would always do what was right. When I asked him about the wheelie bins he told me that some school kids were playing and messing about and he was just standing there. This was happening on the school grounds and it had happened before. A school teacher came out and as he was approaching them, everyone else ran away. Hasib said he was not doing anything wrong and just stood there. Why should he run? When the teacher saw him standing there, he wrote something in his note book and went back into school.

As for the serious issue of writing "Osama Bin Laden Power" on his note book, he had already told his mother about this. Hasib's woodwork teacher always called him "Osama Bin Laden" and he didn't like it. Hasib had told me that he didn't like to be called that name. He told his woodwork teacher that he must stop it but he carried on using this name. The teacher was Jewish and Hasib was certain that he did not like him wearing Arabic dress and he always teased him about it making him angry. This teacher also did not like him being a devout Muslim. Hasib thought he should behave like a teacher as he had no right to say anything about anyone's dress code or religion.

Hasib mentioned another incident where this teacher made a fool of himself. Hasib was in a woodwork class and sat on a chair and there was some wood dust on the table. The woodwork teacher blew that dust from one side of the table into Hasib's eyes. His eyes started to sting and he immediately went to the bath room and cleaned them as much as he could, but some dust still remained in the eyes which became painful for sometime. When he returned the teacher asked with some kind of hate "how are you feeling?" Hasib told him that his teacher should not do these kinds of things to his students. The teacher then said "I was just joking". It made Hasib very angry as this was happening in front of the other students. He said he told his mother about this and she stopped him from making a complaint to the head teacher.

As for the writing on Hasib's exercise book; it is worth remembering that I was familiar with my son's handwriting and I was satisfied with Hasib's answer that he hadn't written it. So off I went to the school meeting. I was a bit nervous and concerned as my son's future was at stake. I was called in to a meeting room and I saw an army of men and women. I said hello and introduced myself to everybody present. Some officers from the local education authority were there, as well as school management, the Head teacher and some others, maybe a deputy head teacher. I was already nervous but when I saw all these people I realised this could be a very tough time for me. The head teacher started. He was reading the letter which had been sent to me a few days ago. I stopped him and told him that although he had invited a team of officers and the teacher involved, where was the accused? The headteacher said that he "does not feel that Hasib's presence is appropriate". I insisted that he "should be here listening to all the accusations and he must be allowed to answer". The Head teacher apologised and made it clear that Hasib was not allowed at the meeting. I told them all his presence was very important as it had been mentioned in the letter that he may be expelled. I made it clear that I would not sit here without Hasib. He must be in attendance and I demanded he be allowed to answer the accusations. I told the Leeds City Education Officers that "this is unfair and illegal because you are not giving Hasib a chance to explain". When they realised that I was not going to give way the head teacher decided to bring Hasib in. At that point I think they realised they were not going to get an easy ride from me!

After a few minutes Hasib entered the room. I stood up, my son was a God fearing and humble young man. He was wearing his Arabic white dress. He knew that I would be attending this meeting this morning. I asked Hasib to sit beside me. I began telling him that he must respect his teachers. It does not matter which religion they belong to or what colour or race they are from, they are your teachers. You must respect them more than your father and mother. You must respect your elders.

After this I turned to the teachers and officers and told them that I had spent 10 years in a Christian Missionary school and I always respected my teachers. All of them were Christians. I respected all of them but they must also give some respect back. If my child is wearing Arabic clothes and it contradicts your school's dress code, then he must be told to dress according to the dress code. If he is allowed to wear Arabic dress, then why were some teachers giving Hasib a hard time? If a teacher is doing anything wrong then he or she must be corrected or made aware of the sensitivity of other cultures and religions. There is no space here for a teacher to act like a fool in front of students.

Hasib started by saying what had actually happened and who was responsible for the wheelie bin incident. He was not aware of any bins which were taken from people's gardens. He said that he had been wrongly accused as he was just standing there and it wasn't fair.

Then I spoke about the "Osama Bin Laden Power" accusation. As mentioned, I can recognise Hasib's writing and I asked the woodwork teacher if he could present the note book where Hasib had written those words. He refused. Then I told him there was no case to answer. They were accusing Hasib of a very serious matter and threatening us both about removing my son from the school, and they weren't even prepared to provide evidence. What kind of justice was this? And what sort of people were they? I demanded to be shown the notebook or I would see my solicitor the next day. After the intervention of the officers he reluctantly put the notebook on the table and accused Hasib of some connections with Osama Bin Laden. He repeated that Hasib had written on his note book "Osama Bin Laden Power" and that's not allowed in school and he wanted to remove Hasib from the school.

I asked Hasib if that was his writing and Hasib replied "no". I requested from the Chair if I could borrow a pen and a piece of paper. I then asked Hasib to write those words in his writing and write it exactly as it had been written on the note book. Hasib then wrote on the paper and I showed it to everybody and asked them if they think, in their honest opinion, if the writing was the same. Of course it was completely different handwriting and the people sitting there were amazed. The woodwork teacher left the room immediately. Later, Hasib told me that the woodwork teacher somehow had access to his notebook and he had written all this to cause trouble and to remove him from the school. He was Jewish and he didn't like Hasib, his Arabic dress, and that as soon as he returned from Hajj, the teacher's behaviour intensified and made Hasib's life hell.

The writing didn't match. The Head teacher was red faced and the officers were also embarrassed. I asked a Leeds Education Officer who would be expelled now, Hasib or the woodwork teacher? Hasib was very angry and told them that this teacher tried to destroy him and he must be sacked. I told Hasib it was up to the officers what they want to do about him. The head teacher and officers told us not to worry and Hasib went back to his class.

Hasib came home after school and told his mother what had happened and told her that he would be happy if the woodwork teacher got the sack. I told Hasib not to push it but he was very determined and decided to pursue his demand. I am not sure what happened to that woodwork teacher. He might have been sacked or transferred to another school, I do not know. Hasib never talked to me about that particular teacher again, but I do know, soon after that meeting, a letter came through from Leeds Education offering me a position as school governor. The head teacher also wrote a couple of letters in apology and to try to persuade me but I always refused. I later became a school governor because I wanted to have an insight into the education system. I attended a lot of meetings but when I realised nothing was happening and it was just a talking shop, I left. Hasib was admitted to college and the school integrated with another school.

I can't say that all Hasib's teachers were narrow-minded. I respect them all from the bottom of my heart. It is sometimes very unfortunate that because of one teacher's personal attitude towards other cultures, religions and lack of awareness, pupils can be subjected to bad treatment. I do not know how much racism plays a part but there are some rotten eggs in the education system that just destroy an innocent child's future. This bad practice and racist behaviour must be stopped to protect all our children as they are the future of this country. I hope tolerance, patience and openness will prevail.

9. DREAMS, SWEET DREAMS!

May the good I have done remain,
May the wrongs I have done be washed away.

*Dreams are very important in Islamic culture. After Hasib passed away,
I had a lot of dreams about him and I still have dreams about him
regularly. There are many kinds of dreams in ones sleep but the dreams
I have of Hasib are purely spiritual. They are very personal but I want
to share them with you.*

ON 26TH JULY 2005, I saw Hasib in my dream. I was
talking to him and asked him why he didn't meet me
before he went to London. I saw Hasib enter our house
through the back door. He said Salam and I was sitting on the sofa.
He took his shoes off. I got up and embraced him. He said. "You
asked me, why I did not meet you before I went. I have come back
to see you." He was smiling and looked very happy. I looked at his
face for a long time and then kissed his forehead. Then he went
back and my dream ended and I got up crying. At the time, just
weeks after the incident, I spent most of my time in bed staring at
the bedroom ceiling with sleep a millions miles away.

On Friday, 29th July 2005, I dreamt of Hasib again. I saw him
coming out from the moonlight. There's a very shiny light around
him and three other boys. All are surrounded by moonlight. The
three men were very young but I had never seen them before. This
moonlight was on Masjid-e-Nabavi in Madina and right on top of
our beloved Prophet Mohammed's (pbuh) green dome and I could
see Hasib's face appearing from the moon. I then got up.

These weren't the first dreams I'd had of my son. On Thursday,
17th July 2005, Hasib was sitting down on a sofa with all the family
members around him. I put my hand on Hasib's head and stroked
it. Hasib said, "I came back, I just went away for a short time." He
was smiling when he was talking to me. Two days later, I saw Hasib
coming out of a car outside our house. His beard was golden and

long. He hugged me and went back smiling.

These dreams came and went but would always leave me an emotional wreck which is why I wrote them down. On Wednesday, 23rd November 2005, Hasib was sitting down on a chair and I was sitting beside his feet on the floor. He was very happy. On Friday, 17 February 2006 Hasib returned to my dreams. He was happy and smiling. I was taking something from the cupboard in our sitting room and suddenly he entered the room. He was smiling and his face was full of happiness. His height was not the same and he looked smaller than normal. His nose was a little round and it seemed that for some reason, his face was burnt or his face looked very innocent like when he was a child. He looked very happy and full of joy.

24th July 2006: Hasib was talking to his mother with his eyes down. I asked Hasib something from but he kept quiet. I woke up soon after that dream and started to cry.

Thursday, 3rd October 2006: Hasib as a little child. He was on some type of uneven ground at the top of the street. Hasib points out his finger to a gold coloured wire. I carried him on my left shoulder. As I was carrying him, I bow down to Allah and cried. When I awoke my eyes were full of tears.

Thursday, 9th November 2006. Hasib would be about 14 or 15 years old. He was wearing blue jeans and boots. He was eating ice cream and walking towards me with a happy expression on his face. I got up immediately after this dream and went into very deep thoughts. May Allah have mercy on him.

Monday, 23rd April 2007. Again he came to my dream. Hasib was about 12/13 years of age. His hands were in his front pockets. He seemed happy. I got up and started to pray for him.

Thursday, 26th April 2007. Hasib was in my dream again. I saw that we were meeting in Kabbah, near to the black stone (Hajr-e-Aswad) on the side of Bab-e-Multizam (Kabbah door). We embraced each other. I asked Hasib how he was? He replied "fine and very happy". I asked him if he could stay with me and tried to sit him down near the black stone but he went back. He returned after a short time and we read our prayers in front of Hajr-e Aswad.

I woke up after the dream and carried on praying for Hasib.

Saturday, 23rd June 2007. I was very tired and went to bed in the afternoon at about 5 pm. In my dream, my wife was with me. Hasib's was about 10/12 years old.. He appeared on television. I told my wife that I have seen Hasib on TV but she was not paying any attention. But I started crying and woke up. He was happy.

Friday, 13th July 2007. In my dream, Hasib was very healthy and chubby. He was wearing a shirt and trousers. He was about 12/13 years old. He carried a cup or pot and he seemed to be eating an omelette. I was sat on a bed and asked Hasib if he could hug me. As soon as he leaned forward to hug me, my dream ended. Hasib had his usual smile and was full of happiness.

Wednesday, 21st November 2007. I was in bed at about 8 pm and in my dream Hasib was about 10 or 12 years old. He was healthy and chubby and he had one hand on his leg and he was sitting down with a happy face with pride and dignity. He was laughing a lot and his cheeks were rosy and fat. He told me that his Bahiya (brother) went to London. I told Hasib that your brother did not tell me that he is going to London. I also told Hasib that you didn't tell me either when you went to London. He was smiling and I touched his cheeks with my hands and kissed him.

Monday, 7th January 2008. I saw Hasib in my dream again. I was on a journey to Makkah and Madina. Hasib was also with me and we sat on a footpath. We were holding cups of tea in our hands. I embraced Hasib and kissed him a lot. He was smiling and said "Father, you had trouble because of me."

Friday, 7th March 2008: I was crying in my dream. Hasib was wearing a shirt and trousers. He was standing on top of a pile of dead boys. My uncle was also near to us. I had no idea what and why but the figures 150,000 and 175,000 were written. I never had this type of dream in my whole life!

Tuesday, 4th August 2008: Hasib was wearing a top quality Arabic dress and playing football. When he kicked the football, I then realised he was not Hasib, but it was his elder brother when he turned his face towards me.

Thursday, 25th September 2008 (25th Ramadan). I was very

tired and my sugar level was playing up again and I was feeling dizzy. I went to bed about 4 o'clock in the afternoon to have a little rest. In my dream, I was taking off my shoes. One shoe lace was opened and the other one was very tight. I was carrying my shoes and running around like a mad person. I was at a very green and beautiful place. The hills were full of flowers. The place I wanted to go was like a hillside and full of trees with a very long walk to a muddy path. I saw a graveyard and some people stood around. In the middle was Hasib's grave. As soon as I saw the graveyard and Hasib's grave, I started to cry. I woke up from my dream and cried like a child.

On 29th Ramadan (2nd November 2005), we buried Hasib Hussain Mir and handed him over to our Creator. I was tired and went to sleep during the day at about 3pm. I saw a text from Hasib on my mobile. The message said, "I'm alive and I am somewhere on the Afghan border".

I answered back to Hasib by text saying, "You stay there where you are, and today or tomorrow I will catch a flight to bring you back here." I told my wife and others that I am going to Afghanistan to bring Hasib home and then I started making the necessary arrangements. Then my dream ended and I was thinking what's happening. Is Hasib alive and living on the Afghani border?

It was 29th Ramadan that day and it was a very strange dream. May Allah have mercy on Hasib and grant him the highest place in paradise.

10. HASIB'S ENGAGEMENT AND WEDDING PLANS

L OSING A CHILD is the most horrific experience in the world. The suffering of the parents is unimaginable. Carrying the body of a child on one's shoulder is the hardest thing a father can ever do. How does a mother cope when she has carried him in her womb for 9 months? Only those parents who have experienced this kind of calamity will know how it feels.

By contrast the most beautiful and happiest time for a parent is when their children get married. Parents cry with happiness. Just imagine then that parents are planning for their son's wedding and suddenly, out of blue, they lose their son forever. If the whole world cries with them, no tears can soothe their anguish.

Hasib was engaged to a girl who he had chosen himself, and we were planning for his wedding after he had completed his studies at university. In 2002 we both went to Pakistan for a few weeks. My wife and I had to go to Pakistan as repairs were needed on my house there.

I have an elder sister who lives in Karachi. Each time I travel to Pakistan, I would fly to Karachi and meet her and the family. I asked my wife if she wanted to go to Karachi and she told me that she hadn't been there for ages and she also wanted to see my sister and her family there. My sister, her husband, their son, daughters, my brother-in-law's brother, wife and children all live in the same house although by this time my brother-in-law was living in Holland and he hadn't been to Pakistan for a long time due to family reasons. We booked our travel arrangements and went to Karachi. We were made welcome there and spent a couple of days. While we were there, my wife's cousin asked if my wife was looking for Hasib's bride or had any plans. My wife told her that we had no plans as Hasib was in school and he was not yet mature enough to get married. The conversation ended there.

Each time I go to Pakistan, I try to see my sister in Karachi, but she rarely comes to see me in Rawalpindi because she is too busy with her children and other things. I always went there and I was happy to do that. Each time I got a lot of care and affection from them. The whole family always seemed very happy to see my wife and I. I was able to stay just for a couple of days because I had my own problems and busy work schedules in Rawalpindi.

I remember paying Rs 1000/- for a return ticket to Karachi in the good old days, and the last time I went it was almost Rs10000/- return. It was not the issue of money, seeing my elder sister was more important for me. We returned to England after visiting my elder sister in Karachi and sorting out the repairs on the house in Rawalpindi.

The next time I returned to Pakistan was 2003. This time I had a very tight schedule and was unable to visit my elder sister and her family in Karachi. I fell ill during this visit and as soon as I recovered, I went to see my other sisters living in Jhelum. Then I went to see my cousin whose sister was living in Karachi. This was the lady who talked to my wife about Hasib the year before. I stayed overnight at my cousin's house in Mirpur. The next day I was supposed to be going back to Rawalpindi as I was due to fly back to England in two days. At breakfast my cousin said something about the Karachi family and this is how this important conversation started about Hasib again. I remembered my wife had mentioned the discussion about Hasib the year before but had thought little about it since. Now my cousin asked me about Hasib and I mentioned to him about my wife's conversation and previous chat about him. I reminded him about this and he was delighted. I told him that the girl's father was in Holland and his brother was responsible for everything. He knew a family feud was on going and her father seemed to have no responsibilities towards the wife and children. They said he was in Holland wasting his time and wouldn't return to fulfil his responsibilities towards his children. I told him that my wife and I had seen the girl in question and we liked her, but I wasn't sure about Hasib, and the other family members including my other children. He suggested I ring my family in Karachi and see what they thought. I agreed but said I must consult with my wife and Hasib first. That morning I returned to Rawalpindi.

That evening I called my brother-in-law in Karachi who was responsible for the upbringing of his brother's children. I asked his opinion of my son Hasib. He was delighted and very happy to hear of the proposal. I told him that initially I had to ask Hasib and his mother, and then his brother and sisters. I may then be able to talk to him because I want to make sure that Hasib is happy. He agreed. Then I rang my wife the same night and felt I should return home when we could talk about it but she seemed happy on the phone. Coincidentally my elder sister was also in Leeds at that time and my brother-in-law told me to talk to her and I would talk to the girl and the girl's mother. In the meantime, he said, I should talk to her father who lived in Holland.

I returned to England the next day. After a few days, I talked to my wife and asked her what her thoughts were about Hasib marrying her cousin's daughter in Karachi. I was aware of the feud which was ongoing between these two families, and I was also aware that it may cause some problems for me and my side of the family, and I certainly didn't want to jump into a burning fire. My wife said she would ask Hasib, although she was very happy about this relationship. It is worth remembering that when I rang my brother-in-law about this he told me that anyone would be over the moon to give their daughter's hand to Hasib because he is the best person in our whole family, who could refuse? He had visited England the year before and met my son.

Now, I left it entirely up to Hasib's mum to talk to him. If he was happy, then okay, otherwise that would be the end of the matter. It is very important that I didn't force Hasib to agree because I believe in God given rights. My wife asked him about marriage to this particular girl. Most parents in this world are not lucky enough to hear their son's most honourable reply. He told his mother, "I will marry a girl who is a practising Muslim, who could look after and give respect to my parents and I leave it to you and my father to choose for me. It does not matter if she is dark or small as long as she practises Islam." His answer might not fit in to other people's descriptions of their ideal bride but I was shocked when I heard his answer through his mother. It was the most honourable answer a father and mother could hear from their son. When I heard Hasib's answer, I told him, "Hasib! That girl is not only a practising Muslim, she has also learnt the Qu'ran by heart. She is brown and little, but beautiful and she would certainly suit you." This proud young man lowered his gaze and replied "I will leave it to you to choose my bride."

There is no doubt that Hasib was very strict when it came to Islam and acting on its teachings but, in my opinion, he was not a fanatic. He was a fundamentalist and I was proud of my son. There is nothing wrong with being a fundamentalist. If someone is practising his religion's basic teachings and people call him or her a fundamentalist, then so be it. I do not care if Hasib was a fundamentalist. There is a big difference between a fundamentalist and a fanatic.

My cousin in Mirpur phoned me to say that my sister in Karachi was very happy about Hasib. I told him my wife and I were also very happy and then I told him about Hasib's reaction. I then talked to the girl's father who was still in Holland. He told me he would agree with whatever his elder brother decides and that he too would be happy. I relayed Hasib's answer to my brother–in-law in Karachi. He told me that his girl and her mother were happy and that I should go and see my sister (his wife) in Leeds to ask her and the rest of the family.

My wife and I went to see my sister who was here from Pakistan visiting our family. My wife asked her if she had a photo of the girl and she provided one. They were very happy and agreed they were very lucky to have Hasib as a son-in-law. My wife and I returned the photo because Hasib would have rejected it straight-away, the reason being that the girl had no scarf on her head, although she was with other girls when the photo was taken. They gave us another photo where she did have her scarf on her head and she was among 7 other girls. I should point out that Hasib had only seen this girl once before in his life. That was when Hasib went to Karachi when he was 9 months old, and the girl at that time was less than 2 years old. We did not talk to my eldest son, his wife or my two daughters, although they were aware that we were looking for Hasib's fiancée, because we wanted to make sure Hasib was happy first before we told everyone about the new bride to be, as we didn't want to spread rumours regarding someone else's daughter. We kept it to ourselves as a surprise.

As per Hasib's permission for us to chose his Fiancée, we brought the girl's photo home, and put it on the table and asked Hasib to tell us which girl we had chosen for him. There were other girls with her but he put his little finger on her and said "she is my bride". I nearly fainted. How on earth did he know that we have chosen this girl for him? He had never seen this girl before in his entire life! It was mind blowing and very surprising for us. It was about 11 pm and my wife was so happy for her son, I have never seen her happier in my life. She was delighted for her "Big baby". That was the last time I saw my wife smiling. She hasn't smiled since Hasib was snatched from us.

My wife called our daughters, my son and his wife to break the good news to them. My daughters were very glad and my son congratulated their brother. He would often call Hasib "Osama Bin Laden" as a joke but my daughter-in-law was not happy at all. This is my own judgement. I may be wrong but I know why she was not happy because actions speak louder than words! I will tell you about this when I write regarding the gifts to Hasib's fiancée.

I found out later that some of our family members were very jealous of this engagement and showed their unhappiness with unreasonable remarks. They kept asking me when he was going to get married and I felt very tense about their funny remarks. Someone said to me that "you should hurry up and get Hasib married as anything could happen tomorrow." These remarks still haunt me today. Why hurry up? Why ask again and again about his marriage? Were they aware that something bad was about to happen? What was troubling them and why were some of my relatives telling me to hurry up? I am still unable to understand this.

I have mentioned before about the family feud but I could

handle that. One remark really upset me however when my cousin, who was in Mirpur, and his mother said "If my own were good enough then we would have kept her hand to give to our grandson." It showed extreme jealousy. I was still unable to understand why people say these kinds of things.

A few days later, my sister and some of her side of the family came to our house and gave some gifts to Hasib for his engagement. My eldest sister was due to return to Karachi so we gave her a jewellery set, make up set and £100 cash for Hasib's fiancée to buy clothes for herself. My daughters sent two gold rings for Hasib's fiancée.

I was very upset and I am still in shock when I remember this. I told my eldest son that we were planning to send some gifts to Hasib's fiancée. He told his mother that he was going to get something. I told him not to buy anything expensive. Maybe £10 will do but he and his wife never gave anything for her or Hasib.

My wife wanted to buy a gold ring for our daughter-in-law to be and she asked me to come with her to a local jewellers. Hasib also gave £250 to his mother to buy something nice for her. When she was in the jewellers, she fancied a very beautiful gold set and I said, "It will be expensive." She said "this is no more expensive than my baby". She took the money out and bought that particular gold set.

My heart bleeds, my eyes cry as though it's a river flowing and I cannot sit in one place when I think about those priceless moments when we were in that shop and the happiness I saw on my wife's face. The woman serving us also became very emotional and kept asking about our son. She was very surprised when we told her that this jewellery was for the engagement. Normally people only give a small ring but this was a full set.

When Hasib passed away my sister wanted to return all the gifts to us but we refused to take them back. We could not do that as we still considered her our daughter and we love her. I wanted to get her married and spend all our money on Hasib's fiancée but unfortunately they never gave me a chance. My Karachi side of the family got her married very quickly while we were still mourning our loss. When Hasib was little and I bought a very beautiful gold set for his future bride to be but that day never came. Hasib was only 6 years old when I bought the jewellery set for his future bride. I have still got it and I cannot let it go because it is Hasib's memory. I'm not sure what feelings he had about his brother and his wife for not giving presents to his fiancée but I tried to not to make an issue out of it. These were the happiest moments in Hasib's life and he was looking forward to his wedding after his education.

Our beloved son Hasib was a very honourable, dignified and remarkable young man. He was a religious person obeying Allah's commands. He was very strict on some of the religious matters. For instance, once he was engaged we had his fiancée's photo and his brother wanted to look at it but Hasib stopped him because she was his fiancée. She was non-Mahram to him. I did advise Hasib regarding this but what he was saying was 100% correct religiously. I did not push it further.

Hasib's fiancée's uncle came to our house and congratulated Hasib and our family. He was very happy and hugged my son, that was almost a year to the day before Hasib died. He later told me that whenever he travelled on the M621, he would always slow his car and pay his respects to Hasib as he's buried beside the motorway in a local cemetery. After Hasib's engagement I asked Hasib if he wanted to talk to his fiancée but he said no. I asked him if he wanted to write a letter to her and he said it is not permissible but he did send some gifts to her on 26.6.2005 through my old friend who was going to Karachi. I was told that she received those gifts about 11 days after 7/7. I wanted to send Hasib's photo which I took especially for her but for some reason I couldn't do that, but after 7/7 when I developed those photos, Hasib's face looked very sad. These two photos are extremely distressing to me. I do not know why he looked sad and fearful in those photos.

After the engagement, my wife and I went to Holland to see the girl's father. He was ill and had recently undergone open heart surgery. We stayed there for 7 days. He was recovering and I told him to go back to his wife and children, but he refused. He was very happy there on his own. He was also very happy for his daughter's engagement. He phoned Hasib from Holland and congratulated him. He also gave us a gift for Hasib. His financial circumstances were not good at all but he still managed to send something for Hasib. Later he came to Britain and visited us. He was living alone in a small village. We took a lot of frozen food for him. Someone told me that he had married again in Holland and that he had even had children but it was a complete fabrication. We never noticed anything like that there. He was alone and there were no signs of any one else living in his house. I also asked some of his friends about his supposed marriage but they all denied this. He was broke.

We went to a local town and he didn't have a single Euro with him and he asked me for car parking money. I also paid some money to him so he could put petrol in his borrowed car. We also bought food for him and other things he liked. I was able to help him, so I did. He was my cousin and Hasib's future father-in-law. I met some of his friends and one of them was from Egypt, he was also called Mahmood. He was very funny and a family man. He had a very successful business in Egypt but had lost everything due to financial difficulties. He was living there with his wife and young daughter. There were a lot of Turkish families running the local businesses. We bought some Turkish bread for him. I also bought my favourite cheese. We came back after 7 days.

I have mentioned earlier about the family feud. This was ongoing between these two families. Due to domestic violence, Hasib's mother-in-law to be left Karachi leaving her three children including Hasib's fiancée and came to Mirpur to her brother's house. Soon after my brother-in-law was shot 6 times; he was left fighting for his life. His brother left Holland and went to Karachi after the shooting. It was a very difficult time for us. I told Hasib what was happening but told him not to worry as it would all settle down soon. I called my eldest sister and told her that I wanted to go to Karachi but she told me to come to Pakistan when going for Umrah and then travel to Karachi. I was very worried regarding this new situation and I was fearful as many relatives were asking me about Hasib's marriage and, of course, some were not happy at all about his engagement. It brought more pressure on me.

My wife and I went to Karachi via Saudi Arabia after our Umrah. The evening we reached Karachi my brother-in-law was discharged from hospital but he was still very ill. His wounds were open, but he survived. We were very fearful and tense in Karachi because we had no idea who had shot him and why. My brother-in-law said he knew who shot him but was not willing to tell me. He hinted but I don't want to write this here. He was very ill and all the family was upset and I didn't want to discuss Hasib's marriage. I really wanted to but couldn't because of the circumstances.

We returned home and then I started to ask my wife if we could take Hasib to Pakistan and get him married. My wife kept it quiet. I was worried as some unknown fear was in my head. When Hasib was engaged, my brother-in-law told us that we should wait at least two years for his school course to finish and I also told him that Hasib was in school so we weren't in a hurry. Now the situation had changed and I wanted to get Hasib married as soon as I could. I asked my wife if she would ask Hasib about it. I had to respect his decision and I did not say anything else to him or his mother. It might be my assumptions but who knew that my brother-in-law would get shot and then 7/7 would happen? And why were some of my relatives telling me "hurry up anything could happen"? Why were they telling me that for? It wasn't their business at all! Perhaps 7/7 would never have happened if Hasib had got married. There are some questions which are disturbing me a lot - my head is spinning!

Hasib wanted to concentrate on his education. I asked Hasib if we could do the Nikah ceremony and come back, but he said that he preferred that it should all be done in one go, then he could bring his bride to England. His future mother-in-law made the situation worse. She could not leave her children and go 1000 km to live with her brother. It was not a wise step. She had lived all her married life in Karachi but if there was any friction with her brother-in-law, then it should be sorted out with reasonable negotiations, not leaving the children and just running away from the problems. Then on top of that, my brother-in-law was shot 6 times. My worry was if this man dies then Hasib's future maybe in jeopardy because the relatives were unhappy with Hasib's engagement. I believe some of them may have had their eye on Hasib's intended for their own son. It was really a difficult situation for my wife and I.

When my eldest sister went back to Karachi in December 2003, she phoned me to tell me that Hasib's fiancée was very happy. My brother-in-law told me that we had to wait another two years for the marriage. That meant that we had to wait till the end of 2005 to go to Karachi and get Hasib married.

By the summer of 2005 Hasib had left college and completed his studies and was planning to go to university. Hasib was aware of what was going on in Pakistan. I talked to my wife to see if we could go there not only could we have a holiday but we may be able to check the situation and ask my brother-in-law to get ready for Hasib's wedding. My wife agreed and we booked our tickets to fly on 20th August 2005 to Pakistan. The reason I booked for 20th August was in case Hasib needed my help to sort out any university matters. He might have needed money or something else. I told Hasib I would pay for his fees and expenses. I was told that he was trying to get a loan but when I found out, I told Hasib I would pay for him so he didn't have to worry about loans. I don't know why my son would even have thought of applying for a loan when I was happy to pay, I don't know why he got this idea. Maybe his cousin was advising him, I do not know. We wanted to go to Pakistan after Hasib's university matters were settled and if there was to be any delay, then we would rearrange our travel dates.

One day at the end of June 2005, I told Hasib that we were going to Pakistan for a short time and we wouldn't go until his university matters were completed. I was very surprised when he asked me if he was going too. I told him no but said if he wanted to come, he was welcome. He said no. The way he asked me "if he was going too" makes me wonder whether Hasib knew what would happen in the near future, how advanced his plans were.

Hasib kept assuring me that going to university would not be a problem for him as he was a good student and he would pass.

He was telling us the truth because on 8th July 2005 and 3rd November 2005, Hasib's college certificates arrived and he had passed his exams with excellent results. I told Hasib that a friend of mine was going to Karachi at the end of June 2005 and did he want to send any gifts to his fiancée. Initially he wanted to send her a mobile phone. He was going to buy her one but I told him that I had a spare but he changed his mind later. He did send some other items for her. I packed the items and he went with me to give them to my friend who agreed to pass them to her. Before he left I invited my old friend for an evening meal and Hasib joined us. This was a couple of days before 7/7. Hasib seemed very happy and my old friend was extremely shocked as what happened a few days later. I asked him after returning if he had noticed anything suspicious or strange in Hasib when we met for the evening meal. He felt he acted as normally as any young man could. Sending a mobile phone to his fiancée was my idea, but maybe Hasib didn't like it, or perhaps he was thinking of something else, in any case he changed his mind. It is worth remembering that I am sure that Hasib would not lie to me. He was a very honest person. He was religiously very strict, that's why maybe he would not want to send a mobile phone as he wouldn't want to talk to her before marriage. My friend took Hasib's gifts on 26th June and I told Hasib on 28th June at about 4pm that we were going to Pakistan.

A young man planning to go to university, planning his marriage after successfully completing his education, sending gifts to his fiancée, learning to drive so he could be a successful business man, telling his mother and I that he was going to see the London Eye and other buildings because he liked it with his friends, keeping in touch, eating healthy food and exercising, and having a very healthy lifestyle and not a single shred of any suspicion in his recent or past life or past. That this very happy and well-liked young man suddenly loses his life in 7/7 does not add up at all. I knew Hasib very well and I put my hand on my heart, and I will express my honest belief that Hasib would never lie to me, to his mother or to his brother and sisters. He was a very honest man. If he was planning anything like that, we would have suspected something. He would not betray us, of that I am certain.

In my honest opinion, Hasib didn't know what was going to hit him. I am not a child. I can tell you that if someone is suffering from a headache and if Hasib was planning something, I would have noticed something strange or out of character from my son, which I never did. I could have read something on his face but he was very clean and without a doubt, an innocent child not knowing what would happen to him.

If a person is planning for his future and the whole world is at his feet why would he suddenly become involved in 7/7? It makes no sense to me at all.

PART 2 – 7/7

MY SON'S FINAL DAYS

Although it is extremely difficult and heartbreaking for me to write about Hasib's short life, it has become equally shattering and painful to write about the unfolding incident. First I put all my thoughts together and handwrote a book in Urdu, then typed it and then I translated into English (hand written again) and then typed it up on a PC. So, I have gone through Hasib's life story four times and as you might imagine, it has not been easy. It is not easy even to write a fictional novel about such events but when the story is true and happens to you it can be almost impossible.

Writing about his last days is unimaginably agonising and upsetting. The only people who know how that feels like are those that have lost sons or daughters in a similar incident. Losing a child in this way brings a lot of pain and suffering and when you cannot do anything about it, it makes frustrated beyond belief. Some people even end up taking their own life. I am hopeful but unable to go through this pain and I do not think I ever will. This is the most important chapter in this book and, of course, to me it is the most agonising part. I have cried for my son, I have also cried for people who lost their lives in 7/7. My Creator knows best why Hasib was taken away from me and I have to obey His commands. This is my hope and my Allah is Merciful.

3rd July 2005

The weather in the summer of 2005 was warmer than usual and I often struggled to sleep. On 3rd July I woke up very early as I had not slept properly all night. It was very hot that morning so I decided to go to the local Car Boot sale in Leeds. I was in two minds as I was very tired and feeling unwell but still I went. I bought a few bottles of mineral water and ice tea and some more of the drinks from the week before that Hasib had liked. After returning home I had some breakfast and returned to bed but I was miles away from sleep. It was too hot and I remember something was disturbing me and keeping me awake. I came down after an hour or so and watered some plants which I had planted a few weeks before. At about 11 or 11.30 am I opened my front door and saw Imran taking something from his car and thought he might be getting ready to go somewhere with his children. I watered the plants by the front door and just then Hasib came out of the house while my eldest son was talking to me. I asked Hasib where he was going. He told me 'nowhere special' and started a conversation. It was not his style but he started talking. Imran soon drove off with his kids soon after and I put my watering can on the garden wall and paid full attention to Hasib.

A few days before my stupid younger brother had phoned me from Pakistan asking for money. He told me he had wanted the money I spent on Hajj for himself and this upset me, mainly because it was not his money and I was not responsible for maintaining his luxurious lifestyle. It was unacceptable to me. Nobody in this whole world can emotionally blackmail me to prevent me going to Hajj. I will not compromise on that. I lost my head when I heard his stupid remarks and shouted at him and told him not to ring me anymore as I was not responsible for him or his family. I was fed up of his stupid, unreasonable and degrading demands. He ended the call by saying, "You just think I am dead to you and I have no relationship with you anymore" and put the phone down. I was paying for this bloody call and he put phone down on me! This disrespect made me angrier and I decided there and then, I'd kick him out of my house when I got the chance. Hasib and his mother were listening to this. It was very obvious Hasib felt it as well and he wasn't happy with my plight. He knew what I had done for my family and that they are the most selfish, stupid and cowardly people.

When Hasib was talking to me outside our house, I discussed this conversation with him. He said he had heard everything and his friends' families were the same. They always made demands and they were also sick of them. I told him "I have a very simple life – I'm ill and I'm suffering. I'm worried about my health and they do not leave me alone." I asked Hasib to ignore them and not to worry about it and to let me deal with it. I would never want my son worried or upset. He was my dearest son and my life. I would give my life to him and would not involve him with any kind of undesirable worries. As we continued talking, I told him about the ongoing problems with my eyes. My sight seemed to be getting worse despite me finally getting control over my diabetes. One eye was worse than the other. The specialist had done laser treatment many times but there didn't seem to be any change and I felt pain in my eye. I was going back to the hospital on 7th July and I asked him to pray for me and my health and then I started crying and said "What would happen if I lose my eyesight, how I would see Kabbah, if Allah called me?"

I told Hasib clearly that I'm very proud of him and that all my friends and relatives were proud of him. "You have given me so much respect and honour. People say very good things about you and you make me very proud and happy. I am very happy with you." I was talking to Hasib and watching his face, at this moment it was shining and an extraordinary light appeared on his face when I said, "I am very proud of you." I will never forget this light on his face. The sun was just peering out from the top of our house as it was nearly midday, and the sunshine on his face and head, and his hair made it look golden brown. Hasib was a bit taller than me and I could see a couple of long hairs from his nose. For some reason I remember thinking he should cut them when he returns home, it's funny the things you remember.

I want to share something which I have never seen before in my life. Hasib's face was full of light, his cheeks were rosy. He was a very unusual, extraordinary and proud young man. I have never seen a person as respectable and dignified as Hasib. Now, you might think I'm saying this because he was my son and that I am praising him unnecessarily. No it's not like that. He was a truly remarkable young man.

Next he said something very important, "Abba (father) I will join university within the next two months and I am planning to take the advanced business course and it will last about 3 years, and I will get married after my education." Hasib himself started talking about this subject and he informed me of his future. I told him, "Hasib Puttar (Hasib son) you don't have to worry about anything. Whatever you feel, whatever your heart says, tell me, you will get married. Do not worry about the marriage at all. You just take care of your education. Just do not worry." I even told him, "Hasib! Engagement is just a promise, but you should not worry about your marriage. Your education is more important for your future. We can wait until your education ends." I always impressed upon my children the need to get a decent education and become respectable community members.

I then told Hasib, "Son, you are doing a business course don't worry about your university fees and other financial matters. I promise you I will give you everything for your education. Even if you need money after university for your business, I will provide it for you just concentrate on your education and don't let me down."

I swear to God, Hasib never let me down. On Friday 8th July, a certificate arrived from his college and he passed with distinctions. When this envelope arrived, I put it on his table and thought that he would open it himself when he came back from London. On 2nd November 2005, the day of his burial, another envelope arrived from college and he had passed the remaining modules of his business course.

After our conversation outside our house he told me he had to go some where. I asked him where he was going and he told me he was going to see his Auntie. As it turned out he did not go there, so he may have changed his mind. As Hasib was walking down the footpath, I noticed that his back was very thin and he looked very weak and skinny. I thought that when he returned I would tell him to stop his extensive exercises, but unfortunately this conversation never took place.

As mentioned above, Hasib told me about his university plans and studying for three years. He told me that he would marry his sweetheart after university but he was learning to drive and was happy with his healthy lifestyle, and I gave him all kinds of support. A young man with a bright future and everything there for him, he was not depressed and he never had any worries at all. He was a very bright, noble, loveable and decent ordinary young man. Suddenly, three days later he's involved in 7/7 and loses his life. This does not make any sense to me. He had everything to live for.

4th July 2005

My youngest daughter lives a few streets away from us so we often go to her house. That Monday night at around midnight Hasib and his mother were returning from her house. As they were passing a nearby shop, Hasib told his mother that he was going to London the next day to see the London Eye and other landmarks with his friends. My wife might have mentioned this conversation to me in the aftermath of what happened but I can't recall exactly when. If I knew that Hasib was going to London, I would have asked him why he was going, with whom and when he would return. This is my nature and obviously I cared for Hasib so much, I did not want to see him in any trouble. In the event Hasib did not go to London the next day as he said his friend's car had broken down.

6th July 2005

At about 9am I opened Hasib's room door very slowly and saw him sleeping and said "Hasib, are you still sleeping?" Then I closed the door. Approximately an hour later I could hear him going to the bathroom. He was wearing a white shirt and pyjamas. I could only see his back as my bedroom door was open. A little later I returned to his room again and asked him if he was staying home and if he was going out then to make sure he locked the doors. I told him that I was going to the town centre for a bit. He said he would lock the doors and soon after he told me that "he was going to London later." When I asked who with, he replied "with friends". I did not ask him anything else because I felt it was inappropriate as he never mixed with people who were not of good character. I was happy, in a sense, that I never had any problems or any complaints about him and his friends, so I felt no need to be concerned. He had been to London before so it was nothing new for me. I was sure Hasib didn't associate with bad boys so I was not worried at all.

At about 12.30 I was ready to go to the town centre and I went to Hasib's room to see him. I asked him "Haven't you gone yet?" He replied that he was going to London later in the afternoon. Then I asked him if he was taking his mobile with him and he said yes. Then I asked him if he had credit on his mobile and said he had. I asked if he had my mobile number and he said "yes." Then I said "keep in touch" and he said "yes". I bid him goodbye saying "Khuda Hafiz" and went downstairs and out through the front door and got in my car.

As I waited at Brown Lane to join the main road I thought I should go back and give Hasib some money (£80) and tell him to stay a day or two more in London with his friends, as he wasn't doing anything but unfortunately, I had to turn right as my car position was in the wrong lane to do this. So I carried on driving towards the town centre. It never crossed my mind that I had just seen my son for the final time.

I was sitting with a friend that day and told him that Hasib was off to London that afternoon and he might have left already because it was about 4 pm. Then I went to a shop with him and bought some mangoes for Hasib as he liked them very much. As we were crossing Cross Flatts Park, some boys were playing cricket. I recognised one person who was from our street but I didn't know the rest of them. Later I found out that Shehzad Tanweer was also playing that day.

My wife said she saw Hasib at about 2.30 pm on Wednesday eating some sandwiches in the basement. She asked him if he needed to take food with him as she would prepare it for him but he said he would buy something on the way. She did not stress because he was going with his friends and they might eat in a restaurant or café. To me, it was very strange because you need food with you because London is not round the corner.

Aqsa is my eldest granddaughter. On Wednesday 6th July, at about 3.25 pm, Aqsa returned home from school with her mother. As Aqsa was taking off her shoes, Hasib came downstairs and she asked him "Chachoo where are you going?" and Hasib replied, "I am going out". That was the last time Aqsa and her mother saw Hasib. The day before Hasib had taken my other granddaughter Bismah along with Aqsa around the streets for a walk. He was a good kid...

Thursday 7ᵀʰ July 2005

TIMELINE FROM THE OFFICIAL ACCOUNT OF THE BOMBINGS - PUBLISHED 11TH MAY 2006

03.58: *A light blue Nissan Micra is caught on CCTV in Hyde Park Road, Leeds, prior to joining the M1 outside Leeds. This car was hired by Shehzad Tanweer and is believed to have been carrying Tanweer, Mohammed Sidique Khan and Hasib Hussain. Hyde Park Road is close to 18 Alexandra Grove – the flat which appears to have been the bomb factory.*

04.54: *The Micra stops at Woodall Services on the M1 to fill up with petrol. Tanweer goes in to pay. He is wearing a white T-shirt, dark jacket, white tracksuit bottoms and a baseball cap. He buys snacks, quibbles with the cashier over his change, looks directly at the CCTV camera and leaves.*

05.07: *A red Fiat Brava arrives at Luton station car park. Germaine Lindsay is alone in this car. During the 90 minutes or so before the others arrive, Lindsay gets out and walks around, enters the station, looks up at the departure board, comes out, moves the car a couple of times. There are a handful of other cars in the car park. A few more arrive during this period.*

06.49: *The Micra arrives at Luton and parks next to the Brava. The 4 men get out of their respective cars, look in the boots of both, and appear to move items between them. They each put on rucksacks which CCTV shows are large and full. The 4 are described as looking as if they were going on a camping holiday.*
One car contained explosive devices of a different and smaller kind from those in the rucksacks. It is not clear what they were for, but they may have been for self-defence or diversion in case of interception during

the journey given their size; that they were in the car rather than the boot; and that they were left behind. Also left in the Micra were other items consistent with the use of explosives. A 9mm handgun was also found in the Brava. The Micra had a day parking ticket in the window, perhaps to avoid attention, the Brava did not.

07.15: Lindsay, Hussain, Tanweer and Khan enter Luton station and go through the ticket barriers together. It is not known where they bought their tickets or what sort of tickets they possessed, but they must have had some to get on to the platform.

07.21: The 4 are caught on CCTV together heading to the platform for the King's Cross Thameslink train. They are casually dressed, apparently relaxed. Tanweer's posture and the way he pulls the rucksack on to his shoulder as he walks, suggests he finds it heavy. It is estimated that in each rucksack was 2-5 kg of high explosive. Tanweer is now wearing dark tracksuit bottoms. There is no explanation for this change at present.

07.40: The London King's Cross train leaves Luton station. There are conflicting accounts of their behaviour on the train. Some witnesses report noisy conversations, another believes he saw 2 of them standing silently by a set of train doors. The 4 stood out a bit from usual commuters due to their luggage and casual clothes, but not enough to cause suspicion. This was the beginning of the summer tourist period and Luton Station serves Luton Airport.

08.23: The train arrives at King's Cross, slightly late due to a delay further up the line. The 4 are captured on CCTV at 08.26am on the concourse close to the Thameslink platform and heading in the direction of the London Underground system. At around 08.30am, 4 men fitting their descriptions are seen hugging. They appear happy, even euphoric. They then split up. Khan must have gone to board a westbound Circle Line train, Tanweer an eastbound Circle Line train and Lindsay a southbound Piccadilly Line train. Hussain also appeared to walk towards the Piccadilly Line entrance.

08.50: CCTV images show the platform at Liverpool Street with the eastbound Circle Line train alongside seconds before it is blown up.

Shehzad Tanweer is not visible, but he must have been in the second carriage from the front. The images show commuters rushing to get on the train and a busy platform. Some get on, some just miss it. The train pulls out of the station. Seconds later smoke billows from the tunnel. There is shock and confusion on the platform as people make for the exits.

Forensic evidence suggests that Tanweer was sitting towards the back of the second carriage with the rucksack next to him on the floor. The blast killed 8 people, including Tanweer, with 171 injured.

At Edgware Road, Mohammed Sidique Khan was also in the second carriage from the front, most likely near the standing area by the first set of double doors. He was probably also seated with the bomb next to him on the floor. Shortly before the explosion, Khan was seen fiddling with the top of the rucksack. The explosion killed 7 including Khan, and injured 163 people.

On the Piccadilly Line, Germaine Lindsay was in the first carriage as it travelled between King's Cross and Russell Square. It is unlikely that he was seated. The train was crowded, with 127 people in the first carriage alone, which makes it difficult to position those involved.

Forensic evidence suggests the explosion occurred on or close to the floor of the standing area between the second and third set of seats. The explosion killed 27 people including Lindsay, and injured over 340.

***08.50 onwards**: Initial confusion over the nature of the incidents with reports of power surges, explosions and suspicious packages at various locations. Local police officers quickly deployed to potential scenes and police Gold Command, already in place for the G8 summit, takes over operational command function leading on security and response to the incidents.*

I got up early today because I had my appointment at 9.25 am. When I got up, I turned on the TV and there were reports of an underground electric fire in London. Some other channels were saying that underground trains had caught fire. All the TV channels were repeating that fire had broken out underground. At this moment I hadn't even thought that as Hasib was in London he might be in trouble. As far as I was concerned, he had gone to

London with his friends sight-seeing. A little later my wife got up and watched the news with me but she didn't express concern about Hasib. We didn't draw a connection between the reported 'underground electric fires' and our son.

Then I went to hospital for my eye check up. In the past few months I had gained good control of my sugar levels because a few weeks before I had very painful laser treatment in my left eye and I had been scared that I might lose my eyesight. The specialist checked my eyesight at about 9.25 and this was approximately the time when the no. 30 bus blew up.

★★★

08.55*: Hussain walks out of King's Cross Underground onto Euston Road. Telephone call records show that he tried unsuccessfully to contact the 3 other bombers on his mobile over the next few minutes. His demeanour over this period appears relaxed and unhurried.*

09.00*: Hussain goes back into King's Cross station through Boots and then goes into WH Smith on the station concourse and, it appears, buys a 9 volt battery. It is possible that a new battery was needed to detonate the device, but this is only speculation at this stage.*

09.06*: Hussain goes into McDonald's on Euston Road, leaving about ten minutes later.*

09.19*: Hussain is seen on Gray's Inn Road. Around this time, a man fitting Hussain's description was seen on the no 91 bus travelling from King's Cross to Euston Station, looking nervous and pushing past people.*

It was almost certainly at Euston that Hussain switched to the no 30 bus travelling eastwards from Marble Arch. The bus was crowded following the closures on the underground. Hussain sat on the upper deck, towards the back. Forensic evidence suggests the bomb was next to him in the aisle or between his feet on the floor. A man fitting Hussain's description was seen on the lower deck earlier, fiddling repeatedly with his rucksack.

09.29*: Metropolitan Police press office confirm, "This has been declared* *as a major incident. Too early to state what has happened at this stage".*

09.30:*The Cabinet Office Briefing Rooms (COBR), the Government's national crisis management facility, is activated in response to the explosions (it was already in place to co-ordinate any response to events in Gleneagles). COBR attended by officials from all the appropriate central Government departments together with the Metropolitan Police Service functions round the clock until 15 July. Seems increasingly likely that this is a terrorist incident.*

09.47: *The bomb goes off, killing 14 people, including Hussain, and injuring over 110. It remains unclear why the bomb did not go off at 08.50am alongside the others. It may be that Hussain was intending to go north from King's Cross but was frustrated by delays on the Northern Line. Another possibility, as he seems to have bought a new battery, is that he was unable to detonate his device with the original battery. But we have no further evidence on this at this stage.*

10.00: *Home Secretary, Charles Clarke, chairs a meeting of COBR.*

10.55: *Home Secretary statement outside Downing Street makes clear that the blasts have caused "terrible casualties" and confirms that public transport has been suspended.*

11.00: *Metropolitan Police Commissioner in a briefing confirms "The situation has been very confused but is now coming under control".*

12.00: *The Prime Minister in a statement from Gleneagles says "It is reasonably clear there have been a series of terrorist attacks in London". G8 leaders add their condemnation.*

I left the hospital in a positive mood, my health seemed to be recovering after a long period of illness and I was happier than I had been for some time. All that came crashing to a halt when I got home...

By now the pictures of the bus bombing were all over the TV. No one knew if this had any connection with the underground fires reported that morning, the city seemed to be in chaos.

My wife and Imran had tried to contact Hasib with no joy. I began to worry that he had been trapped in the underground fires reported on TV, maybe he'd been on the bus... The news was showing people emerging from the underground trains covered in what looked like soot and, in some cases, blood. Panic had started to set in at home. I started to blame myself for not asking Hasib where he was staying. Then I started to get angry with Hasib for not leaving a contact number other than his mobile.

That evening my wife and I paid a visit to some friends to offer our condolences as their relative had passed away recently, all the time I was there all I could think about was my son and where he might be. I was sitting with friends talking to them but my thoughts were in London with Hasib and people could see the anguish on my face. We didn't stay long.

That night my wife phoned London police on the number they had issued on the news. She told the police that Hasib was missing in the city and if police had any information, could they let us know. They wrote down his details but had no idea about Hasib's whereabouts or any other information about him.

That evening the police commissioner appeared on television and announced that an 'electric surge underground' had caused the chaos on the tube. Other national television stations also mentioned that it was an electric surge. Then there was news of the blast on the bus. The television started showing pictures of the bus. There were also a few people who were injured and getting off from the top deck. At this point, I could never have imagined that Hasib was on that bus!

By now I was in despair and convinced that Hasib was stuck underground in the train or perhaps injured and in need of urgent help. I was frustrated and didn't know what to do or where to go or who I should ask about Hasib's well being. Some relatives phoned me and asked about Hasib but I was unable to tell them anything. I could not sit still and kept asking my family about Hasib. I felt powerless to do anything. I was crying and praying for him.

I do not remember exactly if it was same evening or the next day when I went to Leeds train station and asked about train times to London. I got a timetable from the train station to check which train Hasib and the others may have caught from Leeds. I wasn't thinking properly and soon I gave up and stopped reading. I was sinking deeper into depression and my brain was full of suspicions and uncertainty. I rang Hasib many times on his mobile but there was no answer. I was told that the government had blocked all mobile networks in London. I cannot describe what was going on in our minds. My wife and children were extremely worried and believe me, it's out of my capability to describe what was happening to us. I was in a very bad state. I used to put my hand on my stomach and lay down on the floor with severe pains as if someone had snatched a child from its mother. I was devastated and very frustrated because I could not do anything. We were all saying to each other that Hasib might be injured underground and I felt as though he was calling us for help. All these thoughts were killing me and my family.

At this point it was worth remember that the top London police commissioner had announced that the incidents were 'electric surges underground' and not terrorism. It was also disturbing me that if I had not been to Hasib's room on Wednesday morning, I would never have found out that Hasib was going to London with his friends. Hasib had told me that he was going to London but unfortunately I was pre-occupied with other things and I did not ask him which address he was going or anything else about this trip. I missed this opportunity and did not ask Hasib more about his travels as I should have done or, as I normally would.

This day was the most horrible, hurtful and unfortunate day in my entire life. I was very worried and weeping all the time and I was thinking about a lot of dreadful things that could have happened to my son. I was watching television again and again to see if there was any news regarding Hasib.

That night was very painful. I heard my wife call London information centre many times regarding Hasib. I didn't sleep at all that night and spent most of the time praying for Hasib's safety. There were a lot of disturbing thoughts going through my mind and I could not rest and I was going mad really.

My wife and children were in the same situation and struggling to understand what was happening. Most of my family members rang the London emergency number but there was no answer. We were very worried about Hasib and also for the other parents and relatives of those who were on the train. It was on my mind that the next day was Friday and if he was able Hasib would definitely return for Friday prayers, and I would see him at Umar Masjid and we would pray together.

Friday 8th July 2005

As the investigation continues at the sites, the priority is preservation of life and dealing with those injured. The second objective is to obtain evidence. At 23.59, Khan is identified as the account holder for a credit card found at a second scene, Edgware Road.

★★★

I was shattered and very tired. I had been unable to sleep. I was worried about Hasib and hoping that some news would come but we heard nothing. I offered my Fajr prayers. I was crying a lot and prayed for Hasib's safe return. As it was Friday, I was hoping that I would see Hasib at Umar Masjid. I got ready for Friday prayers. I phoned Hasib on his mobile many times but there was no answer. I do not remember how many times I called him, but I remember leaving some messages for him and asked him to contact us, and at one point, I cried. It was also in my mind that Hasib might be in masjid and his mobile phone was switched off. I was hopeful, as it was my last hope that I may see him in the masjid. I dreaded the fact that I might not see him today.

My mind was full of fear and some hope as I went to Umar Masjid. As I reached there, I didn't see Hasib and I became very worried. I thought he may still be in London but my main thoughts again were that we would see each other today at Masjid Umer Beeston as Hasib used to come with me for Friday prayers there but over the previous two weeks, he had stopped coming with me and read his Friday prayers with a friend. When I asked him about this he told me that some Fridays he would be in Dewsbury with his friends and he would read his Friday prayers there. I told him that was okay but that his main masjid was Umar Masjid. So I went alone to Umar Masjid. For some time myself, Hasib and Imran would to go to Abu Huraira Masjid for Friday prayers but Hasib wanted to go to Umar Masjid as he was unable to understand what the priest was saying during his speeches in Abu Huraira Masjid, so we all started going to Umar Masjid. Hasib also used to go to the Islamic Centre when he was at college and he found it useful because the Imam there would speak in English and Hasib could understand what was going on. At Umar Masjid, there was one English speaking Imam and sometimes he used to lead us for Friday prayer.

Now, with his absence at Umar Masjid, all my hopes were dashed and I became very worried and realised that something was very seriously wrong. I was already very weak, and not seeing Hasib there was the last straw for me. When we all stood up for Friday prayer, I couldn't stand, there was no energy left in my body. I tried once but I couldn't lift myself and read my prayer sitting. I was mentally and physically very down. I was shaking and unable to get up. I can't describe what I was thinking, but I can tell you that I was feeling that there was nothing left for me in this world and everything was destroyed, someone had stolen everything from me and I'd lost everything I had. I was alone in this world.

With these feelings, I hardly finished my prayer. My brain was frozen and I became very confused. I kept looking around me for Hasib but my son wasn't there. Somehow I came out of masjid and I looked all over again for Hasib. I stood near the main door outside the masjid where Hasib used to stand with his friends after prayer, but there was no sign of him. I asked a few of the local boys who used to stand with Hasib after Friday prayer but they said that they hadn't seen him today. These young boys always stood beside Hasib after Friday prayers, but today they were not helping me or saying anything about Hasib's whereabouts. I thought it was very odd as they always waited for Hasib outside the masjid and greeted him and stood with him for sometime as I waited in my car for

Hasib to come out but today they had no idea where he was. I thought they were lying to me and hiding something from me. I didn't know them personally but they always adored and respected my son.

I asked some other people about Hasib but no one could tell me anything. Some of them even refused to acknowledge they knew Hasib even though I had seen them with him many times before in front of the masjid. I thought these people were very cruel and mindless. I kept saying to myself "you bastards, you used to greet and hug Hasib and now you deny Hasib altogether! Shame on you, you bastards!"

In a panic I drove off and one of my friends waved at me to stop but I was very upset and carried on driving. I turned right at the end of the street where the masjid is but retuned after a few minutes. I saw a person who is the so-called head of masjid. I stopped my car and asked him if he knew about Hasib. He was very rude to me. I had known this man for a very long time. He suggested something and his remarks were totally unreasonable and stupid. I was horrified and told him to piss off because instead of a simple answer, he suggested something which was inappropriate. I then drove down the same street and turned right again and I stopped in front of a barber shop. There was a book shop in front of the barber shop and once, after we finished Friday prayer, Hasib had taken me to this shop and bought a small bottle of perfume for £2.50. At the time I thought Hasib had so many different perfumes at home, why was he buying this? However I didn't ask him about it as he was very fond of alcohol free perfumes. Now, in a distraught state, I stopped there because maybe I hoped that the shopkeeper may have heard something about Hasib.

The shop was closed so I went into the barber shop and asked the owner if he knew when it would open. He said it should have opened after Friday prayers. I asked him about Hasib and he told me that he saw him a few times with a Bengali boy who lived in one of these streets. I walked on a bit and asked after him to some Bengali people, but they had no idea about this young man. I then came back to my car and this time the bookshop was open. The only reason I wanted to go to the bookshop was in case Hasib might be there. I was very confused and upset and I was searching for my son. I went in to the Iqra book shop and there were two young men inside. One was at the counter and the other was in the back room. I asked the man at the counter if he knew Hasib. He told me that he didn't know Hasib and from his response I knew he was lying. His face was telling me that he was hiding something. He told me that he had no idea where Hasib was. I told him that my son had been missing since Wednesday and could he please let me know if he knew anything about him. The unbearably wicked smile on his face was killing me and I was sure he knew something about my son. I didn't like that young man. I didn't like him because he was not giving me a straight answer. I also didn't like him because his face was full of gloom, wickedness and he had a very unusual Satanic smile.

I asked him again and finally he said Hasib may be with 'Sid'. I asked him who 'Sid' was and could he tell me where could I find him? He then said he may be with 'Kaki'". I almost fainted because I was not aware of either of these people and asked him where to go and how to find them. He told me that 'Kaki' is Shehzad Tanweer and he ran a fish and chip shop at the end of Tempest Road and that Hasib might be there. Then a small but well-built young man came out of the back room and told me that he and 'Sid' live in Dewsbury and he's his neighbour. He also told me that Hasib may be with him. He gave me Sid's address but I couldn't remember it properly because I was very confused and mentally unstable. I never liked the man at the counter and I might be wrong but I believe he knew something about 7/7.

By now I was so confused. I didn't know how to find the fish and chip shop. I started to ask for directions but soon I realised that it was at the end of Tempest Road near the traffic lights. I was very upset and feared that something was very seriously wrong. I was shaking and hysterical and the man in the shop was on my mind and it had disturbed me. I drove to the chip shop, parked my car in the street and went in. A few men were serving food and I asked one of them who was 'Kaki' and who was Tanweer. First nobody answered me and then they told me that they didn't know. Then I asked them again and I think it was Shehzad's younger brother who told me to go to the rear of the shop and then go upstairs. I asked him if he could help me and take me there. He showed me the stairs and I went upstairs. I was thinking Hasib and 'Kaki' may be there together.

I went upstairs and saw two men sitting on old chairs. The room had no carpet and was not in a good shape at all. I saw Mr Tanweer (Shehzad's father) and another man. I greeted them both. Although I had met Tanweer many times, I never knew him personally. All I knew was that he was a local businessman. When I asked him about 'Kaki', he told me that he was his son and when I saw their grim faces, I suspected something was very seriously wrong. I told him about Hasib and that I was looking for him and he was missing from home. He told me that his son was also missing from home and he was very worried about his well being. I told him about Hasib going to London with his friends. I never knew or saw Shehzad or 'Sid' in my life. Mr Tanweer told me that he went to Dewsbury looking for Shehzad but could not find him and he was extremely concerned.

At that point, just looking at them was making me very worried. I had entered a surreal world, a situation that seemed almost dreamlike; it felt as if my soul was coming out of my body. I asked them how and where I might find Hasib, but they had no answer. This was the first time I found out who 'Kaki' and 'Sid' were. Mr Tanweer told me that he knew Hasib as he used to come to his house with Shehzad and on many occasions Hasib stayed there late with him and they were friends. Mr Tanweer said that he had contacted some masjids in Dewsbury but nobody was aware of them or 'Kaki' but that he would try again and go himself to find him. I think at that point Shehzad's younger brother also came upstairs and joined us. He was also very upset and concerned. I gave Mr Tanweer my mobile number and took his number agreeing we would let each other know if we found anything about them. I came home but carried on phoning Tanweer but there was no news.

I'd like to state here that in some media reports it has been mentioned that both my sons knew Tanweer and that they would meet in the front room of our house. I can state categorically that I was not aware of him and had never met him. You can make up your own minds whether the reports are accurate.

When I returned home the family were glued to the coverage on TV. They were showing live pictures of the underground and the bus. Again the London police chief appeared on TV and gave a statement that it was an electric surge and mentioned blasts on the underground. This was his second statement about the electric surge underground.

I was crying over and over again and asking my wife how we could find Hasib. I had no address, no telephone number for him or a phone number of any of his friends or their names. We were all powerless and frustrated. I told my wife and children that I had seen Mr Tanweer and his relatives at the fish shop and I had also been to the Iqra bookshop by chance and found out about 'Sid' and 'Kaki'. Mr Tanweer and his relative informed me that they had been ringing 'Kaki' and Hasib and they weren't picking the phone up and he was very worried because Shehzad left home a few days earlier than Hasib. I also told my wife and children that had I not stopped at the barber shop and gone in to Iqra bookshop, I would not have found out who 'Sid' and 'Kaki' were. At this stage, nobody in our household had ever heard of 'Sid' and 'Kaki' and had never seen them before.

Now everybody was worried sick and we ran towards the phone whenever it rang. Although Mr Tanweer had my mobile number, he didn't ring me and I don't know if he ever went to Dewsbury or any other places to find out about Hasib and Shehzad. This was the second day and I was very concerned about Hasib. I assumed that if Hasib knew we were looking for him, he would contact us immediately. Some of our relatives came and they gave us hope and encouragement that Hasib would return saying it's taking time as he may be underground.

I don't remember who suggested travelling down to London to check various police stations and hospitals because Hasib may be injured in one of them. Some of the young men from our family decided to travel to London with Imran. I told them that this was a good idea and Hasib may be getting some treatment in a hospital and not yet be identified. The police would not necessarily know about him and that's why they were unable to give us any information. My son took Hasib's photo and went to London with the others. We kept ringing the London police helpline but there was no answer.

That night my son and the other men went to London to look for Hasib. They rang me many times to inform me of their whereabouts. They reached London and went to various hospitals and asked about Hasib but there was no sign of him. They checked the injured people's lists but there was no information. They also checked hospital admissions and discharge sheets but there was no mention of Hasib. My son told me that they had passed very near to where the bus was but obviously he had no idea his own baby brother was there at that time! They all returned home empty handed early the next morning. All our hopes had gone and there was nothing we could do except wait and pray.

When these young men came back home, they were very tired yet some went straight to work. It's also worth remembering that each one of them were later interviewed by the police. I still don't see any obvious reason as to why they were interviewed? They went to London to find out about Hasib, nothing else! I do not know how some of my children found out about 'Sid' (Mohammed Siddique Khan) and 'Kaki' (Shehzad Tanweer). Sid's parents and family used to live in Beeston. Sid's brother was living in Beeston at the time of 7/7 and the rest of the family had moved out of Beeston some time ago.

SATURDAY 9TH JULY 2005

Police searching for clues at the bomb sites find items linked to Tanweer and further items linked to Khan. Significantly, items traceable to Khan have now been found at 2 of the scenes – Aldgate and Edgware Road. In reviewing records, it is also found that Khan has previously been picked up on the periphery of another investigation. Tanweer's link to this investigation was identified later.

The nature of these links is covered by the Intelligence and Security Committee's report.

Inevitably in an investigation of this scale, many avenues are pursued, to eliminate those not involved from the inquiry. One initial strand concerned 3 British citizens from West Yorkshire who arrived at Toronto Airport, Canada, on a flight from Manchester, which left around mid-day on 7 July. The group arrived back in the UK on 9 July and were released without charge on 10 July.

The press reported later that a known extremist figure and possible mastermind left the UK shortly before the bombings. There is no evidence that this individual was involved.

There was also interest in another individual who was linked to 18 Alexandra Grove.

★★★

After Imran returned empty handed from London I was fearful. I became very weak, disturbed and confused. It was like a horrible nightmare and I was unable to calm down and put myself at ease. I was shattered and at times hysterical.

Today the Metropolitan Police Commissioner appeared on national television and in response to a press reporter said "we cannot rule out a terrorist attack". Remember the first day (Electric Surge), second day (Electric Surge) and on the third day at evening time he completely changed his statement and said nothing about the underground electric surge. He changed his statement to "we cannot rule out any terrorist attack". It is very important to note a few things regarding his statement. This is a police chief who is not only responsible for his police force but he is also responsible for the safety of the British public. God knows what else his role is but as an ordinary citizen of this country, it makes me very doubtful that it took him three days to find out whether it was electric surge or a terrorist attack underground. This is the highest ranking police chief who is responsible for British security, yet his intelligence was so weak that it took him three days to find out…

That day I went to various masjids in Leeds. I went to the Grand Mosque and asked many people about Hasib. Some of them knew him but could not say where he was. One man said that Hasib was a very good lad and he sometimes read his prayers in this masjid. I then went to another masjid in Leeds 6. I don't remember the name but a Pakistani student guided me to this masjid. At that time they were praying and I sat down on one side until they finished. I greeted them. They were mixed men, young and old. I asked them about Hasib and they all said that he used to come here and read his prayers. Nobody knew where Hasib was but the Imam told me that this young, tall man was very humble and a pious person and he was very happy to see Hasib. Some suggested he may be at the Islamic Centre in Leeds 7 with the group of people who sometimes went out preaching. All the people in the masjid said that Hasib was a very respectful and honourable young man and they all liked him, the Imam said that he was always delighted when Hasib entered this masjid. "We always greeted him and looked after him because he was such a good person, anybody would be proud to associate with him" he said. I told them that Hasib was missing and we were looking for him, but they were unable to say where he was. Their soothing and respectful words were very precious to me but I wanted Hasib. I wanted to know where he was. Again, with great pain and uncertainty, I returned home.

All day I was very worried and tense and unable to keep myself in one place. That evening Mr Tanweer and his son came to our house. They had also gone to different places to look for Shehzad and Hasib but there was no sign of them. We were all very worried and thinking the worst. Mr Tanweer told me that Shehzad was happy at home and he'd had no worries about him. I also told him that we never had any trouble or concern about Hasib and he was a very happy and loveable young man, so why was this happening to us? We were talking about this but we had no idea what had happened. Mr Tanweer and his son left and I think it was that same night when my son told me that Siddique's brother lived in Beeston and he might know something about his brother. I don't know how my son found out about Sid's brother. We went to his house in Beeston. Luckily he was at home. I asked him if he knew anything about his brother and Hasib, but he said he had no idea where either of them could be. He mentioned that since his brother had changed his religious sect, there had been no communication between them whatsoever. I was ashamed when I heard this because changing religious sect does not mean you cut your relationship with your own brother! He also told me that 'Sid' had very little contact with his parents. I told him that it was very important for me to contact 'Sid' because Hasib might be with him. He was very reluctant to give me any more information about Siddique Khan. When I found out his father's name, I informed him that his father used to work with me, and we had a very good working relationship and could he please let me have his contact number, so I can get in touch with him. He then told me that his sister was due in Leeds and he would give the number but I wanted it now. Eventually he agreed and he gave it to me.

Imran and I returned home and I rang Sid's relative. The lady at the other end said she was Siddique Khan's mother. I asked her about 'Sid' and she said she had no idea where he was and she had no regular contact with him. She told me that he didn't come home regularly, sometimes months would go by. She told me if Siddique wanted to come home, he would always ring and let her know he was coming but she hadn't seen him recently. I mentioned about Sid's father and told her that we used to work together in a local firm and he's a very nice person. She said Sid's father came back from Pakistan recently and was very ill. I asked her to let me know if they had any contact with 'Sid'. I think I rang her twice but she said they had no contact with him.

Sunday 10th July 2005

Despite the attacks in London thousands of people, including a great number of veterans, turn out and gather in the Mall for Commemoration Day, marking 60 years since the end of World War II.

Driving licence and other identifying documents in the name of

Hussain found at Tavistock Square. Link made between these and the missing person report.

Police enquiries reveal that Hussain had travelled to London with Khan and Tanweer.

★★★

This was another very depressing and sad day for me and my family. As time passed we became more worried and frustrated as there was no news about Hasib at all. Some family members came to our house and started talking about him and comforted us by saying he will coming home soon and don't worry too much. Someone said he was a very sensible and intelligent person and that he would never do anything to cause any distress to his parents or anybody else. Others were saying he may be trapped underground and maybe the emergency services hadn't reached him and that's why it's taking time. I thought Hasib maybe on the bus and had been hurt and in hospital. Although my son and others had been to London looking for him, they came back home empty-handed. I also thought maybe Hasib was causing us deliberate tension and worry which was strange because he was not like that at all. He would never cause any sort of trouble for us.

These negative thoughts were going around in my head and they were killing me. One of my cousins came to see us. He was over from Pakistan to visit us and other members of the family. He told me that God forbid if Hasib got involved with anything like blasts. He knew Hasib and he told me that Hasib was a very good person and he found him always willing to help as he was a very humble and pious young man. He asked me if I wanted to donate to a certain charity for poor people which I did. Our whole family was very concerned and worried as there was still no news. My wife rang the emergency number again and the person said he would phone later. In a telephone call from London later that day a person asked about Hasib. My wife was telling him about Hasib's age, height, facial description and some other information he wanted from us for ID. I was sat with my wife as she took his call. We gave him all this information because we were desperate to find out about Hasib. He asked for our address and gave us a reference number to keep if we rang back. He told us if we got any information we must let them know. He advised us to keep ringing the emergency number and gave us a reference number. As far as I remember, some other members of my family may have contacted the London emergency number, but I am sure my wife and children were ringing regularly. My daughters were telling me not to worry but my heart was bleeding and I was crying and praying for Hasib. I can't put my pain in to words, any parent can only imagine what happens to parents in this situation.

On TV most channels were still repeating stories about the blast and electric surge, and now there were conflicting stories. They were repeating these conflicting stories again and again, as they had no other news. They still mentioned underground electric surges. The press reports were unclear as to what had happened and reporters were telling the public their own version of events.

Monday 11th July 2005

The Prime Minister updates Parliament on the investigation. He says "7 July will always be remembered as a day of terrible sadness for our country and for London. Yet it is true that, just four days later, London's buses, trains and as much of its underground as possible are back on normal schedules; its businesses, shops and schools are open; its millions of people are coming to work with a steely determination that is genuinely remarkable".

Further information provides a possible link between Hussain and 18 Alexandra Grove.

Last night as usual I was unable to sleep and when I did, it was fitful with horrible dreams. I was more worried today because there was still no news regarding Hasib and I was blaming myself as I had not asked him which address he was going to in London and with whom. I didn't ask for his friend's names or telephone number so I could contact them. I thought I should call the local police but they would have given me the same emergency number. I went to Hasib's room and checked through all his papers but there was nothing, no address or any number to contact. I saw, as usual, some of his clothes neatly laid out on his bed.

In the same upset state I phoned the emergency number and told them that my family members had been ringing but no one had given us any response or any information. I talked to a female and told her that they may be looking for people from London but my son is from Leeds. I asked her to please find out if anyone was there with the name Hasib, and let us know is there any information about him. I again told her that he's from Leeds not from London. The lady told me that she would refer this to the Metropolitan Police and let them know my concerns. She said that the police may come to talk to us and would take some more details. This lady also took our address, name and telephone number to pass on to the police.

It is worth remembering that the staff at the information centre or emergency centre never told us it was a blast, whether the trains caught fire or there had been an electric surge or anything else like that. The only information given to us was that 'an incident had occurred underground'. Each time we rang, they said they were still trying to get information and would let us know.

Not long after I told them that Hasib was from Leeds not London, a policeman and a policewoman arrived at our house. The man said he was from London and the lady was from our local police force. A friend of mine was with me in my house when the police arrived. He went home telling me that police would ask questions and he does not want to be present, despite me asking him to stay with me. My wife was not home when the police came but my son and daughters were.

The police officers sat down in our front room and started asking questions about Hasib. At this point it seemed they didn't have a clue at all about Hasib, his whereabouts, who he was, who he was with and his identity. I told them that Hasib had told both me and his mother that he was going to London. We all saw Hasib on Wednesday. I told them what I knew and said that Hasib went to London sight-seeing. I answered all their questions as I also wanted to know what was going on with my son and where he may be now. One of the police officers later told me that I had made their job very easy, "We would not have known about this incident or who was involved" he said. The female police officer told me that some of them were later awarded by the Queen for their bravery.

The police officers asked some questions about Hasib and I answered them. I told them that I had no idea about Hasib's friends and that he was a fine, very obedient and loving son. He had no problems and everybody at home and whoever knew him liked him very much. All his family was happy with him.

I told the police that on Friday I had gone to the local Umar Masjid where Hasib used to go for his Friday and other prayers, and as I was coming home I found out about 'Sid' and Shehzad. I was told by some people that he may be with them. I told them about the Iqra bookshop and the fish and chip shop where Shehzad's father was very concerned about his son. I told him that I had been looking for Hasib and then I came home. It seemed to me that they had no idea as to who 'Sid' and Shehzad were. I may be wrong but that was my impression. They asked me if I had a recent photograph of Hasib and one of my daughters got me one. It was his passport photo and his face was clear. At this point, they never said anything about Hasib. I just told them what I knew. Then they both asked me if they could see Hasib's room and I led them upstairs.

Hasib's room is very simple and clean. Everything was kept in good order. The lady officer opened a cupboard and put her hands in Hasib's jacket. Then she looked at some books in a plastic container and said to me "he reads Islamic books". I told her "there is nothing wrong with that. Why shouldn't he?" When this lady police officer saw Hasib's room in a very orderly way, she said and I quote from memory, "it seems that this boy is a perfectionist and well organised." She checked some books and opened one. As soon as she opened a book, her remarks upset me and my sixth sense told me that what she was becoming judgemental. I became very concerned and they both seemed to be making an unreasonable profile of Hasib just by the state of his room. I sensed there was something wrong and I didn't appreciate their unreasonable

Islamophobic comment.

By now I did not like the tone of the female police officer, she was becoming very unreasonable. Some people think that because we are a Muslim household that we are from another planet, that they could do and say whatever they wanted. Her face showed clearly what she had in her mind. It looked to me like they had already made their assumptions about a Muslim household. These are my thoughts and I have no hesitation in describing the situation as I saw it. They asked about Hasib's religion. I told them that Hasib was an ordinary Muslim boy. He read his prayers five times a day, went to masjid, fasted during Ramadan and he was a very humble boy. He had performed his Hajj at a very young age and he was a son of whom we were all proud.

They took Hasib's photo. It is the picture still in circulation in the media that is published every time his name is mentioned. Believe me, when these two police officers left, I thought, God forbid, observing their body movements, language and the way they were communicated with each other, I was convinced they had already found Hasib guilty of something.

I am sure, at this point, they had no idea who 'Sid' and Shehzad were. I told them what I had discovered about those two in Beeston. I wanted to know about Hasib and obviously I cooperated and provided all the information I had gathered from my own investigations. As mentioned earlier, the police officer told me that they would have had great difficulty finding out about the four people and I made their job easy. I don't know about making their job easy, but I certainly did my job and acted as a responsible member of the public should. Perhaps I should have got a medal…

Both police officers went away and I told my wife what had happened when she returned home. My children and my wife were very worried and extremely concerned about Hasib's well being. My wife kept her cool, as that's her nature, but I had become very hysterical and felt half dead. It was the fifth day today and there was still no sign of my son. My thoughts were if we stop searching for Hasib what if he returns home and questions why we hadn't looked harder to find him saying "I was injured and you were not there for me?" All these questions hurt me and I cried before my wife and children but we were all powerless.

Many times it entered my mind that Hasib may have left the country but where could he go when his passport was at home along with all his other documents. Why would he leave? Where could he go? He might have gone for a holiday from London with his friends and may not have wanted to tell us but no, his passport was still at home. Had he made another passport? His Pakistani ID card made recently wouldn't allow him to travel without his British passport. We were clutching at straws really and everything failed to make sense.

Despite still being very worried I thought that at least now the police were involved and we would get to the bottom of things. I was very surprised at the police as when they came to our house, at that point, it seemed that they were completely unaware of 'Sid' or Shehzad. I thought that before they left, it looked like they made certain assumptions. I cannot read other people's minds but I suspected something dodgy as they talked to each other. I did not like it at all. I think they had done their homework before they came to our house. At that point, I feared the worst and thought a calamity may have struck. But on other hand, I was also hopeful that Hasib may be injured underground or on the bus and injured and that the police would let us know. We never thought that Hasib may be involved in any way.

Hasib was a very caring and respectable young man. We thought he would never harm anybody. He was a very gentle soul and would help anybody who was in trouble or stress. A person who cared so much for human beings and creatures, we couldn't see how he would ever harm them. That night, we supported and encouraged each other believing that Hasib would be home soon. Any parent can imagine what we were going through and any brother or sister would dread to think of these feelings if anything like this happened to their brother. We were waiting for good news and also may be the shock of our life...

I prayed and asked Allah for help and guidance but He had his own way and wish. I did what I could. I am a very strong believer in my Creator but we are so powerless, we would dare think anything against His wish. I left all to my Allah with great hope that He's very Merciful and will bring good news, and if it was bad news then I still would obey Him and His commands. I begged for my precious son's safety. I cried so much that my eyes became dry until no tears came out. Despite weakness, sleep was a million miles away, I could hear Hasib walking towards me and talking to me. I could hear his footsteps. I could see him sat on a computer chair and I could hear his beautiful voice. I could see him bowing his head and reading his prayers, but I didn't know that Allah had already taken him.

Tuesday 12th July 2005

In the early morning, the police search premises in the West Yorkshire area, including the homes of Khan, Tanweer and Hussain and 18 Alexandra Grove.

A report received that 4 people in two vehicles were seen putting on rucksacks at Luton Station car park. One of the vehicles was now missing but one remained in the car park.

By lunchtime, police working on the theory that there is a King's Cross link to the 3 train bombs, all being broadly equidistant from there at the time of the explosions, identify a CCTV image of 4 men with rucksacks at King's Cross. They recognise Tanweer first from a DVLA photograph.

The police identify CCTV images of the same 4 at Luton Station.

The Micra is found at Luton and examined. 9 controlled explosions were carried out on material found in it. The Brava, which had been towed away because it did not have a parking ticket, is later traced to Lindsay. There had been a report on the Police National Computer that the Brava may have been used in an aggravated burglary and Lindsay was named as the registered keeper for the car.

There was, at the time of the attacks, reports of a "5th bomber". It was thought, because of witness statements and CCTV, that there was a 5th man with the group travelling down from Luton. Inquiries showed the individual was a regular commuter and he was eliminated from the inquiry. Also in the period immediately following the attacks, one man was arrested in connection with the investigation but he was released without charge. In subsequent weeks, a further man who had claimed to be the "5th bomber" was also arrested and later charged with wasting police time. There is no intelligence to indicate that there was a fifth or further bombers.

★★★

I don't remember what time I laid down in bed. I was shattered. There was no energy left in my body. I was thinking about horrible and unimaginable things and feared what might have happened to Hasib. I'm a diabetic and I'd had no proper food for days and lost a lot of weight. My sugar levels kept going down and many times I started to shake and I was close to slipping into a coma but I pulled myself together and ate something to prop up my sugar levels. Many times I was on the brink of losing hope but I never did. I was always hopeful and put my trust in Allah. I was going through a very bad time in my life and always asked Allah for help and sought refuge.

This morning at about 6am I heard some noises and when I looked outside the window, I saw the same two police officers who came to see me yesterday. They were talking to one another. I didn't see Imran but he said later that he had talked to them earlier. My son had gone looking for Hasib again last night and he was outside the house when the police arrived. When I saw the police officers I thought they were here to ask me more about Hasib. As I was in bed but awake, I thought if they wanted to talk to me, then they would knock on our door. I was worried as it was impossible for me to sleep. After a short period of time my son came inside the house and I went downstairs and asked him if he found out anything about Hasib. The police officer also came inside the house soon after my son and he told me that if they wanted to, they could break the front door. I told the police officer that my door was open and that you do not have to do this. If you knocked, I would open it myself.

My other family members came down when they heard the voice of the police officers. My wife also came downstairs. I sat down on a sofa but my wife was standing in the kitchen.

The police officer told us that our house had been surrounded by armed police officers and he had a warrant to search the house. He showed me the search warrant. He told us that "Hasib was near the blast area and we have found his personal documents." I asked him "Is Hasib alright?" He answered "at this point I couldn't tell you". Then he told us "you people take one piece of clothing and a toothbrush and leave this house at once, and you will be searched as you leave the house."

At that time, I cannot tell you how my wife and I felt. Even if I try to I cannot express those feelings or put them into words. I thought it was impossible and I was shocked. I was shaking but conscious. How was my wife feeling about her "big baby"? I thought my son was in deep trouble. My wife and I almost fainted when we heard that Hasib was near the blast.

The police officer told us if we wanted to go to a hotel we could. But we told them that we would go to our daughter's home. We took some belongings as we were told and I handed over my house keys to the police officer and told him "all the internal doors are open and you can search as much as you want, everything is open and there is nothing illegal in my house" and we walked out. As we came out I saw many armed police officers and the street was blocked.

I was thinking that if Hasib was near the blast, then obviously other people would be there too. If that was the case, why did they come to Hasib's house and search the premises? After all, they had come to my house yesterday and they had no idea who 'Sid' was and who Shehzad was and they are missing from their homes too. Yet I am the one who is being pointed out to the police and they knew nothing about it before I mentioned them. It is important to say that these two police officers later agreed with me that they had no knowledge of 'Sid' and Shezad. I only informed them of this because I believed Hasib may be with them.

I wasn't concerned about our house or our belongings at all. I was worried sick about Hasib's safety. I was shocked and in disbelief when I heard all this. I was praying for Hasib.

The police officers took us to my younger daughter's house in a car and around the streets there were hundreds of police officers and a lot of press cameras. All the streets and roads were blocked. At this point I realised something very big and bad had happened. As we went inside our daughter's house, we lost our minds and started shouting. It was madness. It must have looked like a lot of mentally retarded people shouting at each other. It was a surreal situation. As the head of the household I tried to keep calm but nobody was listening and all we wanted to know was what had happened to Hasib. We were all mad. My whole body was shaking. I had no mind, I had lost everything in my life.

The press followed us. I came out of the house and I saw 20 to 30 press cameramen in the street and dozens of relatives. They started to knock at our door and I told them to please go home and come one at a time, but they didn't listen to my request. When I saw so many people and press cameras, I was still unaware as to what had happened and I still didn't know where Hasib was.

I heard on the news that scaffolding had been erected around our house and it was being searched. I asked all the family members if they have anything illegal in our house. They all replied that they hadn't. The lady police officer (Liaison officer) told us that the search would take less than 24 hours and we would be able to return home after that, but I didn't believe her judging from the police's performance so far. My son, grand daughters and daughter-in-law had gone to my younger sister's house. My son-in-law had been at work the night before and he came back home at 7.30 am. We were all in a very confused state. I was thinking about this huge incident and how Hasib was involved. I kept telling myself that Hasib could not be involved. He had told me that he was going with his friends. He may be injured like other passengers have been, but why all the police, searches and press? It was mind-blowing and very distressing. I was unable to comprehend it all.

My daughter's house was small and there was continuous harassment from the press. We decided to shift to another house nearby and we told the police that we were moving. I am very grateful to my sister-in-law who asked us to stay with her. Both police officers told us that we should not believe what the press were saying, they were talking to my son more than us. They also told us that if we like they could stand in front of our door and media can make their films or take photographs. On one hand, they were saying do not believe them but on the other hand, they were saying they would allow the press to take our photos. I couldn't understand the double standard. It was my impression that the officers were trying to get some information from Imran and they told him that the press were using him then you should also take advantage of them.

Meanwhile my wife and I were very upset and just praying for Hasib's safe return.

I asked my children why the police were not telling us what was going on and how come Hasib had something to do with these blasts? My children were very scared. It was not easy for us to stay with other relatives, although we had food and shelter there, your house is your castle but we had no other choice. We had no control over what was going on and we had to adjust to the situation. We stayed awake all night and although I went upstairs for a bit, I could not sleep. My sugar levels had gone down and I had to eat. I had a banana and a drink. I stayed downstairs with my wife and sister-in-law. We kept trying to work out what could have happened? We were guessing but never thought of Hasib being involved in these blasts. That was out of the question. We never believed at that time and my thoughts remained the same for some time. In our eyes Hasib would never harm anybody. He was a very well-behaved, caring person. He would never do such a thing. By looking at his past life and him caring for others, he would never do the slightest harm to others. He was a humble, pious and gentle young man. He had everything he could wish for in this world. He had planned to go to university, start a business, get married and he had a happy and most caring family with him. I was always there for him and his mother loved him so much. He was our "big baby" with a bright future ahead of him.

Wednesday 13th July 2005

Germaine Lindsay's wife informs police that he is missing.

Police search Lindsay's home in Aylesbury.

European Union Ministers assemble for an Emergency Justice and Home Affairs Council and agree a plan of action for EU anti-terrorist co-operation.

★★★

We returned to our daughter's house after staying last night at my sister-in-law's house. We watched television and the reporters were saying that three men were involved with the blasts. There was no mention of any names. A little later these men were identified as Mohammed Siddique Khan, Shehzad Tanweer and Germaine Lindsey. All the TV channels were broadcasting the same news. There was nothing about Hasib at all at that stage but it didn't look good.

The lady police officer who came to our house when I rang the London emergency number now became a Liaison Officer and she took my wife to the police station where she was questioned for 6-7 hours. I was very unhappy and shocked when my son told me that she had been taken away by police. I had gone out with someone to find out what was going on and while I was out the Liaison Officer took my wife away. There was a huge police and press presence and I was unable to understand why us, why my wife and why Hasib since there were only three people involved and he wasn't one of them. Somebody informed me that the police had also raided addresses in Beeston and Dewsbury. The Beeston raid was at Mr Tanweer's house and at Dewsbury probably it must have been Siddique's house. Mr Tanweer's house was on the news and all the traffic to and from Beeston was blocked.

My wife returned home after her long interview. She told us that she was asked a lot of questions about Hasib; about the family history, Hasib's recent conversations with her and his life.

Then other things such as his height, weight and so on. A swab was taken from her mouth. It's obvious that with 6-7 hours of constant questioning my wife was very upset and tired; it was a huge pressure on her, but when she returned, she was fine. She told us that the police had treated her well and questioned her in an air-conditioned room and breaks were given to help her to relax. The police must have made a profile of Hasib then. We provided all the information to the police. I do not remember the exact time when my wife came back home but it was late afternoon.

At around 6.30 pm we were in our daughter's house and thinking what would happen next? I was hoping that as the news said there were only three men involved and they were all in the underground blasts, Hasib must not have been involved and he would be safe but that wasn't the case. We never even imagined that we were going to hear the most horrific news about Hasib. A little later the police came and told us that they wanted to talk about something very serious regarding Hasib. They told us that Hasib had passed away in the London bombing and that he was involved in the bus blast. My wife and all my children were there and we were all shocked. We could not believe this. We all started to cry. I was holding my wife's hand and as she heard this tragic news, her hand slipped away. I have seen tears in my wife's eyes which I dreaded to see. Her baby had gone forever never to return. Anyone on this planet can imagine what was going on in our minds and hearts. I can't put it into words.

Our whole world darkened and everything had been snatched away from us. We were experiencing an unbearable and unimaginable calamity and unable to understand why this was happening to us. There is nothing I can add to this because no word or sentence can explain our heartache. I leave this to my Creator. He has given us the most humble son and now He has taken him away from us. The only thing we could do was be patient and obey the commands of Allah, who is the Most Merciful and knowing.

While we were in a very bad state, the lady police officer asked my wife and I to give a statement to the press. We were already shocked and half dead but she still asked us to give a statement.

I was in a state and felt that we had no other choice but to say yes. It was cruel at this moment. This was the most hurtful and stupid thing to say to us at that moment. My body was numb and my brain was frozen and this stupid police officer asked for us to give a statement to the press. I thought they are pouring salt and chillies on our wounds. They prepared a written statement and told me that this would be in the press very soon. The female police officer (Liaison Officer) was more keen for the statement than our distress. She insisted that the statement must be broadcast by 8.00pm. Our statement read: "We, the family of Hasib Mir Hussain, are devastated over the events of the past few days. We are having difficulty taking this in. Our thoughts are with all the bereaved families and we have to live ourselves with the loss of our son in these difficult circumstances. We had no knowledge of his activities and, had we done we would have done everything in our power to stop him. We urge anyone with information about these events, or leading up to them, to co-operate fully with the authorities. This is a difficult time and we ask you to let us to grieve for our son in private."

Despite the statement, I did not appreciate the demand made by the police for us to make it. It was bitterly inhuman at that time.

The only thing we knew was that Hasib went to London with his friends sight-seeing as he told us. How can a father and mother believe when they are told that their son's involvement in the bombing was real? This was the most horrible and disturbing time of my life.

After hearing this shocking news we went to another house and the TV was full of breaking news. Hasib's photo was on television and it was the same photo which I had given to the police a few days before. Some TV channels were calling Hasib by the wrong name and some said he was 28 years of age. Then they started saying that Hasib was the youngest bomber. Each time I saw Hasib on TV I offered my prayers and Salam. I still do this whenever I see him in any documentary. The past days and then finding out we lost Hasib were unbearable for me, I lost a lot of weight and my eyesight weakened. The press were brutal and told a lot of lies about my son and others. They said whatever they could because they were not answerable to anybody.

We cried all night and nobody could believe that Hasib has passed away. This was like a nightmare. I was asking myself why Hasib, why us? It was around 9.00pm when my mobile phone rang. I did not answer it but very soon another call came and somebody asked my name. I think it was the third time when my phone rang and I answered the call. This was a senior Pakistani police officer and he wanted to talk to me. Again, I turned the phone off. But he kept ringing me and in the end he told me he was calling from Islamabad and he asked me to tell him where Hasib was. He also wanted his passport number and driving licence number.

My family members were listening to me and I told this Pakistani police officer that I had just been told that my son had passed away, and we were very upset and grieving. I did not know where his passport and driving license was, "It may be with the British police because they are searching my house," I told him, "I am not allowed to enter my house and we are living with relatives." If he was a senior police officer, then he shouldn't behave like that. Why was he threatening me? I had done nothing wrong and he had no right to accuse me or my family of anything. I asked him who gave him my mobile number. If the British police gave him my number then he must ask them who employed idiots like him.

He kept asking for documents. I told him that we do not have them and to ask the British police who might have employed you. Then he said that he was asking about documents and Hasib because the British police asked him to do so. I lost my temper and told him to go to hell. I said "we are mourning for our son and you idiots are asking for his passport". I even requested for him to leave us alone. I had no way of telling him about Hasib's passport number or his driving licence, so if he needed more information I told him then to contact whoever he works for. He started to shout and threaten me and said "I will put a rope around your neck". I was furious and upset and told him off as we do in Britain when we are angry. This bastard had no shame at all and kept threatening me and my family. He kept saying that I must let him know Hasib's passport number or I will teach you a lesson. At the end, I told him to go to hell and piss off and said ask your "masters" who put a bone in your mouth. He phoned me again the same night and told me that both my brothers and cousin were in custody in my office. "Now tell me Hasib's passport number and driving licence number." I'd had enough of him and I answered "I do not give a shit what you do with my brothers or cousin, I do not care." I was so upset and angry and told him "shame on you and your mother who brought you in this world and never taught you a word of respect. You said that you are senior police officer. It seems to me that you are worse than a mad dog. You got a pig bone in your throat and now you are acting like one as well. Do not ring me again you pig. You people are so greedy. You would sell your mother for 300 Rupees. You have no dignity and you are not human either. Go away."

The phone was then handed to my brother and cousin who were shitting their pants. I told them that I wasn't in a position to get Hasib's documents because my house had been raided by the police and I couldn't enter unless the search was completed. The next day they were released and I am sure they must have given a bribe to these so called senior police officers. I reminded them, one day no bribe will save you from hell-fire. I honestly think they even believe that. If they do, then there is still time to save themselves.

The Pakistani police must also know their responsibilities and should have acted with dignity and respect. The police officer should have behaved in an honourable way but he acted in a very strange and illegal way. I am ashamed. I have stopped believing in law and justice forever. There is no justice in this world.

★★★

14 July: *Property belonging to Khan found at a third scene, Tavistock Square. Police publicly confirm the identity of Tanweer and Hussain.*

15 July: *Property belonging to Lindsay found at Russell Square.*

16 July: *The police publicly confirm the names of Khan and Lindsay.*

PART 3 - LIFE SINCE 7/7/2005

1. AFTERMATH

THE MORNING AFTER we had been told of Hasib's involvement in the 7/7 bombings the Liaison officer came to see us and I told her about the telephone call from Pakistan. She told me that it was out of her hands and denied the police had anything to do with it. She also handed over some letters from newspapers suggesting we contact them. I said no. She suggested that they we could make millions saying "it's your chance to make some money". I was angry but I kept my cool and told her that I did not want blood money, "My son is not for sale and please do not bring letters from the press any more" I said. She then told me that Imran was talking to them. My wife told him it was up to him, but she was clearly not happy. I had asked my son not to get involved with the press and to make sure he didn't sell his story as it would be "like selling your brother".

My mind was full of suspicion and I was thinking about a huge cover up and conspiracy. I was looking at Hasib's life and his habits. I couldn't believe that he could have done the bus bombing. He was a very simple and straight forward young man. I couldn't accept that he would go to London and bomb a bus. I never suspected him of a thing. I may never truly accept it. My family was shattered and we were thinking about a conspiracy and cover up; everything from Hasib being duped into doing it, to him being part of a terrorism practice operation gone wrong. In reality, thinking back, we did this for our sanity.

A male police officer told me that at that moment there were over 20,000 police officers investigating the case. I told him to do whatever suits him but reiterated that we are law abiding citizens and a respectable family. I was very sure on that point, the police were very clear that we knew nothing about the bombings prior to 7th July 2005. If I or any member of my family had suspected anything about Hasib, I would spoken to him but we never saw anything suspicious.

'ABDUL HASIB'

As mentioned, on Friday 8th July 2005 I went to some masjids to look for Hasib. He used to go to the Islamic Centre, Hardy Street, the Grand Mosque and Umar Masjid in Beeston. Hasib would also go to other masjids, but I was not aware of them. Some people at the masjid told me that they only knew 'Abdul Hasib'. When I described my son's height and age they agreed it was him. One Imam Masjid told me that "we always called Hasib 'Abdul Hasib'". Nobody in our family or household knew that Hasib had added Abdul to his name. I was aware that Hasib's nickname was "CB" but we were not aware of Abdul Hasib.

Hasib never mentioned this name to me, his mother or sisters. I am happy if he added Abdul with his name because Abdul means 'slave of Allah'. It was his choice and I have no problem with that. Whoever I talked to at the masjids they all praised Hasib. One Imam told me that Hasib was very shy, innocent looking and a very dignified young man. They all loved Hasib very much. They told me that I was very lucky to have a son like him. It is very often the case that not many parents are happy with their children, but what I was told by the people was very encouraging. His mother had chosen his name Hasib Hussain Mir after his birth, and before he passed away, he wanted to become the "Slave of Allah". Now this slave is with his Master. I pray for him, may Allah keep him in His highest of the highest place in paradise.

On the morning of 14th July 2005, I mentioned to the Liaison Officer that the Pakistani police had arrested my two brothers and cousin and they had nothing to do with this incident. I was told by a senior Pakistani police officer that they acted on behalf of British police and she said she would talk to her commanders and made me aware that sometimes Pakistani police listen to them and sometimes not. He made it clear to me that the Pakistani police had acted on the orders of the British police. I also found out that there was a huge presence of Pakistani media at our house in Pakistan. I was also told that Pakistani TV channel "Geo" aired the news about 7/7 even before the British media had. I cannot say whether that's true or not.

Now the police started interviewing my relatives one by one. We already told them what we knew and had provided information to the police. It's very important to remember that according to the police and the media, a car was searched in Luton car park and, according to them, they had found more bombs in the car and the bombs were destroyed. I saw long smoky flames on television.

In the meantime our house was still being searched. Our Liaison Officer told us initially that it would only be for 24 hours but the time was extended automatically. When she told us that the search would take longer, I told to her to take all the time they needed and to let us know when they had finished. We weren't going anywhere. When we asked about Hasib, she always blamed him and accused him of the bombing on the bus. She told us that Hasib was on the second storey of the bus and blew himself up. She was continuously asking a lot of questions of me, my wife and children.

From this day (Thursday 14th July 2005) the press started showing our house on television and telling stories about Hasib. Some newspapers were printing untrue stories about myself and my wife. I knew that the police were doing their job and the Liaison Officer was doing hers but I felt a huge pressure from her. She asked me if I needed any legal representation, and I said many times that I had done nothing wrong so I did not need any legal help but I might need it if you take me to court. She always said "No, no, we are not taking you to court." She said many good things about our family.

Personally, I was in a very bad state. I had lost everything; I was shattered, stunned and shocked. I was crying over and over again and thinking why us, why Hasib but I could not find any answers. My wife would cry. Her eyes were searching for Hasib to embrace him, but he had been snatched away from her. Imran was surrounded by big news editors. He was inexperienced and not aware of the media. I told him not to get involved but he was thinking otherwise. He wanted me to talk to the press and I always refused. I told my son that I did not need the money and I did not want to talk to the press. He said there was no harm in meeting with newspaper editors. I explained to my son that we should not talk to any press or TV but he insisted and took me to Bradford.

I was very scruffy and hadn't changed my clothes for days. As soon as I entered the hotel room, everybody might have thought I was homeless because I was homeless! I had nothing left in my life. I was pressurised by my son to come here. While we were in the car, my son told me that he has got small children and after this incident, there may not be any prospects left for him to keep his job because the company who he was working for may sack him. He said that if he took some money from the press, then his financial problems would be sorted. On one hand, I was very upset, but when he told me all this, I said I will try but you keep all the money if they give any as I don't need anything from them. I was very upset with my son's weakness. I was thinking again and again 'why is my son doing this to me?' His mother was upset but he wasn't thinking about her either. I do not know who was pressing his buttons to do this and to get involved in this type of greed. I was dead already but now I was embarrassed too! There must have been someone giving him advice and pushing him for the story.

There were a lot of people in the hotel room. The room was full of cameramen and a few newspaper editors. One of them asked me if I had Hasib's fiancée or more photos of Hasib. I refused point blank to hand them anything. He said "you have to work with us for a few hours and we will print the story on your behalf and we will declare that all the money was given to charity". Of course it was a lie, he was not going to give any money to charity. It was something to do with tax.

He handed me a written contract and he said he was also willing to pay my solicitor fees. He told me all I have to do is sign the contract and he will put my name on the cheque. The others then started to ask about Hasib and his fiancée and I refused to say anything to them. I was aware that my conversation with them may be recorded so I had to be very careful. I could never do this to my son. I had been forced to go there.

I was so upset when they asked for Hasib's fiancée's photo, I immediately turned to my son and asked him how much money he needed and I would give it but "please, my son, Hasib's not for sale". No way would I ever tell stories about my son and I wouldn't do it for money. I would rather die than give a story to the newspapers who would twist and make fun of my son. I kept the photos in my pocket which my son gave to me. I told Imran, "Allah is our provider and it is His responsibility to feed us. I am not begging from those lot". I told him "get up, we must go home". We left the hotel.

They asked me how much money they had to put on the table to get rid of them forever. I asked for a huge amount that they would never agree to pay. The same bunch of senior news editors phoned me many times again but I always refused to talk to them, there's no way I would sell my story despite them offering me a huge amount. While we were travelling home, I thought I may write something about Hasib in the future and that it would be my own version of the story and if I made anything from it I would be honoured because I worked for it but I wouldn't give ammunition to newspapers who would make up false and untrue stories about my son. I believe the collapse of a number of these tabloid newspapers in the last 13 years has proven my judgement correct...

Since 7/7 I have never given an interview to the press and if someone printed anything that was without my consent, I wouldn't allow anybody to say something against Hasib. I also want to mention here something about Hasib's photos which were shown on TV. To my mind, the photos of him at Luton train station, buying a battery and walking near Kings Cross railway station did not make him a bomber. Most of these photos are unclear and they had no value in a legal court, in my opinion. There are huge discrepancies in these photos and I doubted their authenticity.

On 14th July 2005, I was at home and back in my own destroyed world, when the phone rang. My brother-in-law, who lives in Karachi, was at other end. He asked me about Hasib and said he was very sorry to hear this tragic news. Hasib's fiancée also talked to me. I was very upset and could not talk properly. She encouraged me a lot and said it was Allah's wish and told me I should be very brave. I said to her that "I am sorry too and I am unable to do anything and I have lost everything. Hasib was my everything." I was crying and she also cried with me. She asked me to be patient and trust that Allah knows best. But despite all this, I am a father and it's not easy for any father losing his son.

My brother-in-law told me that the Pakistani police had been in his house and his son and brother's son had been taken to the local police station, and at that moment a senior ranking police officer was sitting in my house. I thought, you bastards, what have those innocent children done? Why have you taken them to the police station, they have done nothing wrong. The officer wanted to talk to me so I could tell him what I knew.

The officer greeted me first by saying "Asslam Aleykum". He asked me my name in a very low voice and then asked if I was Hasib's father? I said "yes". He asked me where I lived and I replied "in England". He then told me in a very respectful way that he didn't need any more information from me. I told him "I am here so ask me anything you want about Hasib" but he said "no." He said "thank you" and handed over the phone to my brother-in-law. I heard "Mir Sahib, I am very sorry for your loss and your children will be at home immediately." My brother-in-law told me later that throughout the whole of his life, he had never met a decent police officer like him before. This police officer from Karachi was a decent man. I pray for him, may Allah guide him and give him a healthy long life and forgive his sins, and give him the ability to respect others.

My friends wanted to see me but I was shocked and unable to think properly. I sent a message to them that I would see them but I needed some time to pull myself together. Some relatives came to see me but most of them disappeared. Some sentenced me without judge and jury. A person who I relied upon ditched me and deserted me. I will admit that it was a very testing time for my relatives but they treated me badly. I am ashamed to have those relatives in my life.

The Liaison Officer told me that Hasib's body would be

returned in a few days. My son-in-law took leave from work to help arrange Hasib's funeral, but then the police told me that it would take some time. The police were interviewing our relatives and some didn't miss a chance to make money from the press. One of our neighbours gave an interview to a newspaper praising Hasib as a very decent and well respected young man. He later told me that he used to see Hasib coming out of the front door and going to school and college and always thought that he wished he had a son like him. He cried and said that some newspapers asked him if he had a photo of Hasib and they were willing to pay a lot of money for it. He said "Mr Hussain, I have a mortgage to pay but I would never do it for money. He was like a son to me. I always respected your son," and he cried like his own son had passed away. His wife was also sympathetic and unfortunately they sold their house as it was too big for them as all their children had moved on and had left home. My family is very grateful and we wish them a peaceful future.

As I have mentioned before, more police officers were visiting us and interviewing our relatives and friends. The media was writing about Hasib and the others. Some printed false statements which I had never provided. The media also started a campaign to pay compensation to the victims. They suggested that the government should pay money to the victim's families and relatives for the funerals. A woman appeared on television saying that she has no money for funeral costs but if you look at the background and her house, it was like a mansion. I thought "what a sick joke!"

The Liaison Officer told us that the job of identifying the dead had started and this was a very long procedure. She informed us that DNA profiles would be used to identify dead people; first the victims and then Hasib and the others. It is possible that after this is complete the bodies would be released for the funerals. When I asked her why she had told us earlier that Hasib's body would be released in a few days, she denied she'd ever said it. In the end it took four months! She always accused Hasib of the bombing and when asked about any evidence she said, "Oh! They took evidence with them!" If my wife or I asked any questions about Hasib's ID, she would become very annoyed. Many times she told us that she's our friend and we can talk to her in confidence but we always told her that we were telling her the truth and we were not hiding anything from anybody. We always co-operated with her and her senior officers who travelled up from London. It was our wish to know what happened on 7th July. My wife and I told her that Hasib may be travelling in the same bus as the others and someone else bombed the bus but she refused to accept this. "We have got the evidence" she would say, but when she was asked about the evidence, she always refused to talk about it. We asked if she could send a message to her superiors to ask if we could see Hasib's body and again she refused. I don't think our message was even passed on.

Then one day the Liaison Officer suddenly became concerned about our safety and asked if the police could do anything for our house. I told her that we were not worried and if, God forbid, anything happened to us then we will sort it out ourselves or ask you for help. I asked her if she could arrange to fix iron gates to our front and rear doors or any other type of security, but she said "we cannot afford that". She did agree to fit an iron gate for the basement and I was very grateful for this. When the first and last hate letter came through our letter box, I read it and handed it to police. I was not worried about my house but I think the police were. They said it was likely that a nutter would attack us or the house. This letter came after we returned to our house and I was asked to go to the local police station for fingerprinting.

We could not enter our house because forensic experts and police were still searching. Once I came near to our house and some police officers were guarding the house. I wasn't concerned as there was nothing illegal there and I was satisfied that as a law abiding citizen, I would never do any thing deliberately wrong. Our house was raided on the 12th July 2005 and it was searched for 6 days.

The Liaison Officer was informing us daily but sometimes we got conflicting information. We had no solicitor or legal representation, we relied on her for information. My car was taken by the police and the Liaison Officer took my car keys and said it would be returned soon but it took a month. Obviously, there were some tools and other bits and bats in my car. They were all returned to me in a plastic bag. I was surprised when I read the list. I had a book in my car and I don't remember. I may have put it in my car and forgotten about it. The book was called "Treatment with vegetables" but when it was returned to me it said "Arabic book" but it was actually in Urdu.

On the night of 17-18th July 2005, our Liaison Officer told us that if we wanted to move back to our home we could as the search had been completed. Before that, a man who was searching our house called me on my phone and said there is a little safe in a room and he wanted to see what's in it. I told him that I handed over all my keys when we left the house but I had some other keys if he needed to open it. I told him that I would be there soon and would wait in the street and he can come and take the keys from me. After a short time I came to my street and a police officer stopped me, but when I explained, he let me go nearer. The man came out of our house and I handed over a couple of keys to him and told him, "I am not hiding anything from you and you are welcome to open it." There were some important documents and money in that safe and they were returned to me later.

It was Saturday night when permission was granted for us to return to our house but nobody wanted to go back. Finally at about 1.30 in the morning I went home, alone. It was very hot and all the windows were shut. I saw some papers on the table and I think there were a couple of keys too. The house was very quiet and I wanted to run away from the strange silence. This had once been a happy home and now it was full of sadness. I thought it would collapse on top of me any minute. I wanted to leave but I didn't. Everything was upside down. I was crying and looking for my beloved son but there was no sign of Hasib. My heart and body was sinking and I was shaking and despite the heat, I was shivering. The tears flowed from my eyes but they felt like blood. I went to the basement and most things were upside down and scattered all over. My son's cockatiels started to shout and ask me "Where is our

Hasib?" but I was nearly blind because I could not see properly. I was talking to them like a mental person. I explained to the birds that Hasib had gone to heaven, then they stopped making noises.

I went to Hasib's room. I was talking to him and he wasn't there. Hasib's room was also upside down. His belongings were missing. A piece of carpet had been cut and removed. The room was left in a state as if someone didn't like his "perfectionist" lifestyle. I could feel his presence in his room but could not see him. I came out of his room and went back many times and called "Hasib where are you?" I could hear his voice but was unable to see him. His bedding had been removed as well as a curtain from his cupboard. Most of his belongings had been taken. Some of his belongings have still not been returned such as his wall clock.

I sat in his room for a long time. I was confused and extremely upset. I could not believe it and thought Hasib was still here and would come back very soon. I remember I wanted to run away, not only from Hasib's room but also from the house. I do not remember what kept me in the house. I then went to our bedroom and most things were disturbed and Hasib's computer had been taken away. If I wrote another book explaining how I felt I would not be able to detail my plight in full as it was horrific and very disturbing. I wanted to have a heart attack and die such was my anguish.

In the following days Imran and his family wanted to return. I gave them their keys and they came back as soon as I left the house. I returned to my sister-in-law's house. I became a skeleton and lost a lot of weight. I asked my wife to come home but she was reluctant and said "what home?" I was worried that she might never come back. I was not thinking straight and my wife was also mentally unstable. I asked her sister if she would talk to her and encourage her to return because she could not stay at her house forever. It was very upsetting and I had another hurdle to cross; my wife's refusal to come home. She eventually returned but it was not the same. I can't say how she felt when she returned but any mother can imagine the feelings of loss when she loses a child. My wife was mad, depressed, stopped talking and she lost a lot of weight. She would cry but no tears would drop from her eyes. I became very worried about her in case she may do something silly and hurt herself.

I would cry and call out for Hasib day and night. My wife would try to sleep but every 15, 20 minutes, she would get up again. I was trying to support her through this pain and suffering but she wouldn't listen to me. Many times she argued with me for no reason, perhaps she never thought I was suffering too. Perhaps she blamed me. It was a very tough time for us. She would lose her temper without reason and despite all my empathy and support she would become nasty towards me and I still do not understand why. We both, husband and wife, were in the same boat. We had both lost a child. I was trying very hard to look after and care for her but there was nothing I could do to bring Hasib back. It was also very difficult for me or my wife to think straight but I did not want to cause more problems for her or myself. I had to take some experience from these situations, nobody can do anything for you, and you have to cope with your loss yourself as everyday is a new day. The situation in our house was very fragile and tense. Most times we were so frustrated, we lost our temper and instead of becoming stronger and helping each other, we became very weak and vulnerable. Imran was very upset and crying most of the time but unfortunately his partner was not considerate, and arguments started and I am really ashamed, as parents, we were grieving and they were in their own silly world. I started going to Hasib's room and started to pray on the spot where he prayed and read the Qu'ran. I started to spend my time there. I was trying very hard to keep my family together and wanted to share their emotions and feelings but it is very unfortunate that they took it the wrong way and to be honest with you, I am ashamed again, I was disgusted at their stupid and unreasonable behaviour.

My wife's sisters and brother would come around every day and bring food. I was fine with that as they were comforting her. My brother lives in another city and my sister lives a few streets away. I was very upset as neither of them came to see me and I felt very isolated. I remembered how I spent huge amounts of money to bring them to England. I cared for them and supported them all the time but when my time came, they all ran away. This was not an ordinary situation as they were very selfish and never bothered about me. I thought many times and said to myself, "what an idiot you have been, looking after them most of your life and look what they are doing for you."

It was usual for the Liaison Officer to come to our house daily without any prior warning and she would bring other senior police officers with her. We always welcomed them and told them what we knew. The press was keen to talk to my wife and I but we never did. Many knocked on our door very early in the morning and wanted interviews. My wife and I repeated many times that Hasib went to London with his friends and he told me that he was going to London when I talked to him on Wednesday morning. He was travelling on the number 30 bus and he might have been caught in the blast as others were. The Liaison Officer was keen to blame Hasib and unfortunately she wouldn't listen or provide any answers to our questions.

Most of my relatives stopped coming to our house. I had some contact with a few friends and, although they had nothing to do with 7/7, some of them were a bit hesitant to maintain contact with me but I understood their concerns. I remained isolated and stuck in my house. Some of my friends did try to take me out but I was not comfortable. I went to see my GP a few times. A lady at reception was very nice to me and she held my hand for a few minutes and said "I am very sorry for your loss." I was very touched by her soothing words. On my way home an old lady who lived in our street stopped me and talked about our cockatiels and then she said she was, "very upset at what had happened to you." She nearly made me cry. A young man came to my door and asked me if he could do anything for me, I told him that "I am honoured and happy to see you." He told me that "if anybody gives any trouble to you or to your family, just let us know, we will sort them out". I said "thank you, we are fine". A man in the street suddenly stopped me and cried. I thought he was drunk but he wasn't. He told me that he recognised me as my photo was in the newspaper and I appreciated his sympathy. An Irish lady stopped me once and told me that as an Irish woman she understood the pain and suffering we were going through. Each time I went out somebody was there for me and nobody around Holbeck or anywhere else caused any trouble for me or my family. They never said anything sinister or unpleasant to me. I am very grateful for their sympathy. All my neighbours were very kind to us. As I have mentioned in another chapter, my own community just ran away from me but English people gave me support which remains a treasure for me.

Initially, a police van would come three times a day and knock on our door and ask if everything was fine. They did this for 7 days, three times a day, then reduced it to once a day. I am very grateful for their help. A technician came to our house with the Liaison Officer and fixed a big device in our bedroom, a panic alarm linked directly to the local police station. Despite telling him we didn't need this, he still installed it. We suspected something but we weren't concerned or hiding anything. If it was a listening device, let them listen. He also installed a smoke alarm. We already had 6 or 7 smoke alarms installed in our house, but he said it's better than the others. I asked the Liaison Officer and the officer who came with her, if they had installed any listening devices in our house and they said no. My thoughts are 50/50 as to whether they were listening devices or not. I'm not bothered as we had nothing to hide. Many people told me that our house must have been bugged. We were talking freely inside our home and this bugging device (if there was any) never bothered us at all. The press never got anything from us and they started printing fairy tales about us and our family. Hasib and others were in the newspapers and what they were printing made me very angry but I always kept my cool. I am proud that I was able to handle the press effectively. I would like to say, I have lost complete confidence in the so called free press and I would never believe that what they print is the truth. Freedom doesn't allow you to insult someone or make people's lives difficult. Freedom comes with great responsibilities.

Losing my son in this way was not easy for me or my family and, on top of that, we had to put up with the media's filth. This was a huge loss in our lives. Sometimes, it was impossible for us to cope with it. It didn't matter, I tried very hard but wasn't strong enough to deal with it. The only strength which was keeping me going was my religious belief. It was my faith and divine belief which gave me the power and energy to hold myself together.

It was obvious that anybody in my situation could lose his head with this scale of calamity. My other hurdle was to keep my family together and keep them stable but somehow they had no unity among them. For this reason, I suffered and some made my life worse than hell. I will never forgive or forget.

My sister-in-laws used to come every day and most times they would bring food with them and eat it in my house. That was fine as long as this meeting didn't turn into a party. I stayed in my bedroom most of the time when they were in my house. Sometimes they stayed up till 2am talking to my wife. Many times they laughed and made loud noises. Sometimes my neighbours could hear them. One evening I was in my bedroom and I heard very loud laughs from the basement. I went downstairs and saw them laughing and talking to each other. I asked them to keep their voices low saying "I hope you do it for Hasib's sake". I was very upset as I didn't like their laughter. I told them "you are my relatives and I need you, but please do not do this to me. I do not want to hear any laughter". I was so upset, I told them all including my wife, "Look, my son is still in a freezer and you are laughing. Please keep your voices down." One of them told me "we are laughing about Hasib and the times when he used to pull jokes in front of us. We're talking about his jokes and what he used to do to keep us happy". When I heard the reason, I said again "Can you still keep your voice down."

Sadly, I never knew this side of Hasib. He used to make funny faces and tell jokes to his aunties and others. I never saw him like that. His cousin texted me about his jokes. I cried when I realised he had a funny side. I only knew Hasib's serious side but he was very popular among his relatives. He was always the centre of attention and a very likeable young man. But it was very unfortunate for me because I never knew Hasib's humour.

I would like to share a beautiful and most honourable part of Hasib's life. After 7/7, I think it was August 2005, I was at home alone. I felt very isolated and extremely upset as I was thinking about Hasib and still trying to understand how this could happen. I told my family not to leave me alone in the house and asked them to keep an eye on me. I was unstable and my mind was full of horrible things but unfortunately, nobody listened to me and this time I was home alone. I was up and down and could not sit in one place. I was also thinking what to do with my life now Hasib had gone. The one person who promised to stick by me had left me at a very bad time. My thoughts were along the lines of what's the point of staying here in this world. I was devastated. I was alone in my house, very quiet and nobody was watching me or caring for me I was agitated and deeply depressed. Suddenly, someone knocked on the door. I thought, "not again".

An Indian lady had been pestering me as she wanted to make a movie about Hasib. I told her many times that I had no intention of agreeing to any film and to leave me alone. I don't know how she got my home telephone number but she kept me ringing. She tried to have a chat with me and I thought it may be her again. I decided to tell her not to come to my house again, and tell her off, but when I opened the door a middle aged man and young boy were standing there. The man started telling me that he was a coward and he should have come to see me earlier but he couldn't. He was saying this as if he has committed a crime and he was sorry. He repeated again and again to himself that he was a coward. I asked him, "if he was coward a month ago, then how come you are brave now?" He said "my son was pressuring me to come to see you and I have tried many times to avoid listening to him, but tonight, I gave up and I'm here". I asked them to come in. I asked his name and the reason for coming. I offered them tea but they said refused. The boy was about 10 years old and chubby like Hasib used to be at that age. The man apologised for leaving the visit so late and told me that he was very scared and frightened to come here and mentioned again that his son had wanted to see me and my wife.

I asked the boy why he wanted to see us and did you have contact with Hasib? I was a little bit hopeful that Hasib may appear out of the blue, despite knowing he had passed away. I thought this boy might know where Hasib was or his father would tell me his whereabouts! I informed him that Hasib's mother wasn't at home but that he could talk to me freely. The boy's father told me his name and where they came from but I have since forgotten. As the boy started to talk his father said "Hasib and the others are all innocent" and continued, "I bare witness that they are innocent, very pure and pious young men."

The boy said that Hasib used to go to a swimming pool with him and he also learnt to read Qu'ran from him. "Hasib was not a good swimmer and I often sat on his shoulders while he tried to swim," the boy said, "Hasib taught me how to read Qu'ran and I was teaching him how to swim." This child was telling me things which I never knew about my son and the way he was saying these not only made me happy but also very sad. Many times this child called Hasib "uncle". He said that he was very happy with Hasib as he used to go swimming and so the boy and his father knew him well.

The boy told me "Hasib was very nice to me and I miss him a lot. I wanted to see you and Hasib's mother because I thought Hasib was so nice to me and his parents had to be nice and respectful." The boy used the most beautiful words for Hasib. I cried and it took me a bit of time to control myself. It was very soothing for me to hear again of Hasib's standing in the community. The boy showed a lot of respect for Hasib, he always used the word "Uncle Hasib".

As soon as the son stopped talking, the father said, "I swear to Allah and I am witness to all that happened when I was with Hasib and his friends. One day, Hasib and his friends invited me to go out with them for a meal and I thought 'I am older than them and it wouldn't suit me to go with young men'. I tried not to go with them but Hasib insisted and we all went to a restaurant. They all ate together and without hesitation, they took food from each other's plates and they were eating like brothers. I saw a very unusual and dignified brotherhood bond. I only knew Hasib and Tanweer because they used to come for swimming. I would talk to Tanweer and Hasib at the pool.

"It was sometime after when Hasib invited him again for a meal. I again tried to refuse but they took me to a restaurant again. My reason for refusal was only that they were young boys and they were not my age group, and I felt a little odd among them. Again they ordered the food and ate like brothers. I felt very happy to see them and their unique bond. I thought they are a lot better than other young men who are just wasting their time on the streets.

"While we were enjoying our meals, two beautiful girls came near our table. One girl sat on a chair behind Hasib and the other girl near to Tanweer. It was obvious what they were doing and I became suspicious thinking 'my God, what will happen next'. One of the girl's questioned Hasib and Tanweer wondering why they were ignoring them and then they both came and sat with Hasib and Tanweer. One of them invited the girls to have a meal with them but one said again, 'Why are you ignoring us?' After that, Tanweer said to one girl 'You are very beautiful, you are my choice and I pick you first.' Tanweer then turned to Hasib and told him that he has no other choice but to have the other girl . Tanweer said, 'Look Hasib! My sister is very beautiful.' Then Hasib said to the other girl, 'I have two sisters at home and God is very generous to me. He has given me another sister like you and I'm very lucky that now I have three sisters. If you want to, you could come home with me and meet my sisters.' Both girls stood up and left the restaurant!"

This man again said, "Look brother! Your son Hasib and Tanweer were very pure, decent and pious young men." He repeated the word "pure" three times and said that "I am witness and Insha Allah I will be the witness for them here and after on the day of judgement too. Hasib and Tanweer were the most humble and pure children I have ever seen in my life."

I never had any complaints about Hasib during his life but now he has gone, and people come and tell me about his purity and innocence! It made me feel very proud. Allah says that if two people witness a Muslim being a good person, they will forgive all their sins and they will be entered into paradise. A father and his child were telling me about Hasib's innocence and purity. I had never heard of them before that day! They asked me if I could notify them of when Hasib's funeral would take place but unfortunately I couldn't as it all happened at short notice.

Almost every day, sometimes with notice and sometimes without, the police would arrive at our house with the Liaison Officer for investigations. I noticed that when she was with her senior police officers, she would say nice things but when they were gone, she was a very different person. Most times she would say nice things to my wife and me but when we asked something about Hasib, she would not give us a proper answer. Sometimes she talked about her own children and said that things like "nowadays we cannot trust our children as we don't know what they are doing behind our backs". I told her many times that I always trusted Hasib and I still do. I don't know if it was deliberate but the Liaison Officer asked me about my future in front of my wife. I told her "considering the situation I have no future left. Maybe I might go to Pakistan for a short time, but at the moment, I can't go as I am unable to go alone. I may ask my wife to come with me but I do not know when or if I would ever go in near future." Suddenly, my wife made it clear she didn't want to go to Pakistan. I told her that it was her choice and I wouldn't take her by force! At that moment I had no plans but for the Liaison Officer's benefit I told her it may be a possibility in the future. Unfortunately, my wife misunderstood all this and made an issue of it saying I had given fuel to the Liaison Officer that we had differences. The situation we were in was devastating and because of the frustration, it was obvious that we would show anger occasionally. I am a great believer in openness and communication, but unfortunately, sometimes openness can have negative effects.

Our Liaison Officer wanted to interview me and I told her I didn't have a problem. I was ready anytime. She arranged a day for my interview and I sat with her for a good few hours and I provided all the information about my upbringing, education, work and family history. She told me that these questions were sent from London, they weren't her own. I made it clear that I had no problem at all. She could ask me her own questions if she wanted. She wrote down the answers. At the end of the interview, she told me that she was on holidays the next day and she had no time to read what I had answered and therefore, I must trust her and sign on each sheet. I told her I had given her all the answers truthfully, and if she had written something wrong, then it would be her fault. She asked me to sign otherwise she would be late. I signed all the sheets one by one. I was unable to read each and as she was in a hurry I trusted her. I let her go home early to have a peaceful holiday with her family. After her return, she brought some gifts for my wife and I was grateful for that. Many times she told us that she would be retiring in 18 months.

I was interviewed later by the London police and she was also in attendance. After the interview, she gave me a lift home and whilst sitting in her car, she said, "Mr Hussain in my whole working life I have never seen a more honest, dignified and honourable person than you." I was very grateful for her nice comments.

In the months that followed the attack, hundreds of letters and cards poured in and many people left flowers on our door step. The messages were very moving and I tried to reply but they were too many. I returned some messages in writing. My family and I were very grateful for their sympathy. Each year on the 7/7 anniversary many people send cards and leave flowers on our doorstep. These cards and letters are part of my life and I thank them from the bottom of my heart.

Some of my family members were turning up daily as I have mentioned before but I wasn't getting any help from them because some were very nosey and asked me what the police had taken from our house. I felt very bad about it. Some were asking about

Hasib and his body. It was very distressing for me.

I asked the Liaison Officer about when Hasib's body would be returned to us but there was no response except to say "it will happen soon". I had no legal representation and I do not remember why I went to the local Hamara Community Centre but there I met a young Muslim barrister. He wanted to talk to me. I asked him if he could do something to get the police to return Hasib's body. I didn't know he was already working for another 7/7 family and he offered to act on my behalf for free. I agreed on that basis and asked him if he could see my wife as she also had to give her consent. He came to our house and met my wife and explained what he was going to do, so she also agreed. He and his legal team visited us a few times and asked for more information. He acted on our behalf and helped us as much as he could do but unfortunately, the Justice Secretary rejected our application for legal aid for representation at the Coroner's Court and in the end the lawyer was not prepared to help us for nothing. I understood but that was the time when I needed the help most. We appreciated his help. Most of the victims' families got legal aid and a lot of other legal benefits but we were treated very unfairly and unjustly in my opinion. I will discuss our legal rights in the next chapter.

Most people knew me in Holbeck and a lot were very sympathetic to me, but some of our Pakistani community's behaviour was very disturbing. People would cross the street to avoid me, presumably because being seen with me was "guilt by association" and they probably thought the police would question them. I went to see my GP many times after 7/7, he was very understanding and told me if I needed to talk he would listen telling me that "he would give me more time and help me through this tragic situation." I was very grateful. He referred me to a therapist but she was scared and made it clear she was unable to do anything for me.

Instead I tried to become my own therapist and I am glad I found a very beautiful way to cope with my own problems. There is no harm in prostrating to your Creator and crying for His Mercy. The inner peace, patience, reward and divine help I got from Allah, no one on this planet could provide. I bow down to my Allah any time, any minute, anywhere and He showers me with His mercy. He listens to me at all times. Most man-made laws are unjust and unfair, but His justice is supreme and complete and I know I will get it one day. That day will be judgment day, and there will be no Justice Secretary and barristers, and everyone will be judged on their deeds and punished and rewarded accordingly.

The saga of the post-mortem continued... we asked for a copy of Hasib's DNA profile and our Liaison Officer refused. I was very upset and told her to send her boss a message. I don't know if she passed the message on or not, but a few days later a senior police officer from London came to see us. While he was talking to my wife, he accused Hasib of the bombing and I jumped in, "We do not believe this and do not accuse my son without concrete evidence." I was very angry and told him that next time he comes, make sure he comes with a warrant. I wouldn't let him in without it. He cooled down. The Liaison Officer was very surprised to hear my comments and I also told her that if she wants to come to my house, she has to make sure she comes with proper papers. From then on no one was allowed to come in without the proper papers. I reminded them that we were not responsible for 7/7 and added "you have already searched our house and this house is my property. Tell me if you found any illegal stuff which belongs to me or my wife or any other household member? When you talk to my wife, make sure you remain within your limits."

The top senior police officer then told me his own personal opinion off the record. He said, "It's our government who stuck her nose in to other county's business like Iraq and Afghanistan, we have to deal with it, as it is affecting Britain." I was not shocked when I heard his "off the record" comments. He then told me that it is possible that these four men attacked London because of what is happening in Iraq and Afghanistan. I told him that was his opinion, not mine. I told him he could say what he wanted to say, but until proven guilty, Hasib remains innocent. I was so angry I told him again. "If he behaves like a proper professional, then he's welcome to my house. I will not tolerate any nonsense from anybody. You can always get a summons from court and then talk to me." He apologised and left with the Liaison Officer. He came back again once or twice and was reasonable to us after that.

A lot of people sent me letters and other information to say 7/7 was a set up and tried to prove that Hasib was not responsible for the bombings; evidence on the train times, train cancellations, car parking and return train tickets were unclear. Then there were the unreliable CCTV images of Luton train station, a van parked very near to bus number 30 which belonged to a demolition company and a lot of other information which was conflicting and may have proved that these kids were not responsible for the bombings. People were writing to me declaring that Hasib was not responsible. On top of that, my Liaison Officer and police were telling us not to trust the press and keep away from them but on the other hand, they were encouraging us to make money from them! Surely no sound-minded father or mother would sell their story.

As mentioned, a pretty woman from the Indian film industry was in regular contact. Each time she knocked on my door she was fully made up and always wore a new dress. She said that she was very interested in making a film about Hasib and the Indian film industry were willing to pay a lot of money. She told me to come with her to India and she would travel with me and all that nonsense. I cannot say that I am completely innocent. I am not perfect and nobody is in this world, but I always try to be fair to people. Each time she came, I told her very nicely that I didn't want to go to Bollywood and would she please leave me alone. One day she knocked on our door very early in the morning. She was there wearing full makeup and a nice dress. She asked me if I could talk to her. I replied, "Can't you see the time?" She said, "I am sorry but I wanted to see you urgently." I asked her the reason and she said "I have hired a room in a very cosy hotel and I am inviting you to come and we would talk." Her offer was very tempting of course but I said, "I'm sorry, I am comfortable enough here in my own home with my wife. I am not that sort of a person who would go near this filth. We are devastated and you need to make a Bollywood film." She was upset but I was upset too. I got rid of her eventually by not responding to her telephone calls and not opening the door. It was not my intention to hurt her feelings but I had no other choice. Each time somebody came to my door, I always told them very politely and with respect we weren't interested.

In the months following the attack the newspapers were always inviting me "for a chat". By this time I had received hundreds of letters saying that Hasib wasn't responsible for the bombing. Some blamed internal and external powers for those bombing, others were saying it was a huge conspiracy and a set up. These letters were killing me and I was very upset. I would let my wife know what I was receiving through the post but she wasn't interested. I wanted to make sure she knew what was going on but on the other hand, I was concerned that it would affect her very badly.

In due course a senior officer from London requested a meeting and came to our home on 10th October 2005 at 7.00 pm. Most questions were asked by the senior officer and again we replied according to our knowledge. He asked us if we had any questions. My wife, son and daughters expressed complete dissatisfaction and unhappiness and told him that Hasib wasn't responsible. My wife told him that it's a huge cover up and at that point he become very annoyed. We put forward our own demands but there was not a single satisfactory response from this professional. Our Liaison Officer mentioned a video of Hasib and others when they were travelling from Leeds to Luton in a car and Shehzad Tanweer was arguing at a petrol station with the shop worker. The Liaison Officer had promised to show us that video but the senior officer refused to allow that or give his permission. She told us again, despite the refusal by her senior officer, that she would show us that particular video but she didn't keep her promise and each time she made an excuse.

To me it was all very strange; why would a young man who had everything to look forward to in his life do this? If he knew that he was going to kill himself, why would Tanweer argue with a petrol station attendant over money? If he's going to kill himself then what is the point of the argument? Another thing – I do not understand why they drove an unfit car to Luton filled with bombs. I do not think any sound-minded person would even think taking an old, small car carrying bombs! If they planned the bombing, then why on earth argue over small change and take an unsafe vehicle. What would happen if those bombs went off or the banger broke down on the way? I would not even take my Micra to Manchester because of the fear of breaking down. How come they took this huge risk?

Then there was the evidence at the scene. Why take your personal documents with you and why buy return tickets if you know you have no chance of coming back alive? Why on earth bomb the top deck of a Double Decker bus, why not sit or stand on the first floor and blow the whole bus up? Why go upstairs, sit at the rear of the bus and just blow the top floor out? I do not think a bomber would plan that, do you? Would a bomber buy a battery for his bomb at the last minute? He should have done it a long time ago even before he had prepared his bombs! Would you risk using a cheap battery? Certainly not! It's very strange and extremely surprising for me that the number 30 bus had no CCTV cameras in operation. They were all broken. It's very strange.

These are a few of the mysteries surrounding the 7/7 incident. There's a lot of explaining to do when it comes to proving who was ultimately responsible. Each day, a new mystery and unexplained issue haunts me. Each time we asked the Liaison Officer or senior chief from London for evidence, we were told "they took their evidence with them and I would never be able to get answers." If they took their evidence with them, then how come Hasib and the others were found guilty? You cannot hang someone without concrete evidence! I don't understand the reason why our Liaison Officer first offered to take Imran to London to see the number 30 bus but then my wife and I were told that the bus had been destroyed because there was no place for it to be kept.

Later, when our own Liaison Officer was on holiday, Tanweer's family Liaison Officer and her colleague came to our house and told us that they had made some more arrests in Leeds. I asked her about the bus and why and when they were destroying it? She told us the bus itself is evidence and they weren't destroying it. I reiterated what our Liaison Officer had told that it would be destroyed because there is a shortage of space but she confirmed it wouldn't be. She asked me how I knew that the bus was going to be destroyed, I said nothing to her. This was the last straw for me. I stopped trusting our Liaison Officer. I may be wrong but this is how I felt at that time and I feared for our safety.

At one point, Imran was asked in private to go to London but he refused. Then we were invited to come and see the bus. I suspected something serious and I refused and asked my wife to say the same. We were worried about our safety. Were they trying to get our family's DNA on the bus? I suppose they could do that anyway, it's not difficult. Our requests to see Hasib's body, our request to see Hasib's DNA profile and the video she mentioned were all refused despite the Liaison Officer at one point or another saying all these things would be given to us. In the end she showed she wasn't trustworthy.

Many times I pointed out to the investigating police that the photos of Hasib photos are unclear and a lot of things weren't adding up. They always blamed the press. After the meeting held on 10th October 2005, my son received a lot of text messages and was offered a free ride to go to London and see the bus, and we thought this was not the way to conduct a police inquiry. I thought I have lost my Hasib now something very bad will happen to Imran. I was very concerned about my son and my family.

The forensic team searched our house and took a lot of items with them and three months on they still hadn't provided a list of items taken. I had asked for this many times but when I did get it, some pages were missing. I asked to see Hasib's body and enquire about the time scale for burial but there was never a response. I also pointed out to a senior officer that by law we are allowed to see our son's body as it was mentioned in the Coroner's booklet but nothing was done about it. We asked our Solicitor if he could intervene and make them show us his body but he never came back to us.

When I met my Solicitor at Hamara Centre, it was suggested to me that at first we would conduct our own DNA profile and hire a Pathologist for a small fee. I agreed to pay. Our solicitor was also arranging this for others and he said it was a good idea to have these procedures. My wife also agreed to have this procedure on Hasib's body for her own reasons. We both signed a consent form for this purpose.

Our Liaison Officer told me that the police were prepared to bury Hasib's body and asked me if I would agree to this. I was shocked and angry. I told her, "While I am alive, I will bury my own son." Then I was asked if it would be a private funeral or an open one? I told her, "We haven't decided yet because you are keeping the body. Let me know the date then I will decide what I am going to do." This was very distressing, not only for me but also for my family (by the way my wife paid all the funeral costs for her beloved son). It was suggested to me that I arrange a private funeral as a lot of people might turn up as well as the press. This would put the police in another position as they would have to police it. I was very happy to have an open and public funeral for my son, but my wife and children wanted a private one so I respected their wishes.

A letter was posted to me and a copy faxed to Tanweer's Liaison Officer about releasing Hasib's body. The faxed copy was handed over to me the day after I received the original through the post. The letter from the Metropolitan Police was addressed to me. It was dated 11th October 2005.

The first error on the letter was that it said "your brother Hasib". Hasib is not my brother, he is my son. A responsible officer should not have made this mistake and I do not believe this could have been a typing error.

The letter said that "Hasib's special tests were due to start on 14th October 2005 and these tests were likely to take a number of weeks to complete. Hasib's body can't be released until these tests have been concluded. These tests would greatly assist with the investigation. I have been asked by the Coroner to inform you of your right to employ a legally qualified medical practitioner to attend the examination." I received the letter on 12th October

2005 and the tests were starting on 14th October, how on earth could I arrange for a private medical practitioner within 2 days? This was very short notice and I wasn't capable of arranging that so quickly.

I was told by Tanweer's Liaison Officer on 19th Oct 2005 that the bodies may be released on 25th October 2005. Our Solicitor told me that his Pathologist was in America and he would examine the bodies on 31st October 2005. He had made arrangements for the bodies to be released for burial after the post mortem.

I was informed in writing that the special tests would take a number of weeks to complete but on the other hand the Liaison Officer told me that the bodies will be released on 25th October.

On 31st October 2005 Hasib's body was due to be examined by our Pathologist. Our Liaison Officer came to our house and told me that she was not happy with this arrangement. I told her that I had asked my solicitor to arrange this. I wanted to have a private examination done on Hasib's body so we would have our own results. At approximately 3 pm our solicitor rang me and told me that this examination couldn't take place due to the body's condition and the pathologist would look at photos to determine the results instead.

Our Liaison Officer phoned me that day and told me "your special examination cannot be performed and the tests will take a number of weeks for completion and the body will be released on 25th October." The private tests could not be performed and this unnecessary intervention by the Liaison Officer or senior police made me more confused.

I was not happy at all with this interference. This was a matter between us and our solicitor. I suspected then and now that the people who were investigating were not happy with our private examination.

2. HASIB'S FUNERAL

HASIB'S BODY WAS finally released near the end of our fasting month of Ramadan with Eid just a few days away. The whole Muslim world would be celebrating but for my children, my wife and I we were in a very different and most upsetting environment.

When my father died I was there and I lifted his coffin. When my mother died I lifted her coffin, but this time, it was not so easy. Now I would be burying my youngest son. I was waiting for my own death before I should have the responsibility of lifting his coffin. The whole world knows what a difficult, hurtful and horrendous task it is to bury your son. It is not easy for a father and I was thinking about Hasib and what condition he would be in when I saw him. I had to pull myself together, prepare myself and to be honest with you, I do not know how I found the strength. It was remarkable that I did it. Releasing Hasib's body just before the end of Ramadan and a day before Eid or on Eid day, was like sprinkling salt and chillies on our wounds, but to my family it was a great honour. It was a great honour for my son Hasib. Allah showers His Marcy during this holy month. Hasib was the luckiest person who was given the highest place in paradise in this holy month. I was glad my son would be buried this month.

When we were told that the special examination couldn't be performed and Hasib's body was ready for burial, I asked my Funeral Director, who I had met with a few days before, to arrange to bring Hasib's body for burial. I was told by the Coroner's office to pick Hasib's body on Thursday 3rd November 2005 but I wanted to bring Hasib's body on 2nd November 2005, a day or two before Eid. The Coroner's office agreed to release Hasib's body on Wednesday 3rd November. I was told nobody was allowed to come with the Funeral Director. I wanted to go with him but wasn't allowed as only people from the funeral service were permitted.

The Funeral Director is my relative and he told me that he

would be very happy to bring Hasib's body from London. The Imam Sahib of the same masjid and funeral service was glad to perform Hasib's Janaza prayers. I'm very grateful for their kind help.

I didn't think many people knew that Hasib's body would be brought to Leeds on Wednesday. I kept a low profile and did not want any last minute hiccups. I did not want any police or press. Our Funeral Director sent two people to London on Tuesday night and they were at the Coroner's office at 8 am on Wednesday. I was told by the Funeral Director what was going on and he gave me up to date information.

As I mentioned before, our Liaison Officer asked me a few times whether I wanted a private or open public funeral. She was concerned that if we had a public funeral, then the local community may react angrily and she had to put more police on the street. I wasn't buying that and never believed her. I wasn't scared of anybody. I was not scared of the community. Four months had gone by and nobody in the community had said anything bad about me so I wasn't concerned. At that point, I wasn't bothered about the police or Liaison Officer anymore. I wanted to do things my way. My family had decided to have a private funeral. We told a few family members and asked them to spread the message to come to the masjid on Wednesday just after 12 pm. Only our family knew the arrangements. We also agreed with our Funeral Director that we will bury Hasib on the same day.

It was very unfortunate and upsetting when our funeral service people reached the London office, the officer who was supposed to release Hasib's body refused to do so. I had provided all the relevant documents to our Funeral Director, but the officer said he still could not release Hasib's body. When asked why he said that he had read some statements in the newspapers that Hasib's mother and father had differences, that the father wanted to take the body to Pakistan and the mother would prefer him to be buried in England. It seemed this officer was taking orders from newspapers! He should have done what he was ordered to do and release the body on the order of the Coroner. I was told by my Funeral Director about his stupid refusal so I rang and talked to that officer and told him to release the body, as we had provided all the necessary documents. I also informed him that my wife and I were both happy to bury Hasib in England and he had got incorrect information. I asked if he wanted to speak to my wife and he said no. I then told him we have no differences whatsoever and if he's satisfied then to release Hasib's body for burial immediately. He finally agreed and at 9.00 am these two men put Hasib's body in their car and drove back to Leeds. My Funeral Director was calling me every hour informing me of what was going on. Hasib would reach Leeds Masjid at about 12.00 pm.

My wife and children were clearly very upset but there was nothing they could do except pray for Hasib. They had to be patient. It was the time to see their beloved brother and son Hasib. As time was ticking by, I was getting stronger. I hadn't seen Hasib for 4 months. I was strong but also wondered would I be brave enough to see him? What would happen to me when I saw him? I swear on Allah's dignity and His Mercy and His glory, I saw Hasib with my own eyes and the strength came from my Allah!

We reached Al-Hassan Masjid at about 12.00 pm and Hasib's body was in a private room. My wife, son, two daughters and son-in-law were with me, and most of our relatives were already in the masjid. My wife asked very politely for people not to go to Hasib's room to see him, which was honoured. Hasib's funeral prayers were said soon after Zohar prayer. A lot of people were there and a lot came from the nearby Islamic Centre and other masjids. After the Zohar prayer, my cousin Akhlaq Mir (Funeral Director and Chairman of the Quba Masjid) took us to the room where Hasib was and left the room. My wife, son and daughters were with me in the room. Hasib was in a wooden box covered with a white cloth. My wife opened the coffin. With the grace of Allah, with His given strength, we were the bravest, honoured father, mother, brother and sisters in the whole world. We saw Hasib (May Allah shower His Mercy on him). I kept my son's dignity in my heart, as I do for our beloved prophet Mohammed's (PBUH) dignity, which remains in my soul and heart. Their honour and dignity is the most precious thing to me. I leave everything to my Creator, He knows all and He knows best.

We stayed with Hasib for almost an hour and a half. It was time to take him to the masjid hall for his funeral prayers. Before doing this, I looked at Hasib and faced the Kabbah and read the Dua and said: "O Allah Subhana Ta'ala, You are the Most forgiving and Merciful, You are our Creator and Lord of the day of Judgement. Parents put a beautiful dress on their son and handed over to the bride. O Allah! I put the most beautiful dress on Hasib and am handing over to you. Hasib is now with you. O Allah! Take care of him and shower him with Your Kind Mercy."

Then I lifted his coffin with the other relatives and brought him in to the masjid hall. Our Imam and all the others read his funeral prayers. A lot of people didn't know that Hasib was my son. They were shocked to hear that.

I think somehow the media found out that we had brought Hasib's body to Al-Hassan Centre but the masjid management was tight-lipped and said nothing about it. We then put Hasib's body in another private car and 2 funeral service workers and myself drove to the local cemetery.

There were hundreds of journalists outside the boundary of the graveyard. A lot of my relatives surrounded the grave and we laid Hasib down in his final resting place. I sprinkled some Baqeeh dust on his coffin and handed him over to his Creator. Our Imam Sahib Molana Hassan read his last prayers and all of us read dua for Hasib.

It was 29th Ramadan 2005 and Wednesday 2nd November 2005. Some Muslims were celebrating Eid the next day and some on Friday. I went to Al Hassan Quba Masjid to perform my Friday and Eid prayers.

Our Creator Allah created Hasib and gave him 18 and a half years and with His wishes He called Hasib back in his youth. I accept and honour His commandments. He is the Most Merciful and all Knowing. We all have to return to Him. I leave everything to His hands and with Him.

3. HASIB'S POLICE RECORD

TO RETURN FOR the moment to the female Liaison Officer who started visiting us after the 7/7 incident, this was the same police officer who came to our house with other officers to ask us about Hasib's whereabouts. She told us that she works for the local police and she is a Liaison Officer and has direct responsibilities to MI5 head office. Almost every day she came to our house and interviewed my wife and me officially and was obviously fishing for off hand remarks from us in casual conversation.

Although she was very sympathetic, whenever we asked for something from her she was not very forthcoming with any information regarding the 7/7 incident. We wanted the truth and any information regarding Hasib. One day she told my wife that Hasib had a police record and a DNA profile. She told my wife this in great confidence. When I found out about this I became very upset. I was sure Hasib wouldn't break the law. As we were asking this Liaison officer for information regarding Hasib, we were wondering if she told us this to stop us asking or maybe to have a psychological impact on my wife and I. Later, she told my wife that Hasib had stolen gloves from a high street store. She also told my wife that another boy was involved, but she never told me anything about this.

One day, as I was reading a newspaper, I read an article about this police record business and the theft. They had printed some other stories about Hasib and because there was nothing in my control, I could not do anything. As I was reading these newspaper stories I still wasn't aware that the Liaison Officer had told my wife about Hasib's police record. The Liaison Officer mentioned the other boy's name but no address was provided and my wife wrote these details on a piece of paper and pasted them to the inside of a kitchen cupboard door.

One day I was asking some questions about Hasib and asked

the policewoman how they recognised Hasib's DNA on the bus and so on. She never liked us asking questions. We were co-operating with her and the police to find out anything about Hasib but although she asked us for information she wouldn't give anything away. Sometimes she would become angry if we were asking questions. As mentioned, my wife had noted the boy's name in a cupboard where I keep my medicines but she kept the matter to herself. I must have opened that door hundreds of times without realising what the name meant.

For my part the news about the gloves was tearing me apart and I was very upset to read it in a newspaper. I thought Hasib would never steal a couple of pounds worth of gloves. I always believed my son was an honest, humble and dignified young man who would never do such a thing. I was always there for him if he needed anything, he never had any money problems. He had his own bank account and there was a considerable amount of money in it. He could have more money from his mother. He had access to my money. He was allowed to have anything from the house. Money was no problem at all. So why steal a cheap pair of gloves?

I was unable to find out who the other boy was and where he lived. I was very upset when I found about the police record. Some time later I opened the cupboard door to take my tablets out and, reading the name, I asked my wife about it. She told me how it came to be written down and the significance of it. My wife told me the whole story and told me that this boy was with Hasib when he was accused of stealing the gloves.

She told me that Hasib bought a pair of gloves in the town centre and he kept them in his room and later he changed his mind and asked his mother to return them to that particular store. He had kept the store receipt and she went to the store one day and a refund was given. My wife told me that the Liaison Officer had told her about the police record to deliberately upset her and she kept this to herself and never told me. I then told her that I had read about this in a newspaper and it upset me. I asked my wife if the Liaison Officer had given her the boy's address, but my wife said the officer had told her she wasn't allowed to disclose any information. If that was the case then why did she tell us about it? I could only think the reason behind this was to upset us both and maybe drive a wedge between us.

I believe that the truth will always out. It may take time but our Creator is always watching us and His help is always there. One day my brother phoned me (he lives outside Leeds) and asked me if I had a certain computer lead and if I had, then could I pass it on to his son. I told him I had one. I took this computer lead to his son but unfortunately it was not the right one. Then I went to a local computer shop and bought one for him. I stayed in his son's house for an hour or so. I asked him if he knew this young lad who had a nickname. He said he knew him and that he sometimes lived with his parents and sometimes he went to another city to stay with his grandparents. He didn't know where he was at that time. He gave me directions to his house. He said he had not seen him lately but he knew him. He told me that he had seen Hasib many times with him. My nephew told me it would be very hard to find that boy because he had not seen him for a few months. I came home and decided to go to that address. I wanted to make sure that he was the right person. I couldn't talk to a person who didn't know Hasib. What if I met the right boy and he would not speak to me and called the police or something. He might be in Leeds or somewhere else with his grandparents. I decided to go to that address with great hesitation because I needed to know the truth. While I believed my wife I also wanted to see the boy.

I asked my wife again about the gloves. She told me again that she had returned them to the store after a couple of days when Hasib changed his mind. He gave her the receipt and so on. She took them back to the store and the money was refunded.

So the next day, on 1.12.2005, I went to see the lad and knocked on the door. A boy aged around twenty years old answered. He had a long black beard and after greeting me asked me why I was there. I introduced myself but I think he already knew who I was. I asked him his name and also his nickname and if he knew Hasib. He confirmed that he knew Hasib very well and they were friends. He told me to look at him. He continued to say that "I am here in this position only because of Hasib. I was not a good person but since I met Hasib, I kept my beard and read my prayers five times a day. Hasib changed me and I am a devoted Muslim. Hasib was a very good person and a very good friend who I could rely upon." He praised Hasib so much, I was crying but there were no tears in my eyes.

This conversation took place on his door step. I told him I was here for another reason and asked him if he was able to speak to me. He said he was happy to talk about Hasib. I asked him about the gloves. He smiled and said, "Uncle it was my fault and I should be blamed for it. It was not Hasib's fault," he swore that he was completely responsible for his bad behaviour and actions. I told him that I knew he would never believe that Hasib could steal gloves or anything else. He smiled again and told me, "One day I phoned Hasib to see if he could meet me in Leeds town centre on the way back home from college. Hasib was at Thomas Danby College and he had to change two buses to go to and from college. He had to take a second bus from the town centre. I asked Hasib to meet me at the entrance to that particular store and wait for me. I went inside the store but I had an argument with the shop staff because of their behaviour. To tease them, I came out of the store with a pair of gloves without paying for them. It was not my intention to steal, I just wanted to make a mockery of them. I came out of the store and Hasib was waiting for me outside the store entrance. As I came out, the security officer followed me and grabbed me. Not only did they catch me, they also blamed Hasib as he was waiting outside and grabbed him too. Hasib didn't know what was going on. They arrested me and innocent Hasib. Hasib told them that he was coming from college and he was waiting for his friend but they would not listen to him. I also told them that Hasib didn't take the gloves. It was me who took the gloves to upset staff as they were saying something about his beard. Our finger prints and mouth swabs were taken. Photos were taken at the police station. Hasib protested and told them that he was innocent but nobody listened to him. This incident happened in 2004.

"Hasib was threatened by the police officer and told he would appear in court but then the officer told him that he would not have to appear in court if he admitted to being with me. Hasib become very frightened when he heard about the court appearance and was scared in case you [his parents] found out. He appealed to the police officer to let him off as he had done nothing wrong. But this crooked police officer carried on threatening Hasib to take him to court and forced him to admit to it. Hasib had no choice as he was very scared.

"Uncle this was a stupid act of mine, Hasib had no part in it and he is innocent. I should not have done this stupid act. I'm very sorry. Hasib admitted to this ugly situation to spare you. He was completely innocent and not guilty of any offence." This young man apologised many times and kept saying sorry. He told me that soon after Hasib asked him to keep a beard according to the Sunnah and started reading his prayers five times a day. He told me he was older than Hasib but he taught him how to read Namaz (prayers), how to read the Qu'ran and put him on the right track. "I am very grateful to him but, unfortunately, he is not here anymore." he said.

After our conversation finished outside the front of his house, he asked me if he could come to our house to explain to Hasib's mother. I brought him to our house and he told my wife that it was his fault and Hasib had nothing to do with the theft. It was his fault and innocent Hasib just caught up in the middle. He also apologised to my wife and asked if he could go to Hasib's room. I took him upstairs and he read some Qu'ranic verses then I dropped him back at his house.

It was our impression that the Liaison Officer took every opportunity to upset my wife and I. She would tell us different things then sometime we would argue. I was the head of the household, I tried to keep everything in order but nobody can manage in a tragic situation like this.

Soon after telling my wife about Hasib's police record, she handed us Hasib's photo taken at a police station. Hasib looked under immense pressure and he was clearly worried. It was clear he had been forced to sit in front of the camera. This photograph was published in some newspapers on the 6th anniversary of 7/7 with a copyright mark. How come Hasib's photo came from a police file? Is this crookedness or "in the public interest"? Is it legal for the police to do that? This is disgraceful and utterly shameful. I condemn this action. If it was not taken from police files, then the police should take action and the culprit must be punished.

If this photo came from a safe place their permission or was handed over to a journalist, then this is a very sad time for police and the law. I can only condemn this sort of behaviour.

4. REACTIONS FROM THE COMMUNITY AND MEDIA

AFTER HASIB PASSED away, many relatives and friends offered support to my family and we appreciated it from the bottom of our hearts. Some of my friends were very sympathetic and openly supported me but others ran away. I am very grateful to those who stuck by me despite everything. It can't have been easy with the shocking events and press and media attention. I am also grateful to those who left me for whatever reason as I am sure it was a testing time for them and it is not always possible to succeed under such duress.

That said certain friends and relatives ran away soon after 7/7. I am an independent, self-sufficient person and for most of my life I tried to rely upon myself. If I am able to do a thing, I would do it. I do not hide behind worldly things. These things come and go. Despite my bad health, I do what I can for my family and my community. I lead a very simple life and I am grateful for what I have. I think it was my patience, self-reliance and independence which allowed me to survive this pain and suffering. I was hurt very badly. I was surprised when certain community members dumped me and no one came to see me. I understand 7/7 was a huge event but I never hid anything and some people who had been in trouble themselves perhaps didn't want to get involved as they knew that all the police's focus was on me. Others, who used to associate with me, were interviewed by the police, and they complained that they were troubled because of this.

I would say that prior to 7/7, hundreds of people knew me and a lot of community members knew me very well and I had a good standing as a member of the community. Some of them would come to my house and stay with me until the early hours of the morning but they all disappeared. Some so-called political leaders who used to lick my feet, just disappeared into thin air and never returned.

The meaning of the word "community" is family. But this family left me and I am ashamed of their behaviour. I completely lost faith in my community. I was expecting some support and encouragement from them because they are Muslims and they should give support to fellow Muslims. But I am also ashamed of some people who I thought I knew very well, who never turned up on my door step or said anything soothing to me.

The local English community was more sympathetic and supportive than my own community. I received cards, flowers and supportive messages from the English community. A lot of local English people offered me support. Some came and knocked on my door and asked if I needed anything. Some came and offered me protection and some came to offer me money. As a Muslim and as a Pakistani, I prepared a room and made arrangements for local residents to come to my house and offer me sympathetic support and condolences. I only needed some encouragement and verbal support but nobody came except one or two people. I just sat there alone for 3 months and waited for my community to come but I am very ashamed to say they never did.

I received letters, cards, flowers and sympathy messages from all over the world. I received one piece of hate mail and handed it to the police. To be fair I could understand their frustration but they must not target me or my family as we had done nothing wrong. We were victims ourselves. Apart from that letter, I never received any racial hatred. I am grateful to him too as the hate mail guy reminded me that I am a Pakistani and an immigrant.

A lot of people had written in their messages that they believed my son was innocent and some had written about their own grief and loss. A brother and mother wrote about their loss and how difficult it was to cope with. Of course the media also offered me hundreds of thousands of pounds, but I turned it down as my son is not for sale and neither is my story.

This is the third time I am repeating the word "ashamed" as I really am. I will mention my conduct whenever someone dies in my community; I go to their house specially and make sure the family is aware of my presence. I noticed that many of them felt "ashamed" themselves as they did not come to my door step and offer me a little support. I am there as a reminder for their conduct to me.

For those that offered me a soothing word, a sympathy card, flowers or messages, they are very dear to me and it will stay with me forever. The only thing I can give to them in return is a huge thanks and I will pray for their long life with good health.

I am aware that the media has to sell their story and of course they have to make money. I am also aware that they have a strong influence and whatever they write has an impact on people. Some newspapers printed interviews which I never gave them. I respect the British media whether they are newspapers, television or radio. They are doing their job. It was a very difficult time for me and my family. If any of them printed anything about me or my family it was without me or my family's permission. I have no problem with the media, I just don't trust them.

I spoke to hundreds of news reporters and I always tried to be reasonable with them, but I always asked them to leave in the end. Some tried to provoke me in the hope that they could rustle up a story, others were very pushy with me and my family. I have also seen very good examples where journalists showed me some respect. I wanted to talk to them but couldn't because of mistrust. I will give some examples.

One day, a coach-load of people stopped opposite our house and about 12 Japanese reporters came out. I was looking from the window and two of them knocked on our door. As I opened the front door, all of them bowed immediately and then all the other passengers came out of the coach. They came to our garden and all of them bowed and greeted me with great respect. A very beautiful young lady asked me my name in English and I answered back. She handed me some fresh flowers and a beautiful card with some sympathetic words. The lady told me that they had come straight from Manchester airport to see me. She told me that they were all from Japan and gave me a business card and offered their sympathy and condolences. Their heads were down (as you may know this is their way of greeting). All the others were standing there with their heads down, same as the religious Muslim preachers who come to your door. These Japanese are such disciplined people. They told me that they were there to listen to my story about my son Hasib. They said if I have time to talk then okay, otherwise we respect your privacy. They just came to see me and offer their sympathy.

One of the middle aged men who was with the lady said, "I'm sorry you lost your son in very tragic circumstances but the whole of Japan is with you and we are here on the behalf of our country." My God, I just melted and tears were flowing from my eyes. I told them, I cannot (although I wanted to) talk to you, but may in the future. I promised them that when the time is right, I would talk to them. To be honest with you, the only people I would like to talk openly with will be those people who gave me so much respect. I do not know what the future holds for me but when I get the chance, I will talk to them.

I wanted to open my heart up to them and say a lot about my son Hasib. I didn't want them go away empty handed from my door step. This was the first time I had wanted to talk to the media. I was crying in front of the lady and she noticed my tears. She did not want me to become more upset. As they left they walked backwards, with their heads down and honoured me in a way that I will never forget for the rest of my life. They were great ambassadors for their country and I salute the whole nation. Their soothing and very emotional words went straight in to my broken heart.

A little later two Pakistani brothers who had worked for the media for a long time visited me. I knew one of them but I had never met his elder brother. The last time I had heard of the younger brother he had left Britain because of domestic problems but I didn't know that he had returned to England some time ago. Both brothers were working for the Asian media. I was out and when I came back home, as soon as I turned into my street, I saw a cameraman and another person waiting for me. I stopped my car in front of my house. The cameraman was just going to film me, but he stopped and said "Mir Sahib". I asked him what they are doing here and one of them replied, "We are here to make a film but we didn't know it was you." I told them about Hasib. They put their equipment back in their car and the younger brother embraced me. The elder brother was surprised we knew each other. They said they were very sorry to hear about this tragedy and they were not going to film anything. I invited them to come inside for a cup of tea but they said some other time. I noticed that the younger brother was crying and there were tears running down his cheeks. The elder brother asked me if I would give permission for him to just film the street. I told him I had no problem with that. He is very famous in Asian media circles and is an Asian news reporter. After that they apologised and left.

One particularly shameful example of the media came from the biggest, best know, well-regarded and trustworthy British media organisation – the BBC. They made fools of themselves and brought shame and disgrace onto their company. It also showed how cunning these liars can be. A woman was outside my house. When I came out I saw Imran talking to her. As I came out she stopped me and said "hello, hello" many times. When I realised she was from the press, I didn't bother with her and said nothing. I was not aware that at the end of street a cameraman was filming me. The lady opened her bag and obviously she was recording my voice. Although my son pointed out to me that she's from the press, someone was filming me from the end of street without my permission. Anyway, suddenly an Asian man came out of a car which was parked in our street and he came straight towards me and said, "Your son killed my wife!" I was taken aback but told him, "Look, I have sympathy for your loss. You and me, we've both lost our loved ones. I am also grieving like you are." Then he told me I should apologise. I told him that I didn't need to apologise to him as I hadn't done anything to him, his wife or his girlfriend. I continued to tell him "if he thinks an apology will bring her back, then I have no problem at all, I will apologise to him…".

My son was already suspicious and said "that cameraman is recording you and she is recording your voice." The cameraman was hiding behind a wall at the end of our street. The Asian man started to demand an apology shouting "your son killed my girlfriend". This man first said "wife" and now he was saying "girlfriend." I said, "Look! What evidence do you have that my son killed your girlfriend? Can you provide me with proof? Have the police provided you with proof that my son killed your girlfriend?" At this point, I told him, "Do not blame Hasib, give me the proof and until then I don't want to talk to you anymore."

The next day the BBC showed a documentary hosted and presented by a well known broadcaster. The film and recording was made without my prior knowledge and permission. Then the day after some British newspapers printed a lot of photos and wrote whatever they could manage. The Asian man's interview was printed. I don't know whether whatever he said in the newspapers was his own version or it was twisted by reporters. It seemed to me that he must have made a lot of money. Whatever he said in the newspapers was completely untrue and false. The only thing I can say about this is that he should be ashamed of himself as he made a lot of money by disrespecting his girlfriend's soul. He has lost respect and dignity in my eyes. Money is not everything in this world. I felt very sorry for him. I still don't know if that Asian man was Muslim or not, but he had a Muslim name. It was his problem if he had a girlfriend or wife! How can a person degrade himself and run after money so soon after his loved one lost her life?

I continued to ask the police officers who were coming to our house if they had any proof that my son killed this man's wife/girlfriend and he said "they took their evidence with them." To me, most media have lost their credibility. I will certainly never trust them again and I do not believe what we watch is based on the truth. We have few resources to check if news reports are based on the truth or simply made up to sell papers. I will always be suspicious about the authenticity of press standards for the rest of my life.

5. REACTION FROM MY OWN FLESH AND BLOOD

I LOST MY SON in tragic circumstances. Hasib was everything to me but the most shocking aspect of the aftermath was the troubling behaviour of my own family. I believe that this was a test for me and I should be patient and never lose hope but I am only human.

Soon after Hasib passed away, I experienced numerous difficulties and some of my very close relatives, my own flesh and blood, betrayed me. They treated me very badly and I am unable to describe all this in words. In a previous chapter, I complained about my community but it is impossible for me to tell you about my own flesh and blood and their shameful behaviour towards me. I was left alone and nobody in my family tried to help me. We just separated and there was no co-operation among us. I was in a very desperate situation. My family stopped listening to me and each time I said something, they always argued. It is difficult for me to write about relatives who left me in the dark. I was very lonely and nobody was there for me. I was ashamed, angry, confused and wanted to know why my family was hurting me like this. I think it is better for me not to write anything about them because my anger has now passed, and it is not even worth bothering anymore.

Most of my family left me during August 2005. I begged them not to leave me alone but to stay with me. I was alone at home and imagine, I had just lost my young son and was experiencing a huge uphill struggle. I went to my daughter's house and wanted to tell her that I was in danger and to keep an eye on me but she wouldn't even open her door. I have a brother and sister living in England. I spent my money and time on them and brought them here after their marriages. I paid for their marriages too. When my brother heard about Hasib, he came to see me after four days. My sister who lived very near to us came to see me a couple of times.

All my wife's brothers and sisters are living in Leeds and they would come to see their sister. I was watching all this and felt that I was alone and I was missing my family. Since I became ill I was unable to support them, yet they left me and did not want to know after the money stopped. I decided to go to Pakistan and thought they may look after me or give me some kind of emotional support. I wanted to take my wife with me but she refused and told me that I could go if I wanted to. I was thinking that I may feel better in Pakistan but I got worse there.

I booked my flight. I was alone and sat in the so called "P" class. There were a few passengers and as soon as the plane got airborne I started to panic. I changed my seat and sat with another passenger and told him that I would be fine in a few minutes. He started to talk and after half an hour, I went back to my seat. I became claustrophobic from that day. Hasib was with me all the time. I kept thinking how he lost his life, his suffering and other things. I felt very upset and started to cry. There were two air hostesses in this cabin. I asked one of them if she could sit beside me. She was a very nice lady. She sat with me and asked me what was wrong. I told her that due to my family circumstances, I was not feeling well and asked her to stay with me a little. She started asking me about my family. I did not tell her about Hasib but I found it very helpful. She asked me if I needed some food or drink. She put her hand on mine and she gave me support and it calmed me down. I am very grateful to her. The rest of the journey went without any other further problems. She kept asking if I was okay during the whole flight.

Anyway, I have my own place in Pakistan, but I still did not want to live alone. I thought if any of my family members asked me to stay with them I might consider it. I didn't want to live at my younger sister's house as I brought her daughter to England and she is married to my eldest son. It was a hurtful and very painful experience. It was the first and last mistake I made. No more favours to that family again. I'd had enough.

My younger brother was living in my house and had responsibility for looking after it but actually, he was destroying it. I was paying all his bills and he was getting a lot of income. He used this house as a place of business and some other men also worked in the house as tailors. When I reached home and saw the state of my house, I became hysterical and just cracked up. The house was a mess and there was rubbish scattered everywhere. It looked like nobody had cleaned it for years. It was the first time I had been to Pakistan since 7/7 and he never said a word to me about my son. I was shocked and very angry. I was here to see my brothers and sisters but instead of sympathy he never said a thing to me. He was so arrogant and I thought, "Bloody hell Mahmood! What are you doing here?" He had been using my house for the past 9 years and had made a lot of money and I was paying his bills. And this brother, who never sat with me and said anything about my feelings or my loss, he never even asked how I was coping with my calamity?

The income he was getting from the house was huge and he was managing with his own household bills because he was living in another house and he used my house for his own interests. He never said anything to me. It was a cruel, selfish and the most unimaginable experience of my life. At one time I completely forgot what happened to me. I was shocked and dismayed at what was happening to me now. This younger brother who was putting food on the table for his wife and 5 children, and the worse thing was, she didn't even come to me to say a single word to me!

As for my other brother… I was sat in my younger sister's house when he came in with a well known wicked and disgraceful woman from our area. This is the brother who defrauded me, and sold my land (yes it was my land and I bought it with my own money, it had nothing to do with inherited land, it was purely mine and my children's). After my parents died, I donated it to the masjid but he sold it to a man who used to call my father his "father"! (If some people of Pakistan start doing these sorts of evil things, what would one expect Allah to do with them? The worse calamity will be their fate and it is happening right now in Pakistan.)

I had given away two pieces of land for a masjid. This land is not in a village, it is in the city of Rawalpindi, so it must have some value. Not have I lost money but I have also lost land as has the masjid. Losing all this, my other brother's behaviour and on top of that, I lost my most precious son Hasib. I still thought maybe when I reach Pakistan, my brothers and sister may treat me differently, but I was completely wrong...

When my son Hasib was engaged with a girl from Karachi in Pakistan, Hasib's mother bought gold jewellery for Hasib's fiancé and a lot of other things. Hasib put £250 of his money towards the gifts. Also, I am not sure why, soon after Hasib's engagement, certain family members carried on asking me when Hasib was getting married. I told them "not yet." Some of them told me that I should hurry up as things can change. I was not sure why they said that? This is something that has popped up in my mind often since 7/7, why were they asking me again and again about Hasib? Did they know anything? Or it is just me over-thinking things? The way they were talking about Hasib's marriage it was as though something bad would happen in future. I am sure a few a people were not happy at all.

6. WHO WAS TO BLAME FOR HASIB'S RADICALISATION?

BEFORE I START this chapter, I would like to make it absolutely clear that I am not against all reputable mullahs, molvis, sheikhs or scholars. It is absolutely not my intention to hurt anybody's feelings. I am writing here about those molvis' whose character is disgraceful and their intolerable behaviour in this country. They are using our religion for personal gain. This chapter is about those who brought disgrace on themselves during the 7/7 incident. A big majority of imams are very good people and understand Islam very well, and act upon its teachings and spread their message peacefully. But there are no shortage of black sheep who, in my honest opinion, should not be here and should be kicked out of the country. Some of them are spreading hate and preaching Islam incorrectly and causing a lot of hate amongst our youngsters. It is fair to say that most Muslims would have heard hate speeches in mosques before 7/7. I know that many visionary, well-educated, wise and open-minded noble scholars would agree that there are a small minority of mullahs who have done a lot of damage, not only to Islam but also to their local communities. Their messages have poisoned our younger generation. I hope this chapter will open their eyes.

I respect most Islamic scholars, molvis and imams. I have nothing against them or their sects. However, I am against those who are bad eggs who have no insight into Islam. They are here to fill their bellies and worship their own greed. I had a lot of disgraceful experiences after 7/7 and that's why I have decided to include this chapter.

It is clear that Hasib was radicalised by local preachers and mentors. It seems obvious to me that, as a teenager, he was susceptible to the speeches given in local mosques. In the period between the 9/11 bombings and 7/7 it's clear the atmosphere was very different as the British police and intelligence services did not necessarily keep a close eye on mosques for troublemakers and at the same time there was a sudden growth in the use of the internet by radical groups who sought to brainwash young Muslims. A lot of that information came from beyond our borders but we can surely control who looks after Islam in this country?

As an illustration of how some imams arrived in the UK I'd like to tell you a quick story as an example of how the system works. Once upon a time a very well known Mirpuri businessman had a cloth shop in Bradford. This person died a long time ago but he was famous for bringing farmers and labourers from Pakistan to England. He was very well respected back home in Mirpur. Most of his villagers were young men who emigrated to England leaving only the old people in his village. There was a young boy in the village who unfortunately didn't have the resources to come here. This young boy was a goat herder and all day this poor chap would go to the nearby jungle and feed his goats. One day, he realised that there were only old people left in his village, as almost all the young men had gone to England. He went to see a wise old man and asked him about going to Walayat (England). The old man suggested he should write a letter to "Chowdhary Sahib" who was a businessman in Bradford as he may be able to help him. This young goat herder had never even seen school and was unable to write a thing. He went to the main city post office and asked a munshi (clerk) to write a letter for him. He wrote, "I am a poor goat herder and all the young men have gone to England and I'm the only boy left in this village. Each time somebody from England comes back to this village, I feel very bad because I also want to come to England. Please help me and call me so I can have better life."

The Bradford businessman received this letter and he became bit concerned because as a well known person he could not ignore this boy's request, as almost everybody in his village would know about this letter. There was not much going on in relation to visas because the British government was tightening up immigration rules and there was only one way to bring the boy over – he had to find a bride for him in England and that was very difficult. This businessman had two daughters but he didn't want to get either married to this boy because he belonged to a lower caste, and it was the same with other people. The businessman thought he would write a letter to him and he would soon forget about coming to England as he wouldn't be able to fulfil the requirements as he was illiterate.

At the same time this businessman was having trouble with his local masjid in Bradford where he was chairman and the current molvi had earned his permanent stay in the country and was now threatening to leave. He sent a letter and explained that the situation in Bradford is no good; he couldn't find a bride so there is no way to call you. He asked for him to wait six months and then he'd write to him again. In the meantime the businessman told him to learn basic things about Islam, memorise some verses of the Qu'ran, how to perform prayers five times a day, learn how to lead funeral prayers and how to perform new birth rites. He also advised him to make sure he knew how to control evil spirits because this is a huge tax free business all over England and to let him know when he has learned all these.

This boy received the letter and of course he went to his city Post Office and asked the munshi to read it to him. Learning to read and write would be a very difficult task for the goat herder so he went to his village molvi and asked him if he could teach him. The retired old molvi was counting his days and he thought before he left this world, he would be happy to teach all knew to the goat herder. So the boy started to learn despite it being very hard for him as he had never been to school. Molvi Sahib tried hard and within 6 months he had taught the lad almost everything required by the Bradford businessman. This time the boy himself wrote a letter to the businessman and informed him that he's fully qualified and had learned as required. He confirmed he had also learnt a few extra things like black magic and controlling evil spirits who were causing trouble for Pakistani children and their parents, especially those related to marriage issues.

Meanwhile, back in Bradford, the businessman was having a lot of trouble with his current molvi, he called a meeting with his committee and put a case in front of them. He told them "we can sack this molvi and I will arrange for another molvi to be in place who is one of the best in Pakistan." One night, the current molvi left and he started his own spiritual business earning him a lot more money than his masjid wage. The Chairman had no choice but to call the goat herder, so he applied for his visa from the Home Office saying that they needed a Scholar for "Chowdhury's Masjid". The goat herder was granted a visa and he arrived in Walayat (England) with his fake Islamic degrees and certificates. Not long after he started preaching jihad and told his congregations to kill Jews and filthy English people wherever you find them. As soon as this molvi settled down a bit, he became a "mufti" and the most illiterate and ill-educated people started to come to him to take out bad spirits and have good "taweez" (not proven by Qu'ran) prepared for their children because they weren't listening to their parents. Some were forcing them to marry a boy or girl who lived in a village back home in Mirpur. He stayed with this masjid under the care of Chowdhary Sahib until he got his permanent stay in England, and as usual he also started his own self-employed spiritual business, surely tax free and so the process starts all over again.

In my opinion, these molvis have no idea how to behave in England. They are living here and at the same time, they are preaching very bad things to our children. Before 7/7, each masjid's molvi was crying for jihad but they never preached this message to their own their sons as they were educated in universities to become lawyers and accountants. Why poison others? These illiterate molvis had no idea what they were teaching our children and they have no knowledge of the English language. They have no ability to answer in English to their students. In my opinion, most of them are here to make money and spread their own self-made Sects and to deliberately cause friction in our community. Some of these molvis don't even know their own date of birth and yet they became muftis in this country. These muftis, molvis and illiterate scholars should be kicked out of this country. They are spreading hate instead of harmony, and our new generation is getting the worst deal because of it. You hear every day about Muslims raping children, falling in love with young girls and running away from home. I think the British government must take action against them and they should be deported in cases where there is criminal activity. These "spiritual molvis" are destroying our lives.

Most of them have their own special Sects and mosques and they only preach to their own sects. They are preaching self-made, unproven and stupid stories to our children. We Pakistanis have become a laughing stock in this country because of their behaviour. By preaching their own stupid values and casts, they have done irreversible damage to us. For prayer times, they run behind the British observatory, but when it comes to deciding about Ramadan and Eid, they become blind. They cannot see the moon's appearance! For goodness sake, why can't we celebrate Eid on the same day? What's wrong with you? These molvis throw filth at each other because they do not believe in the same Sect. The only thing I would say is that this government should make sure that our Imams are well educated, not only should they be able to preach in our native language but also in English. Surely, the standard could be raised to be in line with other jobs as they have specific requirements. Why bring an illiterate and saif-ul-malook molvi from Pakistan or a Kashmiri villager who has no insight into our children's needs?

About 500 molvis signed a fatwa regarding 7/7 saying they had nothing to do with it. Of course you had nothing to do with 7/7 otherwise you wouldn't be here! You would be locked up for the rest of your life! You were only worried about your "maseets" (mosques). When everything died down, you revoked your fatwa. Nobody asked you to give a fatwa; I certainly didn't, then why take it back? Why give the fatwa in the first place? That's because you were wetting your pants and worried about your chairmanships, leaderships and that you will be asked to provide masjid accounts! Does the British government know how you built huge mansions and Bungalows back home while you were only getting paid £80-100 a week here?

We certainly don't need these molvis, Imams, Sheikhs and Scholars in our country. They are spreading religious hatred, but some of them have also been found guilty of raping young girls who go to Islamic study classes. Before 7/7, I went to many mosques and at Friday prayer, these molvis were spreading hate against Christians, Jews and any non-believers. After 7/7, I went to a masjid and after the Friday prayer the molvi Sahib, who I wasn't too familiar with, came to me, embraced me and said in my ear, "we are very proud of four who put our heads high and taught a lesson to Kaffers." But the following Friday I saw the same molvi speaking out against 7/7 saying we had nothing to do with the 7/7 incident. I was not only shocked at his double standards I refused to attend this masjid anymore. He was a hypocrite.

I remember in 1969, when the American astronaut Neil Armstrong went to the moon. I was about 12 years of age. My father had a black and white Russian made television set. Nobody in our street had a television. It was our long awaited wish to see an old lady sitting on the moon with a spinning wheel! But on that particular night, we saw some American jumping on the moon with a flag. Some local elder in our street asked my father if he could put the television in the street so the other local people could watch Neil Armstrong on the moon. My father agreed and put his TV on a table, and the street was full of people who watched the one hour programme. Nobody was able to see an old lady with her spinning wheel but we saw Neil Armstrong with his flag on the moon saying "the eagle has landed".

In our street elders were saying that it was impossible to go to the moon because it is too far, and you have to cross seven skies. At this point the trouble started. The next day most molvis issued a fatwa saying the Americans were lying to our youngsters, how could they go to the moon by crossing seven skies? How is it possible to make a very long wire and take it to the moon and then speak from there, it isn't possible, before long each molvi in his masjid started to issue a Fatwa according to his Sect. Now, there were people in Pakistan who believed that Neil Armstrong went to moon and others who didn't. An argument started and it ended in street fighting among them. Some of them started to throw stones at cars and buses, and most local shops shut down as a strike and demonstrations were arranged. A lot of youngsters were injured and a boy was killed by some mobs. The damage to property and business was beyond belief. This all happened because a Fatwa was issued against going to the moon!

Can I ask a question to all molvis? You have a mobile phone – does it have a long wire? Can you ring your relatives in Pakistan or anywhere in the world? How come you can talk to them without a wire attached to your mobile? Obviously you travel to UK but you have never sat on a donkey to come here, it was a plane which brought you here in to England. That plane carried you for almost 8 hours. How did the pilot talk to the air traffic controller? How did the aeroplane find its way to England? Surely you can't even guide our children properly, how could you be guiding an aeroplane this far? Come to the real world. Don't be a hypocritical fool. You should know very well now that what our Creator says in Qu'ran about a human being using his brain? Not only Muslims but also the whole of Allah's creation are allowed to build and make things for their use. The only condition is not to interfere with Allah's business.

In Britain, there are thousands of masjids (according to a 1994 survey there are 1200, but now there will be a lot more) and each masjid is known by some personal name, like Butt, Raja, Mochi, Mirza, Jaat, Jogi. Correct me if I am wrong. Each molvi says bad things about the other masjid and molvi. They call themselves Wahabis, Dewbandis, Brelvis, Shias, Ahl-e-Sunnat, Ahl-e-Hadis, Naqshbandi, Majadadis, Jamatis, and of course there are charity businesses going on television and now, they should call themselves "Kheratis". They are enemies to each other. They blame each other, they say a lot of bad things to each other and the worst thing is they never co-operate with each other. Each molvi is sitting in his hut and making money and calling the other Sects bad names. Why can't they say, "We are just Muslims and we follow Islam and Allah's beloved prophet Mohammed (pbuh), and nothing else"? We have been told to be united in all situations, but what we are doing is completely, utterly wrong and against our own Islamic teachings.

Are these the teachings of our beloved prophet Mohammed

(pbuh)? Of course not. This is the Prophet, on whom Allah himself sent darood. He never guided for anyone to become astray. He showed us a straight path. He never asked us to spread religious or Sectarian hatred. He taught us love and harmony. Doesn't anyone remember our beloved prophet Mohammed's (pbuh) Hajj speech?

Our beloved Prophet (pbuh) suffered. He was stoned and unfortunately, people did a lot of wrong things to him. You should know that he led a very simple life. He sewed his own clothes, he repaired his own shoes. I do not have to tell you all this, but can I ask you, could you do this? You are sitting in a huge mansion, wearing expensive clothes, a long cap on your head and a Mercedes under your feet and you cannot repair your own shoes because you feel insulted. You love your Prophet (pbuh) but you are not prepared to do the things that he did in his own life. Our Prophet Mohammed (pbuh) preached tolerance, harmony, love, and a life according to Allah's commands, so why are you spreading hate and dividing us into sects and castes. Just come out of your mansions and be a Muslim not a Wahabi, Dewbandi, Naqshbandi or anything else. If you want to do jihad, give up all your worldly belongings first and do not teach our children "your kind of jihad" please. Although it is not in my control, if it was, then I would certainly put some molvis on mules and donkeys and kick them back home where they belong.

I was shocked to read in a local Asian newspaper that a molvi spiritual leader raped a 13 year-old Muslim girl. This kind of horrific act brings a lot of shame on our community and I think there should be a law where they must be punished severely and be kicked out from this country forever. If a molvi gives a fatwa to stone adulterers, then why can't the molvi be stoned if he commits the same crime? I think this country is too soft towards these people. They must be regulated. They do not pay any tax on their income as a spiritual molvi. Their income is undeclared and tax people don't know about their personal spiritual business.

When our Liaison officer told us that Hasib's body may be released soon she wanted to check our reaction. She told me that if we couldn't make arrangements for the funeral to let them know so we will be able to bury Hasib. I told her that I am alive and I will do everything for his funeral and God willing, I will pick my son's body on my shoulders. If I am capable of leading my son's funeral procession and read his funeral prayers, then I will do it. I wanted to find a mosque to do this. I needed a place to read the funeral prayers. I went to almost every masjid in Leeds and asked the chairman of the masjid, but they all refused and told me that it was too dangerous. Some of them were so scared; they wet their pants fearing that the police would take action against them. A famous Leeds Imam told me that he needs permission from the police to conduct a funeral procession for Hasib. I was not only shocked but amazed that the British government blindly gave permission to all molvis in this country to say what they want and poison our society by spreading hate, although this has changed following 7/7 and other attacks in the UK.

However prior to 7/7 their crimes were such that they could have been arrested and put away for 40 years but nothing was done. After 7/7, all those Scholars and molvis began to shut their mouths. One molvi told me that "Goray" will target our "Maseets" and we do not want this as it "will affect our livelihoods". I reminded them about their holy duty but because of fear, their "wuzo" (ablution) was broken. This was the molvi who always fixed a price for funeral prayers. This same molvi was so scared, I could hear his stomach rumbling when, with his other colleagues, he issued a fatwa, he was turning away from his holy duties. I have never seen such hypocrisy and double standards in my life. I could imagine their fear but this was a simple funeral, nothing else. One masjid chairman and his committee members shit themselves and completely denied that Hasib had ever read prayers in this "Jogi Masjid". This is the masjid where I used to go with Hasib. Since then, I have never set foot in that masjid again. Allah will curse them severely. These people took personal mortgages out on this masjid building. Shame on you!

I talked to a relative whose business was arranging funerals. He said there would be no problem and he could arrange Hasib's funeral. I'm very grateful to my brother Ikhlaq Mir who helped me to bring Hasib's body from London and then organise the burial.

I am very grateful to the Al-Hassan trust, his management and the very pious Scholar Hassan Sahib, who conducted Hasib's funeral prayers and fulfilled his holy duties without fear, and he proved that he is a true imam and scholar who knows his Islamic duties and how to conduct himself. To become a Scholar and Imam, Alim and Mufti, one must not beg for donations in the name of Allah and maintain to keep their highest honour at each step taken daily.

Finally, I would ask all Muslims to employ young Imams who are aware of British rules and regulations and who can speak English. They should be able to deliver proper Islamic education to more than just their sect. They should also make sure they know the meaning of jihad. To my understanding jihad is a struggle to provide the best education and lifestyle according to our religion and faith to our new generation. Any molvi who is caught spreading sectarian and spiritual wrong doing must be kicked out of the country. Some of these molvis are making millions and sending it back to Pakistan and other countries. They should be stopped. Our Muslim brothers should also keep an eye on donations and should be allowed to see accounts. Most masjid accounts are not regulated and money has been spent on things which are not related to the donation provisions. At this point, I'm reminded of a very humiliating story. A molvi took two hundred thousand pounds to Pakistan and was caught at the airport. He was jailed for a couple of months. This money was donations from poor Muslim people who were giving to charitable causes, but instead he tried to smuggle the money to Pakistan. God knows why, maybe to build his own Kothis or maybe a madrassah to preach jihad?

Masjids and other Muslim schools must be aware that they must deliver a proper Islamic education to our youngsters otherwise we will be a forgotten society. Almost two hundred thousand Muslims came to England after the British Raj left India. One of them was Din Mohammed, who was directly responsible for Queens Victoria's stately homes and he invented a lot of other things for the British people. Tell me, what happened to those people? Where are they now? Where are their generations? If we are not capable of providing a good Islamic education, we will lose a whole generation. So, come out of Sectarianism and think ahead three generations. We certainly do not want our generation to sink like that!

Burning books, making unreasonable demonstrations and building your own "maseets" adorned with your name will not solve these problems. Only good Imams and Scholars can achieve this goal.

7. JUSTICE?

THERE ARE HUNDREDS of questions concerning the 7/7 bombings that I remain baffled by. We haven't been provided with any satisfactory answers to most of them and it's possible that we will never find out the truth. These questions upset me and my family and I believe the British public should also know the truth about one of the biggest events in British history as the internet is full of conflicting stories and unanswered questions regarding the 7/7 bombing, although the presumption is that my son and his friends carried this out.

We received a leaflet from the Coroner's office in London and it outlined our legal rights and also our responsibilities. Although I'm not a legal expert, I have some knowledge of the British legal system. It is the Coroner's duty to inform the next of kin about the time, date and place of the deceased's post mortem in advance. The leaflet also said we had a right to employ our own qualified medical experts to be present when the post mortem took place. In case of an inquest, we have a right to be informed by the coroner of the date, time and place in advance. Our legal representative has the right to ask questions from the witnesses and represent us. Also, we have the right to see the body before release. It is the duty of the Coroner to make such arrangements for the deceased family or next of kin. We have the right to a copy of the post mortem, we may have to pay for this. We have the right to employ our own Pathologist who can examine the body on our behalf but we have to pay a fee.

We asked our Liaison Officer many times if we could see Hasib's body but our request was always ignored or refused. We asked senior officers if they could arrange for us to see Hasib's body but they also refused. We asked for a DNA profile of Hasib, again this was refused. We employed our own Pathologist but professionals were not happy with this arrangement. We were told that Hasib's remains would be released after the tests were concluded and it would take a number of weeks.

Hasib was blamed for the bus bombing. We asked police to show us concrete proof. The only thing shown to us was some very short video clips where Hasib was walking normally and doing nothing questionable in London. These clips don't make him a bomber in my opinion. He was also shown buying something from a store. The image is very unclear and police assumed he was buying a battery. Apart from these we haven't been shown anything which relates to Hasib. We requested a copy of the video clips but again, this request was declined. Most of these clips were circulated in the media anyway. Most photos are also in the public domain.

I was told by the police that they found Hasib's fingerprints in the flat where the bombs were made. It may be possible that his fingerprints were there before somebody started making bombs.

I have stated many times that we co-operated with the police to find out exactly what happened and how Hasib became involved, if he was involved at all, but unfortunately whatever information we asked for was declined. There were a few occasions when we were so scared, we thought our lives were at risk and it was better not to ask anything. We were living in fear, confusion and afraid for our safety.

My wife and I should have been called to the Coroner's inquest as others were called to provide statements, heard by the Coroner, but that never happened. We received no information. It's very sad that we were never told when the inquest proceedings were to take place.

There are many incidents in Britain's history when the government has conducted a public inquiry. If there was a train crash or similar, an inquiry was required but although 7/7 was a huge calamity no inquiry was ordered despite the public outrage and nobody was prepared to want to find out the truth, they just accepted the state's official story. To me, that is suspicious. One reason given was that it would be 'a waste of resources'. The British public knows that over a thousand billion pounds were poured into the banks just to correct bankers' mistakes. Spending a few million on a public inquiry would not make our government poor. To me, it felt like somebody was hiding something and didn't want the truth to come out. We were told that we are law abiding families, but on the other hand the powers that be ignored our basic rights and that does not look good. Worst of all, in place of a proper inquiry where the facts can be established, we have doubt.

We received a letter from the Coroner's office asking which dates we would not available, and we notified them of the dates. We were hoping that we may be called to the inquest and we would be able to say our side of the story but nothing happened. It was my wish to hear the inquest proceedings but I was not called or given the chance. If I was in some kind of danger, then what was the purpose of secure rooms and video links. I think this is not fair at all.

Police officers told us that we are also victims, the same as the other families. We were told we lost our son just like the other 52 families lost their loved ones. Then why this unfairness? Was this all one sided justice? We are victims just like the other families of 7/7 who lost their loved ones in the bombings. We lost our son and brother. The way we have been treated is unfair and in my opinion this was certainly not justice!

All the other family victims were present and family members of victims who were injured were given the chance to put their case or listen at the inquest. The accused, Hasib Hussain Mir, wasn't there but at least his parents should have been present at these proceedings. What was the reason not to call us? We had done nothing wrong. We did not bomb anybody. We are not criminals. We should have the same rights as the others.

I lost my son, the other 52 families lost their loved ones. I feel their pain and suffering. I feel they are like me and they may be feeling some sympathy towards me. My heart goes out to them. I am a human being and a father too. Just think what they are feeling? I am not responsible for their pain and heartache and I have a lot of doubts, considering the huge pile of discrepancies about Hasib's case. If we have done nothing wrong then we should be included in that particular list of families who got legal aid help from the government. But, I'm afraid there was nothing done for us. And they say the law is blind…

According to the British newspapers, TV and internet, our then Justice Secretary decided to award legal aid to the victims' families for free legal representation at the inquest. Now this was a very big case, a calamity which shook Britain. It was in the interests of British Law to award legal aid for those who suffered in 7/7. The 52 families didn't have to fill any legal documents or declare any assets, e.g.. property, savings, earnings, jewellery or any other type of savings. It was commissioned under the banner of "exceptional circumstances". Families were not required to fill any financial assessments forms. If they are victims, so are we. If they received legal aid then we should also be considered under "exceptional circumstances". Our legal aid was refused, the reason given was that we "didn't meet the legal aid requirements". What justice? And the Justice Secretary was the same politician who had a problem with a Muslim woman because she wears a Burqa or veil. I cannot expect justice from him.

The widow of another bomber applied for legal aid. Her case was heard in the High Court but legal aid was refused. For other families it was "exceptional circumstances" but for us nothing. This is not justice at all. When our legal aid was refused, one of the leading legal experts appeared on television and said "This is a very sad day for Britain". If I was called in, even for one or two days, I would have believed in justice but now I have no hesitation to say justice was not served. A person like me, a strong believer in fairness and justice, lost all hope. We were hung from a rope with out any justice or fairness. I was very badly let down by the British legal system. I am really very sad and angry but strongly believe that one day my case will be heard in "The Highest Court" and then justice will be served very fairly. My point is that we, the parents of the accused, had done nothing wrong and we should have been awarded legal help so we could go to court and be legally represented. I don't think it was a huge demand. When our legal aid was refused, our solicitor told me that he was also unable to help me. He did what he could for which I am grateful.

I am very happy for all the 7/7 victims' families who got any kind of help from the government. Good luck to them. At least they were represented at the inquest. My heart goes out to them and I feel their pain and I very much hope that maybe some of them appreciate the pain we are in. Please feel for me and my family. I am also very happy if you got some financial help from the government or any other sources. A lot of money was spent to erect a nice memorial for the 52 victims. I also heard they were given tickets to go to the Olympic Games in London. As mentioned earlier, I was offered a lot of money for my story but I refused to take it as my son was not for sale. If I considered the circumstances carefully then I could call myself the "biggest victim of 7/7". You might have (maybe I am wrong) had some closure after the inquest and are able to move on but I can't. Can you see my pain and anguish?

British newspapers, TV and other press made millions from the 7/7 story. I believe there are a lot of people who lied about my son and my family. The British public is now aware of their conduct. One prominent newspaper has closed down and several others have had their wings clipped following the exposure of the tactics of editors, reporters and special investigators. The phone-hacking of innocent families was one of their most infamous offences and I do wonder if we were hacked at times. Almost every week someone knocks on my door and asks for my story but I feel it is immoral to sell it because it will be twisted and described in the wrong way. I do not believe anything that I see and read. I have lost trust.

Everybody knows that the people who died in 7/7 died in the bomb blasts. The Inquest took place to find out how they died, or perhaps to find out some other details. I have been to another Coroner's court and I noticed that both sides of each relevant party (victims and accused) were present and the Coroner told them that we were not there to blame each other, they were there to find out the facts. In that case a child had died because of careless driving. The driver was present in court and so were the victims' family, mother and father. I know for a fact that if any criminal elements appeared during the hearing, then the Coroner had to report this to a criminal court. Coroners courts all over Britain have the same laws and the same rules. My question is why were we not called to listen to the proceedings even if we were not legally represented? Were the government so concerned about the press reaction that they changed the laws of the country?

The bombers, including Hasib, died in the blast along the victims. The inquest took place for the 52 victims but not for the bombers. If this honourable judge knows victims died in the bomb blasts, how come she didn't conduct the inquest for the bombers? What was the reason? If these 4 died in the bomb blast then what is the point of conducting an inquest for the 52 victims if we already knew they died in these blasts. Did these bombers die in other circumstances? What were the circumstances? If there was no need to conduct an inquest for the 4 bombers, then obviously there shouldn't have been the need to have an inquest for the 52 victims either! None of it makes sense.

I am not criticising anybody, I am just saying what I believe. Why set aside the inquest for the four bombers? To me this is very strange. Somebody suggested to me that the court know the four bombers died in these bomb blasts, but again, my response is, so did the other 52 victims. Why did their inquest take place when there wasn't one for Hasib and the others?

There are a lot of reports on the internet and of course in the newspapers that at the inquest more questions emerged than answers. Some of them said that it was a one-sided decision because the bomber's families were not legally represented.

Apart from all this there are a lot of doubts in my mind. As the father of Hasib, it is natural for me to ask questions. Recently two police officers who conducted the 7/7 investigation came to see me and I put a few questions to them but they were unable to answer any of them to my satisfaction. I was told that I may not find any answers to my questions at all. I am frustrated and it is a one-man struggle to find out what actually did happen on the day of 7/7 and what happened to my son Hasib Hussain Mir? How did he lose his life? What is the truth?

8. CLOSURE

FOLLOWING A *Daily Mail* article on 7th July 2015, showing pictures of me praying at my son's graveside, someone posted a message on the internet that "Mr Hussain is Hasib's father and the father has done nothing wrong and people should be aware of that, and they must not say anything to Hasib's father. The media is printing his photos while he was mourning at Hasib's grave. The media should allow an individual's privacy and dignity should be honoured."

I am a very private person and I have no greed to become famous. Why would I want to be famous? I will be leaving this world and life is a temporary gift. I believe at the end I have to face a Day of Judgment and I should be worried about that, not this world.

As I mentioned in my previous chapter, the families of the 7/7 victims may have found some kind of closure after the inquest but it's possible that some or the majority of them are unable to come to terms with what happened when they lost their loved ones. My sympathies go out to them all.

I know for a fact that I will never be able to cope with my loss. There might have been a very minute element of closure for me and my family if there had been proper legal representation for us, but unfortunately that chance was not forthcoming. Even if this happened then I believe it is still very hard to feel any sense of closure. One of the victim's family members was asked about closure and he said 'there is no closure for me'. I also strongly believe that in my case, there will be no closure at all. I will be in a pitch dark state for rest of my life.

Some of my friends told me that I should move on. I felt very bad about it and told them it's not possible for me because they have no idea at all about my suffering and pain. Not knowing the facts is very painful. No father can move on just like that. You lose your parents and other very close relatives, but losing your own child is something very different, and getting through that pain and heartache is not easy at all. I am Hasib's father and my life stopped after 7/7. I cannot move on. I have nothing to move on to.

People say that time is the best healer but I dispute that. For parents it's not easy. There is some light at the end of the tunnel. I am clinging to my faith and my faith is teaching me to be patient. My only hope is my faith. The whole world can let you down but I am sure my faith never will.

9. LAST WORD!

PEOPLE FROM ALL over the world have said different things about the 7/7 incident and will carry on giving their opinions and views for a long time to come. They have written and will write more in the future. Human brutality, killings, lawlessness and disrespect of basic human rights have continued since Adam's creation. Sometimes human beings behaviour towards their fellow man beings is worse than animals.

We humans can make this world a very peaceful place by tolerance, patience and respect for basic human rights. Long lasting peace and harmony can be achieved without supremacy of a race, religion, or background. We can make this world into a safer and more beautiful place not only for our present generations but also for generations to come by understanding each other's culture, religion and values and communication is a very important key for this purpose.

When a powerful nation does not behave correctly towards a poor nation, when a powerful man does not give the basic human rights to the poor and weak person, it is very likely that a poor nation and a poor or weak human being will somehow stand up and fight for their existence and rights.

Why can't we tolerate one another? Supreme powers have a moral duty for good behaviour towards poor nations. Poor nations and a weak man also have a right to exist. Our history is witness to what happens when a supreme nation attacks or tries to destroy a poor nation, then the struggle begins because the poor will fight back for their fundamental right to existence and this is where the problems starts.

I honestly do not know what the motives were behind the 7/7 incident but I am also struggling to understand how this could have happened. After every large incident, be it a rail crash, school killings, plane crash or social services mistakes there are investigations at a public enquiry. I don't understand why 7/7 was

not so important? 56 people died and over 700 were wou1
There was a huge outcry for an independent public enquiry b1
was refused, the government claiming it was a waste of resou
I don't think this is the reason. I believe it may be that the w1
truth would have come out. I very much hope the truth will cc
out eventually. If not in my life time, then I do not mind if it con
out in the future. We cannot hide the truth forever.

As far as my son Hasib is concerned, I leave this to my Creatoi
He knows the truth. I was given a beautiful present and it was
taken away from me. I am powerless and unable to do anything
when it comes to life and death. I am his father and I know for a
fact that Hasib never gave me any trouble when he was around me,
and never gave me cause for concern when he had gone. To me he
was a law abiding young man.

This book is not meant to cause any emotional distress for
anybody. These are my own words and they are not against anyone.
I have the right to express my views and I have no fear whatsoever
from anybody, rich or mighty, big, small or supremely powerful. I
have said what I wanted to say.

This book contains priceless memories for my children and
grandchildren when I am gone.

My first language is not English and I am not a professional
writer but I am very proud that I have expressed my emotions and
feelings about 7/7 and Hasib. Some people may like it and others
might hate it. I respect both opinions.

I end this book by saying: "And our last call is that all praise
belongs to Allah, the Lord of the worlds, and there is no Might
and Power except with Allah, the High, the Great. And may
blessings and peace be on the most excellent of Prophets and Seal
of Messengers and His family and Companions, all of them. And
we ask Allah for His intercession on the day of judgement."

May Allah make it beneficial for the readers and they approve
it.

Thank you for reading my side of the story.